M000286618

Conscience of the Institution

The publication of
Conscience of the Institution
was greated aided by a generous gift
from the Witherspoon Institute.

Conscience of the Institution

Edited and with an introduction
by Helen Alvaré

St. Augustine's Press
South Bend, Indiana

Copyright © 2014 by The Witherspoon Institute

All rights reserved. No part of this book may be reproduced, stored
in a retrieval system, or transmitted, in any form or by any means,
electronic, mechanical, photocopying, recording, or otherwise,
without the prior permission of St. Augustine's Press.

Manufactured in the United States of America

1 2 3 4 5 6   20 19 18 17 16 15 14

Library of Congress Control Number: 2014950628

∞ The paper used in this publication meets the minimum requirements of the
American National Standard for Information Sciences Permanence of Paper for
Printed Materials, ANSI Z39.481984.

St. Augustine's Press
www.staugustine.net

Contents

Introduction by Helen Alvaré   vii

Chapter 1   Anthony Fisher, Freedom of Conscience and
Institutional Integrity   1

Chapter 2   Christopher Tollefsen, The Philosophical and
Theological Roots of Institutional Conscience   28

Chapter 3   Daniel P. Sulmasy, Institutional Conscience and
Tolerance   47

Chapter 4   Robert P. George, Conscience and Its Enemies   73

Chapter 5   Gerard V. Bradley, Institutional Ministries and
the Church's Temporal Mission   83

Chapter 6   Richard M. Doerflinger, Competing
"Rights" Claims: Defending Rights of
Conscience in the Policy Arena   104

Chapter 7   Anthony R. Picarello, Discrimination in
Discrimination: Confronting Half-Truths in
Anti-Discrimination Laws That Threaten
Institutional Religious Freedom   131

Chapter 8   Michael P. Moreland, Institutional Conscience:
From Free Exercise to Freedom of Association and\
Church Autonomy   151

Chapter 9   Steven D. Smith, The Precarious Freedom
of the Church   178

Chapter 10   Allen D. Hertzke, Implications of the
Domestic Conscience Battle   203

Introduction
Helen Alvaré

By a variety of measures, the United States remains a nation in which religion matters. Prosperity and technological sophistication, both American hallmarks, and both traditionally conceived as the natural enemies of religion, have not displaced religion. References to the links between America's founding and its continuing commitment to religious freedom regularly feature in statements and documents issued both by the state and by private authors. Nearly 71% of Americans generally profess a belief in God. Even among the young cohort called "Millennials," nearly 80% are affiliated with a particular religion, according to the Pew Forum on Religion and Public Life.[1] Politicians of all stripes still feel themselves obliged to interact with religious questions and religious bodies. American religious institutions continue to maintain a high social profile, providing social services, treatment, and education annually to millions of believers and nonbelievers alike. Some receive state funds to carry out work deemed important both to the religious institution and to the state, e.g., health care, or services to immigrants or the poor. The vast majority serve all comers, not only clients sharing their faith.

Tension has grown, however, between the sometimes-denominated "separate spheres" of church and state, with the rise of government intervention into a wide variety of arenas previously occupied more by families, private groups, or religious bodies, e.g., employment, health care, education, and family life, to name just a few. While at one time it could plausibly have been concluded that governmental rules would rarely contradict religious tenets, today this occurs regularly. In many arenas the state now endorses a particular view of the common good—about "human rights," "health," and "equality"—which conflicts with the teachings and practices advanced by one or more religions.

Contemporaneously, many institutions founded by religious actors and bodies grew larger and more complex over the last 60 years, often in response to an increased demand for their services, but also due to requirements imposed by technology, the market, and outside regulatory or accrediting bodies. These institutions also became more likely to hire and serve people who did not share their faith, as a consequence of demographic, social and other forces, as well as religious beliefs in the intrinsic equality and dignity of all persons. Eventually, many religious institutions attracted government funding because of their excellent service records and their willingness to serve the poor and those in underserved geographic areas, both efficiently and with a deep-seated respect for their dignity. From time to time, it has become politically popular for government to seek partnerships with private religious entities. Consequently today, whether because a religious institution is operating in a heavily regulated area, or because it is state-funded, or because it employs and serves the public at large, it is more and more likely to find itself subject to government standards and mandates. This constellation of changes undoubtedly challenges religious institutions' abilities to imbue all aspects of their structures and operations with their founding religious missions.

Current interactions between religious institutions and the government are subject not only to regulations issuing from the legislative and executive branches of the state, but also to prevailing judicial interpretations of the First Amendment's Free Exercise and Establishment clauses. Since the Supreme Court's 1990 decision in *Employment Division* v. *Smith*,[2] states without robust religious freedom laws or strongly protective state constitutions are free to grant less deference to claims of religious conscience than they did previously. They have only to show, in the case of a "neutral law of general applicability,"[3] that the law bears a rational relationship to a legitimate state interest. So long as the law is neutral on its face, even a serious burden on an essential religious practice can stand.

There is also a shifting cultural context for religious freedom claims. While *Smith* left religious bodies free to seek legislative religious freedom exemptions even from "neutral laws of general applicability," legislatures have shown themselves increasingly unwilling to grant generous exemptions. Even religious institutions founded on explicitly religious principles and by religious actors—institutions that still understand their mission as first and foremost religious—are denied legislative exemptions. Both federal and state legislatures are increasingly limiting exemptions to those religious institutions whose purpose is restricted to inculcating religious beliefs. The many religious institutions that hire and serve people who do not share their faith are denied exemptions. The practical effect is that those institutions that might compete effectively against whatever message the state is sending by way of its legislation, are either forced to follow the state's line or exit the scene.

Over the course of American history, different issues have brought religious institutions and the state into conflict. These include polygamy, Sabbath observance, pacifism, and private religious education, to name just a few. Today, there is a great deal of disagreement between the state and religious institutions over the "good" of state contraception programs, sterilization, abortion, and same-sex unions. Governments, particularly the federal government in the Patient Protection and Affordable Care Act ("ACA"),[4] Medicaid, and sex-education policies, have expressed an increasingly sharp preference for birth control, including emergency contraception (which, according to government advisories, can act in some cases as an abortifacient by destroying human embryos), as the answer to the problems of teen births, "unintended pregnancies," and a still-high abortion rate. Federal and state governments are also closely allied with groups—the Planned Parenthood Federation of America in particular—that unfailingly associate easily available birth control and abortion with women's basic equality before the law.

The relatively recent and ongoing campaign in favor of state recognition of same-sex unions has also brought religious institutions and the state into conflict. This campaign is related to the programs discussed in the preceding paragraph, in the sense that both types of programs concern the private and public meanings and consequences of sex. When states decide to recognize a same-sex union as "marriage," they regularly exempt religions from solemnizing same-sex unions (a necessary exemption under the Free Exercise clause), but regularly refuse to offer religious institutions broader protections. Thus various religious institutions serving the public have been required to cease operations, or to change or abrogate their employee benefits structures, as a result of state laws granting recognition to same-sex unions.

The rhetoric on both sides of the current religious freedom debate does not point to a willingness to compromise, to say the least. Criticizing Catholic conscience on abortion, former Speaker of the House Nancy Pelosi charged that Catholics have this "conscience thing," which would effectively let women "die on the floor." She called a bill to amend the ACA to provide more generous conscience protection "savage."[5] In the course of the Maryland debate regarding the legalization of same-sex marriage, the wife of the state's governor publicly called opponents of the law "cowards." [6] For its part, the Catholic hierarchy has repeatedly stated that current narrow conscience exemptions which fail to protect those religious institutions that hire or serve non-Catholics are too narrow for even Jesus Christ to qualify.[7]

When there are conflicts between the state and religious institutions, a great number of difficult and sophisticated questions arise. In 2010, members of the Witherspoon Institute's Task Force on Conscience Protection perceived the need to convene a scholarly consultation specifically focused on "institutional religious freedom." It was clear already that the ACA was fraught with conscience problems. (These remain unresolved at the time of this writing.) The American Civil Liberties Union was at that time entreating the federal government to force all hospitals to perform abortions. Religious social service agencies were closing or reorganizing in the face of same-sex marriage mandates, and the Supreme Court was soon to accept *certiorari* in a case concerning the rights of churches to appoint and remove their own ministers (*Hosanna-Tabor Evangelical Lutheran Church and School* v. *Equal Employment Opportunity Commission*).[8] The task force was more right than it knew, and more right than it wished to be. As 2011 and 2012 unfolded, legal activity affecting institutional religious freedom increased. The Supreme Court issued an opinion in *Hosanna-Tabor*, the Department of Health and Human Services issued a rule that religious institutions had a one-year window to begin providing conscience-violating "health care" services or face debilitating fines, and the Congress repealed the "Don't Ask, Don't Tell" policy on homosexuality in the military, a change leading to disputes about religious freedom for military chaplains and for those religions sponsoring churches on military property.

In June 2011, the Witherspoon Institute convened a meeting of scholars to explore the questions surrounding claims of institutional religious freedom. Scholars from the disciplines of law, theology, philosophy, bioethics, and public policy convened for two days of discussion, centered upon the papers now published in this volume.

The first task was to provide some philosophical, theological, and jurisprudential frameworks for conceiving of a conscience claim, and for distinguishing appeals to *institutional* conscience from those to *individual* conscience. These are necessary not only in order to make more convincingly the legal and social arguments on behalf of institutions' religious freedom, but also for institutions to understand and execute their own collective will. Three papers in this volume pursue these types of questions. Moral philosopher Bishop Anthony Fisher, O.P. (in the paper that set the stage for the consultation) explores the essential attributes of a conscience plea and the general case for according such pleas both moral and legal weight. He also considers the differences between a polity that might properly value conscience, and those that cannot, as well as the shape of current threats and opportunities regarding respect for religious conscience. Moral philosopher Christopher Tollefsen describes the philosophical and theological grounds for claiming that there is such a thing as "institutional conscience." He also proposes the essential conditions for an institution's claim to possess a "conscience," as well as the moral and political implications of such a claim. He acknowledges and describes the elements of the modern struggle to comprehend and to defer to a claim of "institutional conscience." Physician and ethicist Daniel Sulmasy, O.F.M., distinguishes between a correct understanding of conscience and prevailing incorrect notions, and makes the case for the possibility of an "institutional conscience." He further considers the elements of moral arguments for and against compelling an institution to act against its conscience, and the criteria by which a just and tolerant society could mediate competing conscience claims.

Scholars also took up the subject of the particular legal and public policy dilemmas religious institutions face in the near term. Political philosopher Robert George outlines the medical establishment's willingness to cast political and ethical positions in scientific terms, and even to misrepresent the ends of medicine in order to reach a pre-ordained conclusion regarding "reproductive health." He describes in particular the misuse of the language of "abortion," "health," and "health care," for the purpose of achieving specific political and legislative ends in the health care context.

One legal dilemma looms particularly large, and commanded a great deal of attention during the consultation: post-*Smith*, in states lacking either "religious freedom restoration" acts, or strong and specific constitutional protections for religious freedoms, religious actors are often left to win their conscience protections from the legislature. But how to explain "institutional" religious freedom to a lawmaker? Or to the public? Law professor Gerard Bradley suggests an approach. Drawing upon widely shared understandings of human nature, religion, and God, Bradley delineates a new way of speaking to legislators about how institutional religious ministries contribute to the good of individuals, groups, and whole communities.

Even good arguments advancing many reasons for allowing religious exemptions are often shouted down today in the name of "equality," or "freedom," or "health." These are difficult confrontations, as it can seem, falsely, that there is no way to move past competing claims of "freedom" or even "human rights." U.S. Conference of Catholic Bishops (USCCB) official Richard Doerflinger suggests ways to respond to such claims, especially in connection with laws concerning contraception, emergency contraception, or abortion. He offers a variety of arguments demonstrating that these claims are logically and scientifically erroneous.

Anthony Picarello, counsel to the USCCB, addresses the fundamental problem with an important category of laws threatening religious freedom today: legislation claiming to remedy "discrimination," and using purely secular (often ideological) definitions of discrimination to stigmatize and ban traditional religious practices. Lawmakers simply ignore the evidence that the practices they stigmatize are not only constitutive of the religions themselves, but also associated with human flourishing, not the destruction of the common good, as they claim. Picarello describes a response involving better legislative drafting in order to avoid the demonization of various religious practices.

Should religious institutions fail to win a statutory exemption, and fail to win a "free exercise" claim in a post-*Smith* world, some have suggested an appeal to other constitutional doctrines, including the right of association and religions' right to control doctrine and ministerial appointments. Law professor Michael Moreland's essay considers the advantages to religious institutions offered by both avenues, and their potential superiority as compared to claims based on analogies to free exercise claims brought by individuals. Law professor Steven D. Smith is more skeptical of the possibility for successful recourse to alternative constitutional avenues in order to preserve institutional religious freedom. His essay considers the demise of the notion of the "freedom of the church"—the idea that the state ought to leave to religion certain matters acknowledged to be beyond its competence. He argues that this notion is increasingly supplanted today not only by the idea that the state has superior competence on myriad subjects, but also by the emerging conviction that government should strike a balance that preserves society as a "secular space." Smith is not sanguine about the revival of anything resembling the "freedom of the Church," or the possibilities for the success of religious institutions' freedom of association claims. Rather, he proposes ways in which a liberal democratic state valuing individual freedom would be better off recognizing that religion possesses a jurisdiction of its own.

Finally, Allen Hertzke introduces a promising line of reasoning for advancing institutional religious freedom. It is a new body of research indicating the important social value of religious freedom. Various empirical researchers are able to show the link between the presence of religious freedom in a society and a variety of social goods including freedom of the press, the formation of mediating institutions, civil liberties, women's equality, economic development, and peace and stability. Hertzke points out the continuing importance, for the progress of *international* religious freedom, of robust *domestic* religious freedom in the United States.

Together, the essays in this volume treat the leading questions determining the future of institutional religious freedom in the United States. They clarify the essential terminology, gather the extant law and competing arguments, delineate the stakes, and propose solutions. They are offered in the spirit of service to the common good in the United States.

In addition to the authors included herein, many others have been instrumental in the completion of this volume. This includes the staff of the Witherspoon Institute, in particular Professor Matthew Franck. It also includes the membership of the Task Force on Conscience Protection: Professors Gerard Bradley, Michael Moreland, Robert George, V. Bradley Lewis, O. Carter Snead, and Dr. Yuval Levin. Professor Christopher Tollefsen and Dr. Farr Curlin also provided frequent and significant assistance in shaping the consultation.

ENDNOTES

1   See Pew Forum on Religion and Public Life, Religious Landscape Survey, Belief in God or Universal Spirit by Religious Tradition, at http://religions.pewforum.org/pdf/table-belief-in-god-or-universal-spirit-by-religious-tradition.pdf.; Pew Forum on Religion and Public Life: Religion Among the Millennials, at http://www.pewforum.org/Age/Religion-Among-the-Millennials.aspx#affiliation.

2   494 U.S. 872 (1990).

3   *Ibid.*, 879.

4   Pub.L. 111–148, 124 Stat. 119, to be codified as amended at scattered sections of the Internal Revenue Code and in 42 U.S.C.

5   Melinda Henneberger, "Princess Nancy Pelosi" calls Cain "clueless"; vows to do more for childcare, *Washington Post*, 15 November 2011, at http://www.washingtonpost.com/lifestyle/style/princess-nancy-pelosivows-to-do-for-child-care-what-we-did-for-health-care/2011/11/15/gIQACzY1VN_story_1.html.

6   Ruth Fine, "Maryland first lady issues apology for calling marriage opponents 'cowards,'" *San Diego LGBT Weekly*, 30 January 2012, at http://lgbtweekly.com/2012/01/30/maryland-first-lady-issues-apology-for-calling-gay-marriage-opponents-%E2%80%98cowards/.

7   Timothy Cardinal Dolan, "Obama Care and Religious Freedom," *Wall Street Journal*, 25 January 2012, at http://online.wsj.com/article/SB10001424052970203718504577178833194483196.html.

8   That case has since been decided at 132 S. Ct. 694 (2012). In a unanimous decision, the Court held that a Lutheran congregation was within its rights under a "ministerial exception" grounded in the First Amendment's Free Exercise Clause, to terminate the employment of a "called" teacher.

Chapter One

Freedom of Conscience
and Institutional Integrity

Anthony Fisher

Threats to freedom of conscience

*Now the tyrant Antiochus sent an Athenian senator to compel the Jews
to forsake the laws of God and of their fathers. The Gentiles filled the
Temple with debauchery and reveling. They dallied there with harlots
and covered the altar with abominations. A man could neither keep holy
the Sabbath nor so much as confess himself to be a Jew . . .*

*But there was an elderly man of noble bearing named Eleazar. He
was one of the chief scribes. They tried to make him eat pork [which is
against God's holy law]. But he would rather die with honor than live
unholy. So he courageously resolved to refuse, even if it would cost him
his life. Now some Gentile friends took Eleazar aside and urged him se-
cretly to bring his own meat and pretend that he was eating the Gentile
sacrifice, so that he might be saved from execution. But making a high
resolve, worthy of his years and dignity and virtuous life, and in keeping
with God's holy law, he responded quickly that he would rather go to
Hell. "Such a sham would be especially unworthy at my time of life," he
said. "Why, our young people might think that Eleazar in his ninetieth
year has given up his faith! For the sake of living just a little longer, I
would disgrace my old age and lead them astray. Though I might for a
while avoid the punishment of men, yet I shall not escape the hands of
the Almighty."*

*When he had said this, he went at once to the rack. His Gentile
friends now turned against him, for they considered his scruples sheer
madness. As he was dying the old man said, "God knows, though I suffer*

torments in my body, yet I rejoice in my soul to endure such things out of reverence for Him." In this way old father Eleazar died, leaving in his death an example of nobility and a memorial of courage, a lesson not only to the young but to us all. (2 Macc 6:1–31)

Pressures today to act against our conscience are generally more subtle than they were in Eleazar's day. Leaders, senators, and friends may be just as active as they ever were in pressing people to compromise their beliefs, but the rhetoric is now about "providing the full range of mandated services," "anti-discrimination," "reproductive health," and "separation of church and state." The sanctions, too, are more subtle: rather than being literally stripped naked, racked, and skinned alive *(cf. 4 Macc. ch. 6)*, people of conscience may suffer exposure and flaying by media or government inquiry; rather than threats of earthly demise, they may be threatened with professional or institutional oblivion.

From the 1960s, the revolution in Western attitudes to sex, life, marriage, and family played out in the growing tolerance of behaviors previously regarded as immoral. By the 1980s this social, legal, and professional tolerance was increasingly becoming formal recognition and reward. And by the first decade of the new century, this tolerance and recognition were increasingly becoming *intolerance* of anyone who still wants to follow the classical norms. Let me give a few examples.

Abortion was traditionally regarded as abhorrent by the medical profession, but from the 1960s onwards was openly practiced by a few physicians and referred for by many others. Legal toleration preceded a spiraling of numbers of abortions and increased social acceptability, followed by even greater legal and professional toleration, and pressure from powerful lobbies for legalization across the board and easy access. In some places, having performed and being willing to perform abortions has become a *sine qua non* for graduation in or practice of medicine of the Ob-Gyn specialty.[1] In 2008 the state of Victoria, Australia, passed the Abortion Law Reform Act allowing abortion on demand up to birth, requiring doctors who object to abortion on conscientious grounds to refer patients to others without such scruples, and also requiring all health professionals to perform or assist in abortions in "emergencies." *Catholic* hospitals were clearly the principal institutional targets of this law, and pro-life medical students and practitioners the non-institutional targets. Neither that state's Charter of Human Rights and Responsibilities nor the international human rights instruments to which Australia is a party proved any obstacle to making such a draconian law; few citizens understood what was being passed into law and even politicians were bewildered.[2] Meanwhile the Royal Australian and New Zealand College of Obstetricians and Gynaecologists, like its counterparts in the United States, Canada, and elsewhere, acquiesced in the erosion of its members' professional autonomy, implying that physicians should park their ethics outside their surgeries.[3]

Around the same time but on the other side of the world, Britain's Equality Act (Sexual Orientation) Regulations (2007) prohibited "discrimination" on the basis of sexual orientation when it came to a wide range of activities including adoption. The regulations required the eleven Catholic adoption agencies in Britain to mediate adoptions for same-sex couples or at least refer such couples to a willing adoption agency.[4] Despite appeals to the Charity Commission, all these organizations have been forced either to close or disaffiliate from the Church.[5] Similar provisions have been made in other jurisdictions such as the state of Massachusetts, which led to the closure of the Boston Catholic Charities adoption service. The new regulation in Britain came around the same time that a Christian couple was fined for refusing to rent a double-bed room to a same-sex pair in their hotel, and a Christian doctor was sacked from the UK Advisory Council on the Misuse of Drugs because he had previously said that while most homosexuals are not pedophiles, a disproportionate number of pedophiles are homosexual.[6] Not only are such views, however conscientiously held, no longer tolerated, but people with such views may now be denied a livelihood.

In the meantime, across the Atlantic, a nurse working at Mount Sinai Hospital in New York City alleges she was forced to participate in a late-term abortion, despite her prior written conscientious objection. When she filed a grievance, hospital management apparently tried to coerce her into signing a consent to participate in future abortions. The federal court held that despite various conscience protection statutes, the nurse had no remedy at law.[7]

Some believe that the unwillingness of administrations and courts to enforce conscience protections found in international, national, and state laws has rendered them effectively null.[8] In its dying days, the Bush administration sought to strengthen and ensure a process for implementing these longstanding laws, but the Obama Administration has now rescinded that regulation. President Obama insists that his administration intends to "increase awareness of the conscience statutes, work to ensure compliance with them, and require that government grants make clear that compliance is required."[9] But the rescission of the 2008 regulation has only increased the determination of some to enact additional legal protections against "bureaucratic assaults" on the conscience of health workers, such as the No Taxpayer Funding for Abortion Act,[10] the Protect Life Act,[11] the Abortion Non-Discrimination Act[12] and the Respect for Rights of Conscience Act.[13]

Late last year the Parliamentary Assembly of the Council of Europe moved in the opposite direction from President Obama by restating and strengthening the right to conscientious objection in medical care already clear in many member states' legislation. Resolution 1763 provides, "No person, hospital or institution shall be coerced, held liable or discriminated against in any manner because of a refusal to perform, accommodate, assist or submit to an abortion, the performance of a human miscarriage, or euthanasia or any act which could cause the death of a human fetus or embryo, for any reason."[14] However, the same resolution includes the two increasingly customary exceptions to conscience protection in abortion: that the health professional with a conscientious objection to abortion must personally participate in cases of emergency and must otherwise refer to someone who is willing to provide the service.[15]

At the heart of such resolutions is the idea of *conscience* and the *rights of conscience*. But what do we mean by *conscience*? I have examined the history and meaning of conscience at length elsewhere.[16] Here I offer the summary definition that conscience is the ability of the human person to reason to identify relevant moral principles and apply them to a particular situation so as to yield a concrete judgment of what must be done, must not be done, or may be done. By distinction, in popular culture, many believe conscience is about being true to yourself and making your own decisions. So you can be "in good conscience" even while doing some rather bad things. I simply tell myself that such things are not really *so* bad, don't *feel* so bad, or are not so bad *for me*, or not so bad *by comparison* with what other people do. I might also conclude that they lead to good results, or that I am still a good person *deep down*. Anyway, it's no one else's business to judge, and there's no agreed standard by which anyone could. My conscience is "clear" so others had better get used to it. In this usage, *conscience* becomes little more than a high-sounding name for *willfulness,* just another instance of liberal modernity's project of asserting freedom from every constraint.[17]

The idea of "collective" or "institutional" conscience will be examined by others in this volume. While it is an analogous use of the word, it does apply where joint decisions, projects, and activities are engaged in by groups, especially groups established over a long period with a particular mission. In popular usage, however, talk of institutional conscience can be as vacuous as the common uses of "individual conscience"; it is identified as mere strong preference, with the added difficulty that it is not clear who is making the decisions and how, or who bears the moral responsibility and so whose conscience is at stake. But Church institutions, for instance, do from time to time seek to rely on their religious credentials so as to be excused from some duty imposed on other citizens or institutions. In a "post-Christian" world, where external pressures to behave otherwise are common, such retreat to appeals of institutional conscience may be increasingly commonplace.

But the question remains: why on earth would we take each other's consciences so seriously? Why is an appeal to *conscience* often a conversation-stopper and even an excuse for not doing what is otherwise required by law, custom or funding policy? What is the proper reach of pleas of conviction? What are we to make of the contemporary trend to restrict freedom of religious belief and moral conscience and to require everyone, without exception, to abide by the reigning ideology with respect to easy access to sex, contraception, sterilization, abortion, IVF, adoption, drugs, gender reassignment, assisted suicide, euthanasia, a new definition of "marriage," and so on? How are we to assert the rights of religion and conscience both for individuals and institutions, against the tsunami of dogmatic secularism sweeping the West—especially at a time when many believers are as confused as everyone else about these matters? In the rest of this chapter I will identify eleven aspects of a plea to conscience that might, individually or together, highlight for supporters and skeptics alike what is at stake in our current context and on what basis one should evaluate such pleas.

1. The right to conscience as part of or associated with *freedom of thought, religion, belief, and practice*

In the world of human rights talk, appeals to conscience and to conscientious objection are common. The First Amendment of the United States Constitution seeks to limit government interference in the freedoms of religion, speech, press, and assembly, and there is a long jurisprudence about how this might ground effective pleas of liberty of religious and moral belief and action. The Universal Declaration of Human Rights declares, "Everyone has the right to freedom of thought, conscience and religion; this right includes freedom to change his religion or belief, and freedom, either alone or in community with others and in public or private, to manifest his religion or belief in teaching, practice, worship and observance."[18] The International Covenant on Civil and Political Rights,[19] the European Convention on Human Rights,[20] the Canadian Charter of Rights and Freedoms,[21] the Charter of Fundamental Rights of the European Union,[22] and the state of Victoria's Charter of Human Rights and Responsibilities[23] all provide for freedom of thought, conscience, religion, and belief, including the freedom to have, adopt, change, demonstrate, practice, and teach such beliefs, free of coercion. While all these documents focus on the rights of individuals, they may also have application to associations of individuals, including health care, welfare and educational institutions.

Thus international law and the natural law philosophy underpinning it propose a fairly robust doctrine of moral conscience and the respect that it is due. This is closely associated with liberty of thought, religion, and belief. Conscriptions for military or abortion service are the two most commonly recognized situations where people have successfully made pleas of conscientious objection.[24] Though commonly associated with opposite poles of politics and society, the pacifists and pro-lifers run together to the altar and say the word "'conscience," hoping to receive sanctuary. Should they? When and why?

2. Conscience pleas are *moral* claims

Whatever conscience means here, it cannot mean refusing to do my job when I don't like it, or even when I very, very, very much dislike it. To plead the right to do what others do not want us to do, or not to do something others want us to do, *on conscientious grounds* is a different kind of plea from an aesthetic one or a statement of taste or preference, or an objection due to inconvenience, discomfort, or even abhorrence. Rather, to plead conscience in these situations is to plead a *moral* reason for wanting to do what others do not want us to do or for not wanting to do what others would have us do. This is the most important aspect of individual and corporate pleas of conscience properly understood.

Thus Eleazar reasoned that to do other than what he believed to be right would be to act against God, bring dishonor on himself, compromise his ability to give witness to the young, confirm malefactors in their wrongdoing, lead others into evil, and invite God's just punishment. In the First World War, conscientious objectors were expected to show that their objection was not cowardice or treason, by giving an account of the *principles* by which they concluded they could not fight, and demonstrating a course of conduct consistent with those principles; for example, that they had attended Quaker meetings even before the war started. The European Court of Human Rights pointed out in 1982 that a plea of conscience will only be taken seriously when the conviction or belief that motivates it proceeds "from a sufficiently structured, coherent and sincere system of thought."[25] Likewise the House of Lords held in 2005 that for pleas of religious or moral belief to be taken into account, they must be "consistent with elemental standards of human dignity" and be grounded in a coherent system of beliefs.[26]

3. Conscience pleas presume a certain *moral anthropology*

All of this only makes sense if one has *a fairly high view of conscience*. The Christian tradition holds such a high view of conscience, for reasons that I have elaborated at length elsewhere.[27] This high view of conscience, however, itself presumes a particular theological or philosophical *anthropology*.[28] Following the teachings of St. Thomas Aquinas,

Blessed John Henry Newman, and others, the Second Vatican Council taught that:

* human dignity consists in being creatures who by nature have the God-like ability to reason and choose; thus human beings are bound to seek, embrace, and live the truth faithfully;[29]

* every normally functioning human agent has the capacity to know and apply the fundamental principles of conscience, that inner "tribunal" that mediates a universal moral law that is externally given rather than privately invented;[30]

* thus conscience summons persons to inscribe the moral law in every aspect of life by seeking good and avoiding evil, loving God and neighbor, keeping the commandments and universal norms of morality;[31]

* to follow a well-formed conscience is not merely a right but a duty; persons are judged according to how they form and follow particular judgments of conscience;[32]

* whether due to their own fault or not, agents may err in matters of conscience;[33] thus Catholics should seek to conform their consciences to the divine law mediated by the Church's teaching office;[34]

* pressures from personal preference, civil laws or superiors, the market, or community expectations do not excuse a failure to abide by the universal principles of conscience;[35] and

* freedom of thought, including moral conscience and religious belief, should be respected by civil authorities, and people should not be coerced in matters of religion.[36]

While eschewing the religious basis of these claims, international and national human rights instruments likewise assume a particular philosophical anthropology: of the human being as born equal, with intellect and free will. Thus the very first article of the Universal Declaration of Human Rights declares that "[a]ll human beings are born free and equal in dignity and rights. They are endowed with reason and conscience and should act towards one another in a spirit of brotherhood."

A lower anthropology of human persons and their ability to reason about what is right for them to do is unlikely to yield such a robust view of conscience and pleas of conscience. At best, a kind of "live and let live" tolerance is proposed, at least until the old-style "liberal" political philosophies are superseded by the more dogmatic secularist and relativist worldview. For the time being, liberal respect for conscience may look like the classical view of the human person and the respect due to moral agency, but, in Alasdair MacIntyre's terms, this is merely a post-moral-holocaust fragment, and so is very insecurely grounded.[37]

4. Conscience pleas are usually acts of resistance to perceived evil

Though conscience talk has a long and noble history, it received particular attention after the Second World War, in which many people had been pressed to conform to grave evils or suffer terrible consequences. Thus the 1948 Universal Declaration of Human Rights recognized that "disregard and contempt for human rights have resulted in barbarous acts which have outraged the conscience of mankind, and the advent of a world in which human beings shall enjoy freedom of speech and belief and freedom from fear and want has been proclaimed as the highest aspiration of the common people."[38] This points to a fourth aspect of pleas of conscience: that while they may in principle be raised to seek opportunity or permission to do that which conscience counsels, they are more often raised against pressures to do that which conscience counsels *against*. They are, thus, *acts of resistance* to some perceived evil. So Eleazar refused to do that which the state commanded and his fair-weather friends counseled him to do—not out of stubbornness or convenience, but on the basis of his best moral reasoning about what morally he could and could not do.

5.   Conscience pleas are *the price of one's "soul"*

People do not plead conscience against being asked to work an extra half hour on a busy day, even if this has moral aspects. Rather, as the House of Lords observed in 2005, people normally make public pleas of conscience only with respect to "fundamental problems" that have a "certain degree of seriousness and importance" and not to "trivial questions."[39] Thus a fifth dimension of conscience pleas is that they are made in the face of what the agent believes is fundamental, a matter that goes to heart of that person's or institution's identity or "soul," what the Second Vatican Council called the "inner sanctuary" or what even doyens of secular liberalism such as Ronald Dworkin might call "the sacred."[40] There are some aspects of our world and ourselves so precious, mysterious, and awe-inspiring that they can evoke a kind of genuflection even in the atheist and ground for them some "I would never do's," whatever the consequences. To ask me or my institution to do *that* would be to ask us to cease to exist as ourselves. It would really amount to requiring us to shut down. We expect all human beings to grasp the seriousness of this.

But what would one *never* do? What goes so deeply against our sense of who we are? Eleazar would rather die than do what he thought would effectively "un-Jew" him. Before him, Socrates thought some wrongs were so grave that we must be willing to suffer them rather than perpetrate them.[41] His contemporary, Hippocrates, in defining the medical profession, swore by all the gods: "I will do my best to prescribe only what is good for my patients and to harm none. So I will prescribe no lethal drug, even with consent, and never give a woman an abortifacient." Hippocrates, Socrates and Eleazar all foreshadowed what Christ taught about purity of heart (*Mt* 5:8), not being a *skandalon* to the little ones (*Mt* 18:6) and, if need be, forsaking one's very life in order to save it (*Mt* 16:24–26; *Lk* 9:24–25). For Jews and Christians, as for the best of pagans, refusal to engage in abortion and infanticide would, among other things, distinguish them from their neighbors.[42] They were willing to suffer economic disadvantage, professional diminution, public humiliation, even criminal penalty rather than do such things. What made physicians medical *professionals* rather than hired guns or witch doctors was not their techniques, which were often similar, but rather their *profession* to do no harm whatever the pressures of the market or the bosses.[43] So appalled was the world that doctors had turned coat on this profession of faith and morals that they were held to account at the Nuremberg trials alongside the politicians, judges, and generals.[44]

6. Conscience pleas are *claims for exemption*

I have suggested that pleas of conscience mean exercising moral agency in resistance to strong external pressures to commit what one reasons are grave moral evils, especially in matters going to a person's or institution's religious or professional "soul." They commonly involve a sixth element: a claim for exemption from being compelled to do the act and a hope for immunity from sanction for refusing to do so. Thus those conscripted for military service who can show that they are genuinely religiously or morally opposed to military action have often been exempted from service, though they might be required to contribute to the common good in this emergency in some other way. In part this tolerance might reflect the fact that soldiers who are actively opposed to war do not make good soldiers and may undermine the confidence of others. But there is also a willingness to exempt people from acting contrary to their deepest beliefs in such a serious matter.

Thus not only did traditional medical and nursing ethics require doctors and nurses to abstain from abortion, euthanasia, and public executions, but even societies that condoned such practices have normally exempted health professionals conscientiously opposed to such practices from taking part without suffering penalty. Indeed, until recently even those most vocally committed to abortion "rights" did not seek to compel others to be involved; rather, they sought to ensure that those who wanted to have an abortion be free to approach those who were willing to perform them. Hence the rhetoric of "pro-choice."

Having an ethical objection on a serious matter tolerated as an "exemption"—indeed a kind of social eccentricity—is hardly ideal, but it is better than nothing. In the face of the advancing "culture of death," the Catholic Church has in recent years sought to ensure that, at the very least, there be some exemption for those with conscientious objections.[45] Popes, bishops, and curia have taught that abortion and euthanasia are homicides no civil law can legitimize; that same-sex marriage and adoption are direct attacks upon marriage and family; that while we might sometimes obey unjust laws for the sake of the common good, the good of the community could never be served by killing its most innocent and vulnerable members (the unborn and the dying), or by undermining its most basic cell, the marriage-based family; that there is a grave obligation to oppose, reform, or at least ameliorate laws permitting or promoting such wrongs; that professionals are bound conscientiously to object when they are pressured to engage in such practices; and that any state or profession worthy of the name should recognize their right to do so.[46]

7. Conscience pleas are claims for exemption from wrongdoing *and also from unethically cooperating* in someone else's wrongdoing

In some places the look of liberalism is maintained by saying no one is forced to perform abortions or mediate same-sex adoptions or whatever; rather they are expected to refer people seeking such assistance to someone else who will. This draws attention to a seventh aspect of conscience pleas: the person who makes them usually objects not only to engaging in the particular activity as principal agent but also objects to participating in formal or unethical material cooperation in the same activity. When Eleazar's gentile friends suggested that he avoid eating the unkosher and sacrilegious meat by engaging in an elaborate ruse, he recognized that keeping clean hands and a (formally) pure heart were not enough: he must also consider how even (materially) cooperating would endanger his own soul and those of innocent bystanders. If the Gestapo come to the door asking where the Jews are, few would find satisfactory the answer "I won't tell you where they are, but I'll tell you someone who will." It is no consolation to those who believe some activity is deeply immoral that they will (for now) be free not to do it as long as they delegate it to someone else who will. Medical referral for abortion is usually formal cooperation in evil and always at least impermissible material cooperation.[47]

Why do I say that institutions or individuals who refer for abortion usually cooperate formally in evil—something that is never ethically permissible? Consider the case of a hospital whose staff refers a patient to another institution for some unambiguously *good* procedure such as a heart transplant. Why would the institution do that? Presumably so the proposed intervention can be better provided by that other institution. The management and staff referring the patient therefore share in the object, end, or will of those to whom they refer the patient: they will be thwarted if the other institution fails to do the procedure or provide for some suitable alternative. The same is normally so when those working for an institution refer a patient for a morally dubious intervention.[48] This is true even if those doing the referring say they are personally, even publicly, opposed to abortion, would never have or perform one themselves, find the very idea abhorrent, etc.[49]

Someone might claim that such referring is merely material cooperation: the referrer's object, end, or willing would in no way be thwarted if the referee failed to perform the abortion. But if the referral is *for abortion* to a doctor who they know will perform or facilitate an abortion, this is hardly credible. Even *were* this merely material cooperation it would not in my view be permissible.[50] Given that the foreseeable results would include the death of an innocent child, the moral and spiritual damage to the abortionist and collaborators, the additional physical and psychological damage to the woman, the moral scandal to those who follow this example, and the compromise to the referring doctor's ability to witness to the Gospel of Life, it is hard to see what good reason would suffice to warrant even merely material cooperation of this sort.

8. Duress is no exception

The debate over conscience pleas serves to highlight the illogic of those who believe an institution may ethically act contrary to moral norms if that institution is suffering "duress" from law or insurers. Conscience pleas involve precisely the recognition that there are things an institution (or individual) cannot do, whatever the pressures, without ceasing to exercise agency with integrity. Following the Congregation for the Doctrine of the Faith's 1975 prohibition on Catholic hospitals performing direct sterilizations,[51] the U.S. bishops' 1994 Ethical Directives originally included an Appendix on cooperation that allowed material cooperation in procedures such as abortion and sterilization in the face of these sorts of pressures.[52] Following criticism from theologians and the Vatican, the U.S. bishops directed an appendectomy of the Directives and the inclusion of two new directives that made it crystal clear that Catholic health-care institutions, whatever legal, financial, or other pressure they are under, may not cooperate with such practices.

A few academics continue to assert that duress gives Catholic hospitals leeway to cooperate in wrongful activities.[53] But given that Catholic hospitals experience pressure at every point where their ethics differ from those of contemporary culture, the duress exception would, if admitted, invite the abandonment of anything distinctively Catholic in the identity and morality of Catholic health-care institutions; it would excuse acquiescing completely to the culture of death. It would amount to the loss of soul and identity—the death—of the institution. Similar concerns apply to pressures to abandon the erstwhile reservation of sex to marriage, of marriage to a marriageable and consenting man and woman, and of family-making to married couples.

9. Conscience pleas presume a certain kind of *moral polity*

This highlights an eighth aspect of conscience pleas: they presume a certain kind of polity, one that acknowledges deeply held moral and religious convictions as important, permits differences in these matters and, as far as reasonable, allows expression of those differences in actions or inactions on conscientious grounds, without sanctioning those concerned. The state is not, in this view, the ultimate arbiter of good and evil, and is willing to concede that people must obey God before Caesar. That is why the various human rights instruments and the political philosophies that underpin them recognize not only a right to hold different religious or moral convictions, but also rights to express them, not to be compelled to act against them, to be protected in this by the state, and not to be denied this by powerful ideological or economic interests or even the views of majorities.

Such conscience pleas are only likely to carry weight in a morally decent culture, a community of virtuous persons or a polity that aims to make men moral.[54] The classical tradition of natural law, as expressed in the international rights instruments, regarded freedom of thought, conscience, and religion as essential not just to individual human fulfillment but also to the flourishing of communities. A view of the state that puts the human person first, and seeks to serve the common good by ensuring access for all to the necessities for human flourishing, will allow conscience a sort of centrality in law rather than a merely marginal or "exceptional" status, and will exercise a certain flexibility in accommodating serious religious and moral differences.[55] This is not to say such claims will always be trumps: the centrality of the human person and the common good that grounds respect for conscience may also mean that some religious practices, such as child sacrifice, will be forbidden. In a corrupt or tyrannical state, however, such accommodation of dissenters is uncommon and the very idea of conscientious objection is unlikely to work: only a moral entity will condone exemptions for a *moral* reason.

Some liberal political philosophers, from John Locke and John Stuart Mill to John Rawls,[56] while agnostic about the good life, the virtuous person, or the morally decent community, nonetheless favored maximizing people's freedom, especially in the face of deep and apparently irresolvable moral disagreements. If a person's actions, based upon his deep convictions, seriously threatened the common good or the like freedom of others, he might have to be restrained, but otherwise compulsion should be minimized. Traditional liberalism would, therefore, leave Catholic institutions or individual practitioners free *not* to offer certain services, while allowing others to offer those same services. In this view the state should remain neutral on matters such as abortion, neither prohibiting nor compelling it;[57] the "right to (choose) abortion" requires an equal right not to choose it, for pregnant women, health professionals, and health-care institutions.

However, liberalism's diffidence about morality means that in postmodernity, having and following *principles*, internally consistent and embraced over a long period, is not only uncommon but seems "dogmatic" and therefore dangerous, as well as constrictive and unimaginative. In such a context it is harder to explain and maintain earlier liberalism's respect for pleas of conscience. At best we are left with a desire to "get along," leaving each other space to "do our own thing"; at worst we are left with a skeptical or indifferentist denial that there is any truth about things like war and abortion and so we should just "leave well enough alone." Reverence for conscience then reduces to respect for personal tastes—a kind of respect that can be hard to sustain.

10. The kind of moral polity presumed by conscience pleas may be *in decline*

Some say it is the logical unpacking of an earlier liberalism and others that it is a repudiation of the liberal tradition: either way, the examples with which I opened this chapter suggest that contemporary "liberal" democracies are moving in a decidedly *anti-choice* direction that will brook no exemptions for people's convictions. This is an example of a trend that Blessed John Paul II suggested can make democracies no better than tyrannies.[58] Eleazar lived under the imperium of Antiochus IV, who ruled the Seleucid Empire, including Maccabean Israel, from 175 to 164 BC. He knew about democracies and their corruptibility, as it was an Athenian senator that he sent to stamp out Jewish scruples. Antiochus styled himself *Epiphanes*, Manifest God, which cynics mispronounced *Epimanes*, the Mad One. Many mad ones since have made similarly bloated claims for the state's authority over people's beliefs and behavior, made unconscionable demands of institutions and professionals, and followed through with equally cruel punishments for those with principles.

Several ideas conspire to support the view that state-guaranteed abortion or gay "rights" are just too important to allow institutional or personal exemptions. Authoritarianism sometimes likes to dress up in liberal or feminist clothes. Market thinking tells us "the customer is always right," and if there's a demand there should be a reliable and unlimited supply. Medical professional associations, so compromised by decades of collusion in the culture of death, are impotent to protect their own members' professional autonomy. Secularism now proposes an all-embracing state and culture that will not abide any whiff of incense, such as the "sanctity of life" and "sanctity of marriage" ideas that previously informed law and practice. Thus conscientious objection falls victim to the culture wars that now rage over objective truth, faith and reason, religious liberty, human life, dignity, autonomy, sexuality, and the rest. While pleas of conscience may still be allowed from time to time as a kind of concession to oddballs, the very idea of conscience will be marginal at best and often deplored as anti-social. The Bad One wants abortions in Catholic hospitals as much as the Mad One wanted Jews to eat pork: neither will admit any exceptions.

11. Conscience protection is *more necessary* and *less likely* in such societies

If I am right that the kind of moral polity presumed by conscience pleas is in decline, then efforts to entrench respect for conscience in law and social policy will be more necessary than in the past but also less likely to be effective. We should, of course, try to ensure respect for the consciences of health institutions and professionals against being forced to participate in practices such as abortion, of welfare institutions and professionals against being forced to assist in same-sex adoption, and of churches and ministers of religion against being forced to solemnize, as marriages, relationships that are not. But this is largely a fallback position, and we should not be content with the radical decline in the understanding of life, health care, marriage, and family that means Christians must have recourse to playing the "conscience card" on such matters. Because conscience pleas are seen as exemptions or exceptions, we must be aware, also, that the more often we play that card, the less likely others may be to respect it. Hence the attempts to enshrine conscience protection in an ever more solemn, and one hopes effective, series of laws.

The growing need for conscience protection clauses also serves to highlight the greater need to evangelize cultures and educate communities about the moral positions that those pleading conscience are seeking to protect. Until that is more successfully pursued, pleading conscience will often be a sign of the declining influence of Judeo-Christianity, a kind of last gasp. Courts, administrations, professional bodies, and employers will thus continue to feel free to ignore, minimize, and marginalize the very rights conscience clauses seek to protect.

A prayer

Sometimes we have to choose: will I resist doing that which I judge on reasonable grounds to be unethical, and if need be go against what others direct, or will I suspend my judgment, compromise my very identity, and go with the flow of power or opinion, wherever that leads? Eleazar and Socrates, like Christ and the martyrs ever since, *could* have escaped; the plea of *conscience*, properly understood, shows why they *would* not.

I have argued that conscientious objection only makes sense to those with a high view of the human person's ability to reason to and enact the good, a deep reverence for "the sacred" broadly understood, and a willingness to tolerate some moral differences for the sake of the common good. Tyrannies, secular "liberal" ones included, lack such understanding and so are unwilling to allow many pleas of conscience. In denying institutions and professionals the right to raise conscientious objections to performing or referring for abortion, sterilization, same-sex marriage, or same-sex adoption, supposedly liberal societies undermine their grandiloquent talk of "freedom of thought, conscience, and religion."

Yet we must not despair: genuine democracy has not entirely evaporated and might yet return with its Judeo-Christian or at least natural law underpinnings. The rhetoric, at least, has proven very resilient, and the ideals of true democracy still have the power to inspire. In telling the story of Eleazar, the sacred author of Maccabees concluded with a prayerful hope: "I urge those who read this story not to be depressed by such calamities, but to recognize that these trials are designed, not to destroy us, but to direct us. For the Lord never withdraws his mercy from us" (2 *Macc* 6:12–17).

ENDNOTES

1   Maureen Kramlich, "Coercing conscience: The effort to mandate abortion as a standard of care," *National Catholic Bioethics Quarterly* 4:1 (Spring 2004): 29–40; Nikolas Nikas, "Law and public policy to protect healthcare rights of conscience," ibid., 41–52; Margaret Somerville, "Respect for conscience must be a social value," *Mercatornet*, 17 October 2008.

2   Julian McGauran, "Labor's attack on conscience," *Quadrant* LIII:10 (October 2009).

3   See Royal Australian and New Zealand College of Obstetricians and Gynaecologists, "College of Obstetricians and Gynaecologists Backs Victorian Law Reform Commission's Abortion Report," Media Release, May 30, 2008; Margaret Somerville, in "Respect for conscience must be a social value," notes that the Ontario Human Rights Commission has put on record that: "It is the Commission's position that doctors, as providers of services that are not religious in nature, must essentially 'check their personal views at the door' in providing medical care." Robert George, "Aborting

conscience," *Public Discourse*, 9 December 2008, offers a devastating critique of the position of the Ethics Committee of the American College of Obstetricians and Gynecologists; see also his chapter in the present volume.

4   Equality Act (Sexual Orientation) Regulations (2007) Section 15. Rebecca Millette, "Last UK Catholic adoption agency loses appeal over gay adoption," *LifeSiteNews*, 4 May 2011.

5   Adoption by same-sex couples is now legal in Andorra (2005), Argentina (2010), Belgium (2006), Brazil (2010), Denmark (2010), Iceland (2006), Netherlands (2001), Norway (2009), South Africa (2002), Spain (2005), Sweden (2002), United Kingdom (2005 & 2009) and Uruguay (2009), and in various states of Australia (WA, ACT, NSW), Canada, and the United States (DC, NJ, NY, IN, MN, CA, CN, IL, MA, OR, VE, FL). In some but not all of these jurisdictions adoption agencies are forbidden to discriminate on the basis of sexual orientation when allocating children to adopting or fostering parents.

6   John Flynn lc, "Rights versus religion: No tolerance for Christianity," *Zenit* 13 February 2011.

7   *Cenzon-DeCarlo* v. *Mt. Sinai Hospital*, 626 F.3d 695 (2nd Cir. 2010).

8   James Cole, "Have US conscience clause protections been eviscerated?" *MercatorNet*, 29 November 2010.

9   *CNA/EWTN News*, 18 February 2011; *Zenit*, 22 February 2011.

10   H.R. 3, 112th Congress, introduced by Rep. Smith (R-NJ) and Rep. Lipinski (D-IL) and 226 others: to enact the policy of the Hyde amendment on abortion funding, and the Hyde/Weldon amendment on conscience rights, into permanent law for all federal departments and all avenues of federal funding. Approved by the House of Representatives, 251 to 175, on 4 May 2011. Also introduced into the Senate as S. 906 by Sen. Roger Wicker (R-MS) and 28 others.

11   H.R. 358, 112th Congress, introduced by Rep. Pitts (R-PA) and Rep. Lipinski (D-IL) and 141 others: to apply longstanding federal policies on abortion funding, and conscience rights on abortion, to the Patient Protection and Affordable Care Act. Approved by the House Energy and Commerce Committee, 33 to 19, on 17 March 2011. Also introduced into the Senate as S. 877 by Sen. Orrin Hatch (R-UT) and 31 others.

12   H.R. 361, 112th Congress, introduced by Rep. Fleming (R-LA) and Rep. Boren (D-OK) and 78 others: to enact the policy of the Hyde/Weldon amendment into permanent law, by amending the section of the U.S. Code (§238n) that prevents governmental discrimination against ob/gyn

residency programs that do not provide abortion training. Also introduced into the Senate as S. 165 by Sen. David Vitter (R-LA) and 3 others.

13 H.R. 1179, 112th Congress, introduced by Rep. Fortenberry (R-NE) and Rep. Boren (D-OK) and 19 others: to amend the Patient Protection and Affordable Care Act to preserve the right of insurers to negotiate a plan excluding items that are against moral and religious convictions, in the face of new federal "mandated benefits."

14 Council of Europe Resolution 1763 of 2010 on "The right to conscientious objection in lawful medical care," article 1. The resolution also provides that member states must provide appropriate mechanisms for raising conscientious objection, including "a comprehensive and clear legal and policy framework governing the practice of conscientious objection by health-care providers" (article 3) and "comprehensive and clear regulations that define and regulate conscientious objection with regard to health and medical services, and which guarantee the right to conscientious objection in relation to participation in the medical procedure in question" (article 4.1).

15 The Assembly expressed itself "concerned that the unregulated use of conscientious objection may disproportionately affect women, notably those with low incomes or living in rural areas" (article 2). It thus required member states to ensure that "patients are able to access lawful medical care in a timely manner" (article 2), that "the interests and rights of individuals seeking legal medical services are respected, protected and fulfilled" (article 3), that "patients are informed of any conscientious objection in a timely manner and referred to another health-care provider" (article 4.2) and that "patients receive appropriate treatment, in particular in cases of emergency" (article 4.3).

16 Anthony Fisher, OP, "Moral conscience in ethics and the contemporary crisis of authority," in Elio Sgreccia and Jean Laffitte (eds.), *Christian Conscience in Support of the Right to Life* (Vatican City: Libreria Editrice Vaticana, 2008), 37–70.

17 On the problems with this aspiration see, for example, Blessed John Paul II and Benedict XVI both before and during their papacies on the necessary connection between freedom and truth. See also Allan Bloom, *The Closing of the American Mind* (New York: Simon & Schuster, 1987); Robert Bellah, *Habits of the Heart* (New York, Harper & Row, 1985); Robert George, *The Clash of Orthodoxies: Law, Religion, and Morality in Crisis* (Wilmington: ISI, 2002); Stanley Hauerwas, *Dispatches from the Front: Theological Engagements with the Secular* (Durham: Duke University Press, 1994); Christopher Lasch, *The Minimal Self* (London: Norton, 1984); Joyce Little,

The Church and the Culture War: Secular Anarchy or Sacred Order (San Francisco: Ignatius, 1995); Alasdair MacIntyre, *After Virtue*, 3rd ed. (London: Duckworth, 2007); Michael Novak, "Abandoned in a toxic culture," *Crisis* 10 (1992), 16–17; Servais Pinckaers, OP, *The Sources of Christian Ethics* (Washington, D.C.: Catholic University of America Press, 1995); Jeffrey Stout, Alasdair MacIntyre, and Stanley Hauerwas, *The Flight from Authority: Religion, Morality, and the Quest for Autonomy* (South Bend: Notre Dame University Press, 1981); Jeffrey Stout, *Ethics After Babel: The Language of Morals and Their Discontents* (Boston: Beacon, 1988); Charles Taylor, *A Secular Age* (Cambridge: Harvard University Press, 2007).

18 Universal Declaration of Human Rights (1948), Article 18.

19 International Covenant on Civil and Political Rights (1966): "18(1) Everyone shall have the right to freedom of thought, conscience and religion. This right shall include freedom to have or to adopt a religion or belief of his choice, and freedom, either individually or in community with others and in public or private, to manifest his religion or belief in worship, observance, practice and teaching. (2) No one shall be subject to coercion which would impair his freedom to have or to adopt a religion or belief of his choice. (3) Freedom to manifest one's religion or beliefs may be subject only to such limitations as are prescribed by law and are necessary to protect public safety, order, health, or morals or the fundamental rights and freedoms of others." This right may not be waived even in emergencies: Article 4(1).

20 European Convention on Human Rights (1953): "9(1) Everyone has the right to freedom of thought, conscience and religion; this right includes freedom to change his religion or belief, and freedom, either alone or in community with others and in public or private, to manifest his religion or belief, in worship, teaching, practice and observance. (2) Freedom to manifest one's religion or beliefs shall be subject only to such limitations as are prescribed by law and are necessary in a democratic society in the interests of public safety, for the protection of public order, health or morals, or the protection of the rights and freedoms of others."

21 Charter of Rights and Freedoms (Canada) (1982): "2. Everyone has the following fundamental freedoms: *(a)* freedom of conscience and religion; *(b)* freedom of thought, belief, opinion and expression, including freedom of the press and other media of communication; *(c)* freedom of peaceful assembly; and *(d)* freedom of association."

22 Charter of Fundamental Rights of the European Union (2000): "10.1

Everyone has the right to freedom of thought, conscience and religion. This right includes freedom to change religion or belief and freedom, either alone or in community with others and in public or in private, to manifest religion or belief, in worship, teaching, practice and observance. 2. The right to conscientious objection is recognised, in accordance with the national laws governing the exercise of this right."

23   Charter of Human Rights and Responsibilities (Victoria) (2006): "14 (1) Every person has the right to freedom of thought, conscience, religion and belief, including (a) the freedom to have or to adopt a religion or belief of his or her choice; and (b) the freedom to demonstrate his or her religion or belief in worship, observance, practice and teaching, either individually or as part of a community, in public or in private. (2) A person must not be coerced or restrained in a way that limits his or her freedom to have or adopt a religion or belief in worship, observance, practice or teaching."

24   On the history of the conscientious objection idea see: Constance Braithwaite, *Conscientious Objection to Various Compulsions under British Law* (York: Sessions, 1995); Charles Curran (ed.), *Conscience: Readings in Moral Theology No. 14* (New York, Paulist, 2004); Juan Navarro Floria, *El derecho a la objeción de conciencia* (Buenos Aires: Abaco, 2004); Felicity Goodall, *A Question of Conscience: Conscientious Objection in the Two World Wars* (Allan Sutton, 1997); Jean Laffitte, "A history of conscientious objection and different meanings of the concept of tolerance," in Elio Sgreccia and Jean Laffitte (eds.), *Christian Conscience in Support of the Right to Life* (Vatican City: Libreria Editrice Vaticana, 2008),112–139; Margaret Levi, *Consent, Dissent, and Patriotism* (New York: Cambridge University Press, 1997); Michael Noone (ed), *Selective Conscientious Objection: Accommodating Conscience and Security* (Boulder: Westview Press, 1989); Martha Nussbaum, *Liberty of Conscience: In Defense of America's Tradition of Religious Equality* (New York: Basic Books, 2008); Ignasi Durany Pich, *Objeciones de conciencia* (Pamplona: Navarra Grafica Ediciones, 1998); Anders Schinkel, *Conscience and Conscientious Objections* (Amsterdam UP, 2007), esp Part III; Michel Schooyans,"L'objection de conscience en matière de santé: le cas des homes politiques," *Revue de la Recherche Juridique* 2005(1), 505ff; Harold Schulweis, *Conscience: The Duty to Obey and the Duty to Disobey* (Woodstock, VT: Jewish Lights, 2008); Hitomi Takemura, *The International Human Right to Conscientious Objection* (New York: Springer, 2008); Rafael Navarro-Valls and Javier Martínez Torrón, *Conflictos entre conciencia y ley: Las objeciones de conciencia*" (Madrid: Editorial Iustel, 2011).

25 *De Jong, Baljet and Van Den Brink* v. *the Netherlands* (1982) Strasbourg Application no. 8805/79; 8806/79; 9242/81 (Eur Comm. H.R.).

26 *R. (on the application of Williamson)* v. *Secretary of State for Education and Employment* UKHL 15; [2005] 2 A.C. 246. *Cf.* Navarro-Valls and MartínezTorrón, *Conflictos entre conciencia y ley.*

27 Fisher, "Moral conscience in ethics and the contemporary crisis of authority." Other recent writers on conscience include Joseph Ratzinger, "Conscience and truth," *Values in a Time of Upheaval,* trans. B McNeil (New York: Crossroad / Ignatius, 2006), 75–100; and "Conscience in its age," *Church, Ecumenism, and Politics* (New York: Crossroads, 1987), 165–79; Eric D'Arcy, *Conscience and Its Right to Freedom* (London: Sheed & Ward, 1961); Germain Grisez, *The Way of the Lord Jesus,* vol 1: *Christian Moral Principles* (Chicago: Franciscan Herald Press, 1983), 73–114; William E. May, "Conscience and our moral life," *An Introduction to Moral Theology,* 2nd ed. (Huntington: Our Sunday Visitor, 2003), 57–64; Martin Rhonheimer, "Natural moral law, moral knowledge and conscience," in Juan Correa and Elio Sgreccia, eds., *The Nature and Dignity of the Human Person as the Foundation of the Right to Life* (Libreria Editrice Vaticana, 2003), 123–59; Thomas Williams, *Knowing Right from Wrong: A Christian Guide to Conscience* (New York: FaithWords, 2008).

28 Tom Ryan, "Conscience as primordial awareness in *Gaudium et spes* and *Veritatis Splendor,*" *Australian ejournal of Theology* 18(1) (2011), for instance, suggests "participation in divine value through affective connaturality" underpins much of the conscience tradition.

29 Vatican II, *Dignitatis humanæ:* Declaration on Religious Freedom (1965) §§ 1 and 2.

30 Vatican II, *Dignitatis humanæ*§3; *Gaudium et spes:* Pastoral Constitution on the Church in the Modern World (1965) §§ 16 and 41.

31 Vatican II, *Gaudium et spes* §§ 16, 43, 74, 79; *cf. Lumen Gentium:* Dogmatic Constitution on the Church (1964) § 36; *Apostolicam Actuositatem:* Decree on the Apostolate of the Laity (1965) §5; *Dignitatis humanæ:* Declaration on Religious Freedom (1965) § 3; *cf.Catechism of the Catholic Church* § 1777.

32 Vatican II, *Gaudium et spes* § 16; *Dignitatis humanæ* §§ 1 and 11; *cf.CCC* § 1778.

33 Vatican II, *Gaudium et spes* §§ 8, 16, 43, 47 and 50.

34 Vatican II,*Gaudium et spes* §§ 31, 50, 87; *Gravissimum educationis:* Declaration on Christian Education (1965) § 1; *Apostolicam Actuositatem* § 20; *Inter mirifica:* Decree on the Means of Social Communication (1963) §§ 9 and 21; *Dignitatis humanæ* §§ 8 and 14.

35 Vatican II, *Gaudium et spes* § 79; *Dignitatis humanæ* § 8.

36 Vatican II, *Dignitatis humanæ,* esp. § 3;*Gaudium et spes* § 79; *Gravissimum educationis* §§ 1, 6, 8.

37 I here refer to MacIntyre's famous analogy in *After Virtue.*

38 Universal Declaration of Human Rights (1948), Preamble.

39 *R. (on the application of Williamson) v. Secretary of State for Education and Employment,* UKHL 15; [2005] 2 A.C. 246.

40 Ronald Dworkin, *Life's Dominion: An Argument About Abortion, Euthanasia, and Individual Freedom* (New York: Knopf, 1993). On the extension of conscientious objection from religious to secular moral refusal, see: Charles Moskos and John Whiteclay, eds., *The New Conscientious Objection: From Sacred to Secular Resistance* (OUP, 1993).

41 Reported in Plato's *Gorgias.*

42 John Connery, *Abortion: The Development of the Roman Catholic Perspective* (Chicago: Loyola University Press, 1977); J. H. Channer, ed., *Abortion and the Sanctity of Human Life* (Exeter: Paternoster, 1985); Daughters of St. Paul, eds., *Yes to Life: Source-book of Catholic Teaching on the Sacredness of Human Life* (Boston: St. Paul, 1977); Dennis Di Mauro, *A Love for Life: Christianity's Consistent Protection of the Unborn* (Eugene, OR: Wipf and Stock, 2008); Michael Gorman, *Abortion and the Early Church* (Eugene, OR: Wipf and Stock, 1998); Society for the Protection of Unborn Children, *Love Your Unborn Neighbour* (London: SPUC, 1994).

43 Leon Kass, *Toward a More Natural Science* (New York: Free Press, 1985);

44 See George Annas and Michael Grodin, *The Nazi Doctors and the Nuremburg Code: Human Rights in Human Experimentation* (New York: Oxford University Press, 1992); Robert Lifton, *The Nazi Doctors: Medical Killing and the Psychology of Genocide* (New York: Basic Books, 1986). The Nuremburg Courts thought that all people were subject to (and implicitly knew) divine laws or laws of practical reason that specify certain acts as ones no one should ever do. Thus much of the natural law, including the human rights tradition, made its way into international and national law after the Second World War, if it had not already.

45 On conscientious objection in areas such as warfare, civil laws on divorce, homosexuality, and adoption see John Paul II, "Address to the Roman Rota," 28 January 2002; Benedict XVI, "Address to the New Ambassador of the Slovak Republic to the Holy See," 13 September 2007; Congregation for the Doctrine of the Faith, *Considerations on Proposals to Give Legal Recognition to Unions between Homosexual Persons* (2003), § 5; Synod of Bishops, *Justice in the World* (1971), § 65.

46 On conscientious objection to anti-life practices, see John Paul II, "Message for the XXIV World Day of Peace: If You Want Peace, Respect the Conscience of Every Person," 1 January 1991; *Evangelium Vitæ: Encyclical on the Value and Inviolability of Human Life* (1995), § 73; "Address to Italian Catholic Doctors," 25 November 1995, § 4; "Address to a Congress of Catholic Doctors," 7 July 2000, § 3; "Address to the International Congress of Catholic Obstetricians and Gynecologists," 18 June 2001, § 3; Benedict XVI, "Address to an International Congress of Catholic Pharmacists," 29 October 2007; "Address to the Members of the Diplomatic Corps," 10 January 2011; Congregation for the Doctrine of the Faith, *DonumVitæ: Instruction on Respect for Human Life in its Origin and on the Dignity of Procreation* (1987), Part III; *Dignitas Personae: Instruction on Certain Bioethical Questions* (2008), § 35; Pontifical Council for Health Professionals,Charter for Healthworkers (1995), § 144; Pontifical Academy for Life, "Final Declaration by the 13th General Assembly" (2007); Catholic Bishops Conference of England and Wales, *Cherishing Life* (London: Catholic Truth Society, 2004), § 52, 205–207; Catholic Health Australia, Code of Ethical Standards for Catholic Health and Aged Care Services in Australia (2001), §7.19. While the United States Conference of Catholic Bishops, *Ethical and Religious Directives for Catholic Health Care Services*, 5th ed. (Washington, D.C.: USCCB, 2009) does not specifically address conscientious objection and conscience protection, it repeatedly asserts the right and duty of Catholic institutions and professionals to refuse to engage in activities that are unjust, anti-life, anti-family etc.

47 On cooperation in evil see: Anthony Fisher, OP, "Co-operation in evil: understanding the issues," in Helen Watt, ed., *Cooperation, Complicity and Conscience: Moral Problems in Healthcare, Science, Law and Public Policy* (London: Linacre Centre, 2005), 27–64. Other recent writers on cooperation include: Benedict Ashley OP, Jean deBlois, and Kevin O'Rourke OP, *Health Care Ethics: A Catholic Theological Analysis*, 5th ed. (Washington, D.C.: Georgetown University Press, 2006), 55–7;Peter Cataldo, "A cooperation analysis of embryonic stem cell research," *National Catholic Bioethics Quarterly* 2:1 (Spring 2002): 35–41; Germain Grisez, *The Way of the Lord Jesus,* vol 3: *Difficult Moral Questions* (Quincy, IL: Franciscan, 1997), esp. 871–98; Cathleen Kaveny, "Appropriation of evil: cooperation's mirror image," *Theological Studies* 61 (2000): 280–313; Albert Moraczewski, OP, "May one benefit from the evil deeds of others?" *National Catholic Bioethics Quarterly* 2:1 (Spring 2002): 43–7; Alexander Pruss, "Complicity, fetal tissue, and vaccines," *National Catholic Bioethics*

Quarterly 6:3 (Autumn 2006): 261–70; Russell Smith, "The principles of cooperation in Catholic thought," in Peter Cataldo & Albert Moraczewski OP, eds., *The Fetal Tissue Issue: Medical and Ethical Aspects* (Braintree, MA: Pope John Center, 1994), 81–92; Russell Smith, "Immediate material cooperation," *Ethics & Medics* 23:1 (1998): 1–2.

48 See CHA, *Code* § 8.8 and 8.9.

49 Several writers have shown that those who disapprove of an activity may nonetheless formally cooperate in it: Orville Griese, *Catholic Identity in Health Care: Principles and Practice* (Braintree, MA: Pope John Center, 1987), 388; Grisez, *Difficult Moral Questions,* 391–402, 892; Germain Grisez, *The Way of the Lord Jesus,* vol. 2: *Living a Christian Life* (Quincy, IL: Franciscan Press, 1993); Matt McDonald, "The limits of cooperation," *Catholic World Report* 10:11 (Dec 2000).

50 The issues parallel in many ways those that followed the June 1995 legalization in Germany of abortion in the first twelve weeks of pregnancy provided that the woman had a certificate that she had attended a *Schwangerschafts-beratungsstellen*—an approved counseling center. The German bishops and Rome came increasingly to see this as involving illicit cooperation by Church counselors in the practice of abortion: see John Paul II, "Letter to the German Bishops of 11 January 1998," *AAS* 90 (1998), 601–7, and the subsequent interventions by Cardinals Ratzinger and Sodano. What seemed to have been decisive here was (a) the gravity of what was at stake, i.e., innocent unborn human lives, (b) the witness the German bishops and their counseling agencies were called to give to the sanctity of life, and (c) concern about the corrupting effects on church workers, pregnant women, and the culture, of even this much material cooperation in abortion.

51 Congregation for the Doctrine of the Faith, *Quæ cumque sterilizatio* (also known as *Haec sacra congregatio*): Response to the American Bishops on the Question of Sterilization in Catholic Hospitals (1975).

52 Catholic Health Association and U.S. Conference of Catholic Bishops, *Ethical and Religious Directives for Catholic Health Care Facilities* (4th ed, St Louis: CHA, 1994).

53 James Keenan, SJ, "Collaboration and cooperation in Catholic health care," *Australasian Catholic Record* 77 (April 2000), 163–74, at 171: "Immediate material cooperation is always wrong, except in very rare occasions of duress. . . To capitulate or not is a question that the CEO, the bishop and others must consider. The principle gives them some lee-way to decide… " Similarly Thomas Kopfensteiner, "The meaning and role of duress in the cooperation in wrongdoing," *Linacre Quarterly* 70:2 (2003), 150–8.

54 See the considerable corpus by Robert George, such as *Making Men Moral* (New York: Oxford University Press, 1995) and *In Defense of Natural Law Theory* (New York: Oxford University Press, 2001).

55 See Navarro-Valls and Martínez Torrón, *Conflictos entre conciencia y ley*.

56 For example John Locke, *Essay on Toleration* (1667) and *Second Essay on Toleration* (1686);John Stuart Mill, *On Liberty* (1859); John Rawls, *Political Liberalism* (New York: Columbia University Press, 1993), 212–47; Nussbaum, *Liberty of Conscience*. Jean Laffitte, "A history of conscientious objection and different meanings of the concept of tolerance," in Sgreccia and Laffitte, *Christian Conscience*, 112–139, at 117, observes that Locke's vision of tolerance of religious opinion was vast: he intended to open civil society not only to Jews and Muslims, but even to pagans; only Catholics and atheists would be excluded from tolerance. See also Patrick Thierry, *La tolérance, sociétédémocratique, opinions, vices etvertus* (Paris: LivresPuf, 1997), 35–57. Some problems with Rawlsian liberalism are identified in John Finnis, "Public reason, abortion and cloning," *Valparaiso University Law Review* 32: 3 (1998): 361–82.

57 This position presumes, of course, that abortion is not the killing of a human person. If one accepts, as I believe one should, that there is indeed (or there may well be) a human life at risk, then liberalism should not tolerate abortion: it is a radical failure to extend to one person or class of persons (the unborn) the same liberty and protections afforded to others.

58 John Paul II,*Centesimus Annus: Encyclical on the Hundredth Anniversary of Rerum Novarum* (1991), 46; *Veritatis Splendor: Encyclical regarding the Church's Fundamental Moral Teaching* (1993), 99–101; *Evangelium Vitæ: Encyclical on the Value and Inviolability of Human Life* (1995), 18, 20, 69–71; "Address to the Bishops of Texas, Oklahoma and Arkansas on the Occasion of their Ad Limina Visit, 27 June 1998.

Chapter Two

The Philosophical and Theological Roots of Institutional Conscience

Christopher Tollefsen

In this paper I argue that there are philosophical and theological grounds for identifying as real the phenomenon of institutional conscience. This reality must be understood by analogy with the paradigm case of conscience, that of an individual, but given certain facts about the constitution of social realities, the phenomenon will be seen to admit of various instantiations. In most cases of social realities, the strength of the analogy that justifies attributions of judgments of conscience is somewhat weak. In other cases, the strength of the analogy increases considerably, and in these cases, I shall argue, judgments of institutional conscience are quite robust. So one extended line of argument in this paper is a defense of the claim that there are strong cases of institutional conscience.

What are the ethical and political consequences of this argument? I will argue that at the ethical level, the most important consequences concern the correlative concept of institutional integrity: weak cases make weak, and strong cases make correspondingly strong demands on the integrity of the institution in question. I take this conclusion to be significant for the internal deliberations of members of apostolic health-care ventures in particular, and I suggest that such ventures are largely failing to meet these ethical demands.

What about at the political level? Here the question is whether judgments of conscience made by institutions should be afforded political consideration just as such—that is, just because they are expressions of institutional *conscience*, given that freedom of conscience is taken to be an important value. For example, when a Catholic hospital judges that some particular procedure or intervention is impermissible, should that judgment be privileged against laws of general applicability *primarily* or *precisely* because it is a judgment of institutional conscience? Such a privilege would parallel one given to individuals opposed to performing abortions under certain conditions.

I will argue that the existence of a judgment of institutional conscience that runs contrary to the mandate of recognizably *just* laws of general applicability can be a consideration raised against the universal application of such laws, and that a request for a conscientious exemption can be reasonable, and reasonably granted. Given the Supreme Court's rulings in *Smith* and *Flores*, such exemptions will need, except in cases of federal law, to be granted by state legislatures.[1] However, these are not the cases of most current and pressing interest. Of more importance right now are cases in which the laws are seen as a form of overreaching, or as positively unjust. Simply appealing for an exemption can seem an inadequate response. I argue that the appeal to conscience for relief against such laws must often be supplemented in at least one of three possible ways, and the making of such an appeal or exemption carries certain risks that must be borne in mind.

I. The Paradigm Case

Judgments of conscience are our "final verdict on how we are to constitute ourselves."[2] Our practical reasoning is governed by concern for human goods, intelligible aspects of our own well-being and fulfillment, which, because they promise genuine benefits to us, underwrite the reasons for action we recognize in various options for action.[3] The chance to work on a paper in my office today, as opposed to the opportunity to stay home with my family, would be no option at all were it not for the ways in which both possibilities appealed to goods that could be realized in choice and action. But some choices, even while promising real benefit, are nevertheless not as reasonable as others, and thus are deficient as regards both the perfection promised, and the perfection of choice; an agent who chooses wrongly chooses badly, and is worse off, both in his orientation to real goods and as an agent who constitutes himself through choice. Similarly, an agent who chooses well succeeds in two, and potentially three ways: he succeeds in choosing an adequate orientation toward those goods that perfect us and, if successful in action, further succeeds in realizing those goods toward which he is uprightly oriented; and he succeeds, thirdly, in being a good chooser, a good constituter of self.

What, from the standpoint of a practical agent possessed of reason and freedom, could be more important than success of these three sorts? Yet success is impossible if the agent is not possessed of the skills to deliberate well, and the freedom to deliberate, to choose, and to act on the basis of deliberation and choice. So conscience, which in act is the judgment itself, and in capacity is the power of reason that carries out deliberation, is rightly accorded a laudable status among those features of the human person that deserve protection from whatever stunts, thwarts, or perverts it. An endless propaganda of lies or a deliberately imposed paucity of resources for deliberating responsibly; a coercive or tyrannical public authority; or the seductive voices of temptation, self-rationalization, and special pleading, are all offenses against conscience, and thus offenses against the dignity of the human person, just as are more coercive attempts to induce individuals to act contrary to their conscience.

Deliberation, judgment, and choice are paradigmatically acts of individuals. So conscience is paradigmatically a reality of the lives of individuals. This suggests, however, that an analogy can be extended to groups to the extent that more than one individual are, in whatever way, capacitated to become somehow one, a unity, of which not just deliberation, but judgment, choice, and action may all be predicated. I turn next to the ways in which this possibility is ordinarily realized.

II. Authority and Collective Judgments of Conscience

Consider the paradigmatic way that a group can engage in common deliberation and choice; namely, when that group is disposed by the wills of its members toward some common good, and is united under a common authority whose decisions are thought by group members to be defeating of other possible reasons for action. That is, such authoritative verdicts do not simply enter into the members' deliberations as one more reason to be weighed among others, but operate so as to remove from consideration various reasons that were previously available to group members as the basis of deliberation and choice.[4]

The mutual willing of the common good and the acceptance of practical authority are related. The existence of an authority for a group of any size and complexity is essential for that group's successful pursuit of its common good, even in a community whose members are generally of good will and moral character, for there will often be multiple acceptable ways of pursuing the common good. Absent authority, the group will not settle upon one way, and the pursuit of the good will be hindered. And so it is reasonable for the group to take some individual's judgments as authoritative and hence as normative.[5]

In such cases, there will typically be preparatory deliberations, which can be distributed in various ways across the members of the group: for some decisions, all or almost all members will voice an opinion; for others, some smaller subset, perhaps including experts, will enter into the deliberation. There need not be a precise overlay of the agents deliberating and the agents deciding, though sometimes there will be. Similarly, a decision having been rendered by the authority, the carrying out of that decision will also be distributed across different agents. Viewing only the behavior of individuals will thus often not leave the impression that those individuals are deliberating, judging, choosing, and acting *as one*.

But agents mutually joined in the willing of a common good, and bound together by an authority whose decisions bind those agents, form a community—a common unity of agents. They are indeed, insofar as they are so joined, one.[6] So there is a ground for speaking of a collective deliberation, collective judgment, and collective action: considered just as something singular, the group is capable of deliberating, judging, and acting *as a group*.

Let us focus on the group's judgment, rendered by the group's authority. As the group's final verdict on how it is to constitute itself, that judgment is a group, or collective, judgment of conscience. That it is the group's judgment of conscience is not vitiated by the fact that the proximate agent of that verdict is that authority; rather, the authority's verdict *is the group's judgment*. Moreover, this final verdict can be, as an individual's judgment of conscience is, robustly moral, for group deliberations often take on board fully moral concerns, and some options are then authoritatively accepted or rejected precisely because of their moral character. Indeed, the decision may be *narrowly* moral: it might be a judgment only that *this*, which is judged by the community in the person of its authority to be morally impermissible, is to be avoided.

However, in most cases, the domain over which an authoritative judgment may be taken as a group's judgment of conscience is limited; and there are numerous opt-out possibilities for the individuals in the group. For example, the common good of most groups and institutions is tightly circumscribed: it extends over a narrow range of the goods that are pursued by its members across the entire domain of their lives (for its members will typically pursue many other goods); and it extends only over a narrow range of the forms of those goods it takes as common (for its members come together primarily to pursue a very specified form of good). Further, a large component of a group's deliberation typically concerns external instrumentalities. The common good of a musical performance group, for example, extends primarily to the aesthetic good, among all the possible goods pursued by its members; and it extends, among all the forms of the aesthetic good, only to the common understanding and performance of the rather limited range of music within its repertoire. Moreover, the group's deliberations are likely to be taken up to a considerable degree with a concern for empowerment and coordination: ensuring that they have adequate funds, making sure that practice and performance times are well-known, and so on.

If these are the constitutive aspects of the common good for the music ensemble, though, then however authority for the group is constituted—a manager, a leader, majority rule, unanimity—nevertheless that authority will be greatly constrained relative to most of the group members' lives: the authority will not extend to most of the areas in which group members must make choices, such as whom to marry, what religion to belong to, what causes to support, what other goods to pursue, how to raise children, etc. Moreover, many of the other aspects of a group member's life will be more important, whether always or occasionally, so the normative claims of the collective conscience over the individual will be subject to many defeating conditions. For example, commitments to spouse and child will need to take precedence, where necessary, over the group. Finally, individuals who are part of groups do not rightfully cede to the authority the normative power to make and carry out unreasonable and immoral judgments. A musical group's decision to plagiarize from a competitor is thus not genuinely binding on any individual within the group.

In all these ways, the group's ability to speak, deliberate, choose, and act for its members will be limited. To the extent that we should speak of institutional judgments of conscience, or collective conscience, these will be *weak* forms of this reality.

What are the ethical and political consequences of the fact that such groups are capacitated to make corporate judgments of conscience? At the ethical level, the *notion* of collective conscience as such should not play a large role in the deliberations of the associations in question, for "conscience" is not itself a substantive moral consideration, but is rather transparent for the deliberations and judgments that are exercises of our capacity to reason. Yet the notion of collective conscience does seem to be correlative to the notion of group, collective, or institutional *integrity*, and this is a concept of substantive importance for any association aimed at a common good.[7] For any such association can come undone in ways detrimental to its common pursuit if, for example, its members kick or rebel at authoritative judgments without good reason; if their personal commitments are not well coordinated with the commitments of the group; or if the group's deliberations and decision-making are sloppy, ill-informed, or deficient in some other way. Maintaining its own morally upright integrity in the face of life's challenges is thus crucial to a group's existence and excellence. In maintaining its integrity, a group maintains its capacity to make collective judgments of conscience.

At the political level, I suspect that concern for most such groups will not need to give much thought to the *claims* of institutional conscience. The particular judgments made by most groups are not important to the state simply by virtue of being collective judgments. What *is* important is fourfold. First, the continued existence of such voluntary groups as music associations, or larger groups such as businesses or charities, is essential to the common good. Voluntary social groups precede the existence of the state, which is necessary, *inter alia*, precisely in order to make possible and stable these worthwhile forms of association. So a state must make sure that the sorts of groups that are capable of institutional conscience are given the freedoms and encouragements they need to flourish. It is in this indirect way that their judgments of conscience will be respected, since a state that repeatedly restricts such associations from carrying out their decisions in fact makes it impossible for such associations to exist as forms of community. I will return to this point later.

Second, the state will need to ensure that the authority of such groups does not extend to the point of defeating a right of exit for its members. Third, the state will need to ensure that the associations in question are not, by virtue of their joint endeavors, seriously damaging to the common good, as they would be if their purposes were violent, or corrupting of the youth, or fraudulent, and so on.[8] Finally, the state will need to make sure that those judgments *it* makes regarding what is necessary for the political common good, and which thus call for legislation affecting the ability of individuals and groups to constitute themselves, are neither erroneous and substantively unjust, nor outside the authority of the state, nor pursued for reasons that are not themselves motivated by the common good. But these are just the set of conditions that the natural law tradition takes to be essential to the state's just use of authority.[9] And so, when states make unreasonable and unjust demands for what they allege to be the sake of the common good, the appropriate response, in most cases, it seems, will not be to fall back on a right to collective conscience, but to offer a first-order critique of the injustice of these demands.[10]

III. Churches and Apostolic Ministries

So institutional conscience is a reality found wherever a group exists by virtue of its shared willing of a common good, and its obedience to some recognized authority charged with making decisions for the sake of that common good. I have discussed some examples of this that we might consider weak. Institutional forms of conscience are weak when the common good, and the corresponding authority of the institution, are limited. But then, might it not be the case that a form of institutional conscience is stronger when the institution's common good is basic, and encompasses more fully the reality of its members' lives? I will now consider some potentially much stronger forms of institution and institutional conscience, asking again about the moral and political implications of the picture.

The Christian church, by its own self-understanding, is the kind of reality that is the subject of strong forms of institutional conscience. Moreover, certain forms of ministry within the Church are similar to the Church itself in that they too have the capacity to be subjects of strong forms of institutional conscience. After explaining these claims, I will briefly discuss their moral and political implications.

John Finnis has recently argued that any constitutional theory that sees religious commitments as no different in kind from other "deep" concerns and commitments distorts badly the good at stake and is "lethal to religion." Finnis writes:

> Religion deserves constitutional mention, not because it is a passionate or deep commitment, but because it is the practical expression of, or response to, truths about human society, about the persons who are a political community's members, and about the world in which any such community must take its place and find its ways and means.[11]

It would be difficult to find truths more essential to the project of choosing and living well. Accordingly, religion as the practical response to such truths occupies a unique position in the normative economy of human choices. For the practical responses called for by the truths of religion are, centrally, gratitude for all that has been given us by God, and a will to cooperate with God in all that we do, none of which will come to fruition without His willing it. Thus, religion as that practical response requires a will that is in a sense architectonic over all other actions, commitments, and choices an agent makes: all must be made with gratitude and cooperatively. Religion, adequately pursued, is an all-encompassing good.[12]

It is also a basic good: to choose to cooperate with, and express gratitude to, the divine merely for the sake of benefits to be gained down the road is to fail to act cooperatively or gratefully. In making a religious commitment, human beings are participating in a relationship that is fulfilling just as such—and more so to the extent that the propositions accepted achieve the fullness of truth that is possible in this domain.

Institutional religions can exist for a wide variety of reasons, and religious institutions can decline in their reasonableness and integrity. But a community of religious believers, all bound by mutual commitments to a common set of truths about persons, societies, and the world, and a common appreciation for the mode of response demanded by those truths, is a very strong community. And its unity will be strengthened if its members recognize an authority as necessary for their pursuit of the common good of worship and praise of, and cooperation with, the divine, and even further if they recognize that authority as also epistemically privileged, so that the authority's deliverances on doctrine and morality are also treated with deference. A religious institution that demonstrates these marks will approach more the unity of a family, perhaps, and less the unity of a string quartet, university, or political state.

The Christian religion notably goes further even than this, for it takes the entire mission of Christians to be a participation in the mission of the God-man, Jesus Christ, for the redemption of the world, and the bringing about of the kingdom of heaven. It sees the grace required for that common task as provided for in baptism by the sharing of the Christian's life in the divine life of Christ in union with His Father and the Holy Spirit, the sharing of the bodily life of Christ in the Eucharist, and the sharing in the lives of all other Christians in the Church, which is itself the mystical body of Christ.[13]

These claims need not be accepted by someone in order to recognize that, for those who do accept them, their own self-understanding of their unity with other Christians is *much* more akin to, say, the unity of spouses than the unity of a quartet; and if Christians who take themselves to be such a unity recognize as authoritative the judgments of certain individuals or groups of individuals—call these ecclesial and magisterial judgments—then such Christians will think of the judgments of such authorities as their own, will defer to such judgments without hesitation, and will consider such judgments to be judgments of the conscience of the one body of which all Christians take themselves to be parts.

Christians are called to carry out the work of Christ here on earth. That work can be described as apostolic, and the work can be specified into particular domains, and carried out with sets of persons smaller than those constituting the entire Church. Historically, one such field of apostolic work has been that of the health-care ministry. Typically headed by members of religious communities, apostolic health-care ministries such as Catholic hospitals have not seen themselves simply as weak institutions, capable of making weak institutional judgments of conscience, as secular hospitals are. Rather, seeing their mission as the mission of the Church as a whole, but *in* the field of health care, such apostolic agents have pursued the good of health in the broader context of devotion to Christ and His Church, and to carrying out Christ's salvific ministry in the domain of health care.[14]

There is much to be said about the nature of such health-care apostolates; here, I will simply quote John Paul II's exhortation to consecrated persons in health-care ministry:

> [A] part of their mission is *to evangelize the health-care centres* in which they work, striving to spread the light of Gospel values to the way of living, suffering and dying of the people of our day. They should endeavour to make the practice of medicine more human, and increase their knowledge of bioethics at the service of the Gospel of life. Above all therefore they should foster respect for the person and for human life from conception to its natural end, in full conformity with the moral teaching of the Church. For this purpose they should set up centres of formation and cooperate closely with those ecclesial bodies entrusted with the pastoral ministry of health care.[15]

Taken together, these tasks form the common purpose, or mission, and hence the common good, of a health-care apostolate, along with whatever instrumentalities and forms of coordination are necessary in order to pursue this common good. And it is evident that in its robustness, such a common good must, to a degree unlike that of a secular health-care institution, require such a depth of commitment on the part of its members as to permeate much if not all of their lives. They are strongly unified communities, capable in principle of strong judgments of conscience significantly analogous to the judgments of individuals; these judgments are even more strongly unified by the very robust form of authority under which Catholics, and Catholic health-care ministries, operate, viz., the authority of the Pope.

This is, to be sure, all too brief a discussion of the nature of a Catholic apostolic health-care ministry, but it suffices to raise the ethical and political questions with which I have been concerned in this essay.

I have argued elsewhere that the conception of institutional integrity that arises from the description of the institutional mission and unity of, for example, a Catholic hospital is extremely robust. A Catholic hospital cannot possibly hope to be what it is supposed to be if it is staffed largely by non-Catholics, or uninterested Catholics: a large majority of members must be Catholic if the hospital's institutional integrity is not to be a sham. I do not see how a truly Catholic hospital could have a non-Catholic as its head, or any significant number of non-Catholics among its governing members. I do not see how institutional arrangements could be entered into with other hospitals that would permit those other hospitals, even at arm's length and with great dividing buffers, to perform acts forbidden by the Catholic Church. I do not see how such institutions could fail to make a special effort to reach out to the poor, and to local Catholics, or to be in close contact and cooperation with their local ordinaries. I do not see how such institutions could bill the uninsured at rates significantly higher than those at which they bill the insured, forcing some of those uninsured to pay for what other uninsured patients will be unable to pay. And, frankly, I do not see many Catholic hospitals meeting these demands of institutional integrity.[16]

Can Catholic hospitals, any more, be constituted in ways that will sustain their apostolic work and thus their institutional integrity? This is a matter for debate. Truly apostolic work in the health-care field might require creativity and imagination in creating new forms of health-care ministries, perhaps on a smaller scale than the hospital, and characterized by a significant degree of separation from state funding and affiliation with non-Catholic entities. The upshot is clear: the ethical demands of institutional identity and integrity that result from an apostolic health-care ministry's being a subject of strong judgments of conscience are themselves very robust, and are, I have suggested, only inadequately realized in practice.

Whether these ethical norms are being sustained or are capable of being sustained, health-care institutions designated as Catholic exist, and political questions follow, since these institutions are typically Catholic *enough* that they set limits to their willingness to cooperate in procedures or other actions that are recognizably incompatible with Catholic integrity, such as abortion, or are arguably incompatible, such as the provision of emergency contraception to rape victims in the absence of an ovulation test. These and other demands are articulated in the Ethical and Religious Directives for Catholic Healthcare Services, which provide a template for Catholic identity in health care.[17] In these and other cases, the institution might judge that it cannot provide patients with these procedures, nor can it refer for them. It is precisely this sort of judgment that has come under criticism, in cases involving abortion, emergency contraception, and sterilization, among others, as various individuals and groups have suggested either the removal of federal funding from institutions that refuse to provide such procedures, or even the passage of laws mandating that all hospitals provide some or other of these procedures under certain conditions.[18]

IV. Conscience and Institutional Integrity

In the remainder of this paper, I suggest the following possibility: that institutional conscience is where one, but not the sole, focus should be in defending, for example, Catholic health-care institutions from the sorts of demands that are of most concern: demands to provide or refer for abortions; demands to provide contraceptive insurance coverage to employees; demands to provide emergency contraception without adequate safeguards to rape victims; and so on. I first give three reasons why appeals to institutional conscience will not do all the work that might be hoped of them, and then I discuss three additional considerations that must be brought to bear on the difficult cases.

Here is a first difficulty, which I consider superable: Catholic and other religious health-care institutions rely, for their self-understanding and some practical judgments, on a variety of theologically grounded considerations. Such considerations can be appreciated externally as important to the self-understanding of participants in a Catholic health-care ministry, but they are not entirely, or at least easily, available from a political standpoint. I will return to this point momentarily.

A second and more important point is that even if a direct appeal to institutional conscience is potentially helpful here, the strength of such an appeal is rather weakened by failures in the institutional integrity of Catholic health-care institutions. Catholic hospitals staffed primarily by non-Catholics, in occasional cases by abortionists who ply their trade elsewhere, or which allow, for example, sterilizations and prescription of contraceptives on their premises, are simply not in a position to rely effectively on claims of institutional conscience, for they lack the internal unity necessary for such a claim.[19] Such institutions almost invite, by their deficiencies in witness, the sorts of meddling that occur when legislators require that a hospital's insurance plan, for example, provide contraceptive coverage to all employees. Such demands are initiated in some cases by the very employees of such institutions, a sure sign that things are amiss.[20]

A third difficulty is brought out by consideration of the way that appeals to judgments of institutional conscience *should* work for religious institutions. Just now I noted that one reason for being dubious of the efficacy of appeals to institutional conscience was that the self-understanding of a religious health-care institution involves claims that are theological, a matter of revelation. However, the underlying motivation for creating such apostolates is religious: it is grounded in recognition of a good, knowledge of which *is* available to us through natural reason, and pursuit of which is essential to individual flourishing and to the common good of a political society. In consequence, while the state should not take cognizance of the theological judgments of this or that religious institution, it must, for publicly available reasons, make available the social space in which such institutions exist and thrive. This, however, cannot be done if the state is too quick to pass laws that in fact have the effect of making it impossible for these institutions to act as they judge fit and right. And the primary data to which the state must attend are those publicly promulgated judgments of *policy* by which religious institutions govern themselves.[21]

Cognizant of these, lawmakers should, I believe, carve out exemptions when their otherwise just legislation threatens to infringe upon the space for making and living in accordance with policy that is essential to religious institutions, if such exemptions do not threaten the general effectiveness of the law.[22] And such institutions should draw attention to these matters of policy when it can be foreseen that otherwise reasonable laws of general applicability do so threaten. This appeal to policy *is* an appeal of sorts to judgments of institutional conscience, though at a certain level of generality. But in the ordinary case, such an appeal makes no real objection to the general justice of the law in question. For example, Orthodox Jews seeking an exemption from laws that require them to move their automobiles on the Sabbath, or Christian schools seeking a ministerial exemption from laws designed to create more just conditions for the disabled, do not question the justice of these laws—they simply point out that their ability to form and act on their publicly stated policy is threatened by the universal application of these laws, and reasonable legislators and, in some cases, courts, acknowledge the justice of this concern.

However, in the cases that are of most contemporary concern, such as the Health and Human Services contraceptive-coverage mandate case, or the requirement to administer emergency contraceptives without an ovulation test, or the possible future demand that hospitals provide the full range of reproductive services, including abortion, to some or all of their clientele, appeal to institutional conscience is not enough, for that appeal, as I have noted, operates within a presumption of the justice of the law against which appeal is made. And so I will now in closing suggest three further forms of protest to which appeal to institutional conscience must be joined.

First, perhaps the single greatest failing of recent debates regarding health care in the United States and elsewhere is the continued claim that abortion, contraception, and sterilization are aspects of health care. If we assume, as I shall, that health care concerns constitute part of the political common good—that is, the set of goods for which the political state has some responsibility—then it can be reasonable for the state to concern itself in some way with widespread deficiencies in the provision of health care. But the state makes a substantive error, an unjust one in many ways, in folding abortion and contraceptive rights into the idea of health care. Many of the conscientious objections of Catholic health-care institutions would be resolved *without* appeal to institutional conscience were this failing remedied, but appeals to conscience in the absence of making the larger point about the common good is both a failing of witness, and possibly an injustice to those Catholics, for example, who run private businesses and who are therefore not in a position to be able to lean upon the appeal to institutional conscience that is available to members of a Catholic apostolic ministry.

A second domain in which further push-back is necessary concerns the scope of state action. In the ordinary case, appeal to institutional conscience does not amount to a protest against the state's authority to make laws regulating the matter in question. But in some problem cases it is worth asking whether the state is exceeding its proper authority in its demands even apart from the justice or injustice of what is demanded. In particular, is it legitimately part of state authority to require, when putative goods such as contraceptives or other reproductive services are not forthcoming from existing voluntary associations, that such associations provide these goods? The state can establish institutions for the purpose of meeting otherwise unmet and fundamental needs—as it might establish orphanages to meet the needs of children otherwise not served by existing agencies. And it can regulate the provision of goods by existing institutions to ensure that these institutions are not, in fact, causing harm or otherwise damaging the common good. But it seems a problematic extension of the state's power for it to *assign* the task of meeting unmet needs to institutions or individuals not currently in the business of serving those needs for whatever reason—granting the legitimacy of those needs, as I think we should not in this case.

The underlying reason for my skepticism here has to do with the state's entire reason for being in the first place, as a supplement to the efforts of individuals and groups to live flourishing lives in overlapping sets of communities. Such overlapping communities are inadequate, in the absence of political authority and the law, to the task of protection against outside threats and internal miscreants, to coordination of their common lives, and to the provision of some necessary benefits to individuals who might otherwise not be cared for by those with obligations to do so. The state exists in part to make possible the self-determination and coordinated lives of the various communities that it serves, and such self-determination requires latitude on the part of such associations to decide for themselves what goods, and for whom, they will pursue and provide—hence the earlier emphasis on judgments of policy for religious institutions. For the state to take over the direction of such associations, with a view to determining whom they shall benefit and how, begins to erode the very possibility of such associations, for whose sake the state exists.

A third and related protest to be made here addresses one of the core reasons that the state does seem to extend itself unreasonably, and thus to intrude unjustly upon the autonomy of religious institutions. What is at stake in this third protest concerns the mapping of the social space within which voluntary associations, especially but not exclusively religious institutions, serve the common goods for which they exist. How should the relationship between those institutions and the authority of the state be understood?

I suggest here that recent attempts in liberal theory to answer this question are deeply problematic, and that a more adequate answer will again relieve much of the pressure being put on Catholic and other strong institutions. These include not only health-care institutions, but other Church ministries, universities, adoption agencies, and even the institution of marriage.

One possible liberal response to my question, in very broad outline, is that the social space accorded to voluntary associations must be governed by an absolute notion of non-discrimination: non-discrimination respecting which patients are served and how, which staff is hired and how, who is allowed to adopt, who is allowed to marry, and so forth. "Non-discrimination" here takes on the sense that all must be treated *alike*. But this conception, I suggest, is incompatible with the continued and robust existence of voluntary associations whose foundational motivations are based in basic human goods such as health, religion, and marriage. For projects, commitments, institutions, and ways of life oriented to such goods *require* discrimination: they require judgments that such and such ways of acting are incompatible with a true understanding of the goods in question, and that other ways of acting are required by a true understanding of the goods in question. Such judgments inevitably rule out certain ways of acting and certain forms of cooperation with certain people. They cannot remain indiscriminately non-discriminatory by their very nature.

The state must, in one sense, promote the idea of non-discrimination. It must ensure certain forms of fairness and protect against arbitrary forms of mistreatment. But it cannot pursue an ideal of absolute non-discrimination, and it must, in order to allow for the continued existence of robust voluntary associations and worthwhile pursuits of the good, allow many forms of behavior that are discriminatory in the sense that they do not treat all alike.

Appeals to institutional conscience are vitally important. Equally important, to support and supplement such appeals, is an adequate understanding of what is and what is not health care, and an adequate understanding of the limits of state authority. So too do we require an adequate understanding of what is unfair discrimination, because it is arbitrary and irrational, and what is *not* unfair discrimination, because it is predicated upon a genuine understanding of the demands of human goods. Adequate appreciation of these truths and of institutional conscience will probably stand or fall together.

ENDNOTES

1 See *Employment Divison v. Smith*, 494 U.S. 872 (1990); and *City of Boerne v. Flores*, 521 U.S. 507 (1997). See the discussion in Richard A. Garnett, "The Political (and Other) Safeguards of Religious Freedom," *Cardozo Law Review* 32 (2011): 1815–1829.

2 Christopher Tollefsen, "Conscience, Religion and the State," *American Journal of Jurisprudence* 54 (2009): 93–115.

3 For the general theory of ethics adopted in this paper, see Germain Grisez, Joseph Boyle, and John Finnis, "Practical Principles, Moral Truth, and Ultimate Ends," *American Journal of Jurisprudence* 32 (1987): 99–151.

4 For this conception of authority, see Joseph Raz, *The Morality of Freedom* (New York: Oxford University Press, 1986); for the relationship between authority and the common good, see John Finnis, *Natural Law and Natural Rights*, 2nd ed. (New York: Oxford University Press, 2011).

5 "Individual" here and in the subsequent paragraphs of this section should be read as encompassing groups of individuals.

6   Cf. John Finnis, *Aquinas: Moral, Political and Legal Theory* (New York: Oxford University Press, 1998).

7   I have dealt at greater length elsewhere with the notion of institutional integrity; see Christopher Tollefsen, "Institutional Integrity," in Ana Smith Iltis, ed., *Institutional Integrity in Health Care* (Dordrecht, Netherlands: Kluwer Academic Press, 2003), 121–138.

8   Some toleration might be politically appropriate, however, of groups whose purposes were, while not consistent with the political common good, nevertheless not a serious threat to that good.

9   See, e.g., Finnis, *Natural Law and Natural Rights*, chap. XII.

10 This claim, which I make elsewhere as well, may be too strong in the following way: appeal to institutional conscience may provide a useful way to articulate the charge that the state is, in some way(s) illegitimately trespassing into the domain of legitimate self-constitution of individuals and groups.

11 Finnis, *Natural Law and Natural Rights*, 31.

12 For further discussion of the good of religion, see Boyle, 1998.

13 See, for these claims, the Dogmatic Constitution *Lumen Gentium*, of the Second Vatican Council.

14 For an excellent discussion of the nature and role of the Catholic hospital, see Anthony Fisher, "Is There a Distinctive Role for the Catholic Hospital in a Pluralist Society?" in Luke Gormally, ed., *Issues for a Catholic Bioethic* (London: Linacre Centre, 1999).

15 John Paul II, *Vita Consecrata*, "Apostolic Exhortation on the Consecrated Life and its Mission in the Church and in the World" (1996), no. 83.

16 For a description of the bleak state of Catholic health care, see Leonard J. Nelson III, *Diagnosis Critical: The Urgent Threat Confronting Catholic Healthcare* (Huntington, IL: Our Sunday Visitor, 2009).

17 The Fifth Edition of these Directives is available on-line at: http://www.usccb.org/issues-and-action/human-life-and-dignity/health-care/upload/Ethical-Religious-Directives-Catholic-Health-Care-Services-fifth-edition-2009.pdf.

18 For example, Conn. Gen. Stat. Ann § 19a-112e (Enacted 2007) mandates the provision of emergency contraception to victims of rape subsequent only to a pregnancy test, not an LH, test; the starkest statement of the claim that health-care professionals must be willing and ready to provide the full range of legally permitted options is to be found in Julian Savulescu, "Conscientious Objection in Medicine," *British Medical Journal* 332 (2006): 294–297.

19 See Patrick B. Craine, "Doc at Catholic Hospital: I Perform Abortions Because I'm a Christian," *LifeSiteNews*, July 22, 2011. Available at: http://www.lifesitenews.com/news/doc-at-catholic-hospital-i-perform-abortions-because-im-a-christian.

20 See David Neipert, "Guest Post: Another View on Belmont Abbey," *The Baltimore Sun*, October 19, 2009. Available at: http://weblogs.baltimore-sun.com/news/faith/2009/10/guest_post_another_view_on_bel.html.

21 I intend for "policy" here to be taken quite broadly. The Ethical and Religious Directives are certainly parts of policy for Catholic health institutions. But so are kosher and Sabbath laws for groups of Orthodox Jews, even if they are not put out explicitly as the policies by which such Jews will govern themselves.

22 For a defense both of this normative claim, and of its compatibility with the *Smith* case, see Garnett, "Political (and Other) Safeguards of Religious Freedom"; he presupposes throughout that the laws against which reasonable appeal for exemption may be made are otherwise just.

Chapter Three

Institutional Conscience and Tolerance

Daniel P. Sulmasy

Conscience is a widely invoked and poorly understood concept. What conscience is and how it works are subjects rarely probed in any depth. In this essay, I discuss several unsatisfactory accounts of conscience and provide an account that I argue is more robust, justified, and credible.[1] I then argue that this account of conscience applies as readily to institutions as it does to individuals, not merely metaphorically but actually. I then define the notion of tolerance in light of this account of conscience. I next discuss the complicated nature of the relations of tolerance and conscience among citizens, professionals, institutions, and society. I advance an equivalence thesis: that in a tolerant society, one may justifiably override the conscience of a professional or an institution if and only if the issue is one over which one may justifiably override the conscience of an individual citizen. In the web of conscientious equivalence, no citizen can make demands contrary to the conscience of a professional or institution that could not be made justifiably of any fellow citizen; no institution can make demands contrary to the conscience of a citizen or professional that could not be made justifiably of another institution; and no professional can make demands contrary to the conscience of a citizen or institution that could not be made justifiably of a fellow professional. I conclude by exploring several practical examples.

Some Erroneous Views of Conscience

Intuition and Conscience
One very common view of conscience is that it is a distinct mental faculty, an intuitive moral sense that determines the rightness and

wrongness of actions. This "faculty" perspective is probably the notion of conscience operative in the mind of the average person on the street

The faculty view has been proposed by several serious philosophers. Bishop Butler, for example, understood conscience this way—as a faculty by which each of us "pronounces determinately some actions to be in themselves evil, wrong, unjust, [that] without being consulted, without being advised with (sic), magisterially exerts itself . . ."[2]

I would argue, however, that this faculty view is inadequate as a theory of conscience. Conscience is not an infallible little voice whispering to each of us about what we should do. There is no faculty of conscience that is distinct from our beliefs, attitudes, reasoning abilities, and emotions. If conscience were nothing other than a sort of perfect perceptual intuitionism, all moral conversation would grind to a halt. The only statement moral philosophy could possibly make would be "follow your conscience."[3] I think we need to say more.

Act intuitionism, the sort of moral theory invoked by such a conception of conscience, is a weak theory of ethics. Intuitions often differ about particular cases, and if they do, we can conclude nothing more than that our intuitions differ. According to the theory of moral intuitionism, these differences could neither be explained nor challenged. This leaves open too many possibilities. My intuitions about what is right and what is wrong differ from those of the Taliban. I want to reserve the right to challenge the intuitions of the Taliban. I want to reserve the right to challenge, respectfully, anyone's moral intuitions. The deepest form of mutual respect for moral agency actually demands a reciprocal willingness to challenge and to be challenged with reasons.

Intuition does have an important role in morality. It is not, however, the direct way we discern right from wrong. Intuition is involved in what the medievals called *synderesis*. Peter Lombard, Bonaventure, and Aquinas all distinguished between *conscientia* and *synderesis*. The latter was understood to be the capacity to apprehend the most basic moral principles—those principles that are not fully justifiable on the basis of other, more fundamental moral principles, but will be self-evident at least "in the sense that a person who reflects upon his nature will see that certain things are good for him and certain things are bad for him."[4]

By *synderesis*, one might intuitively judge the truth of a very fundamental moral premise, such as, "that good is to be done and evil avoided."[5] One might intuit that knowledge is a human good, or that play is a human good. These intuitions are not acts of conscience, however, because while the object of *synderesis* is a form of basic moral knowledge, a way of acquiring basic moral beliefs, the object of conscience is particular moral judgments.

Affect, Motive, and Conscience

Neither is conscience merely a set of feelings. Mill, for instance, considered conscience to be a complex set of feelings that prevent us from doing wrong.[6] Anticipating Freud, he seems to have foreshadowed the concept of the super-ego—the irrational set of negative feelings that punish us in order to prevent us from violating the rules that have been set up by society to prevent our fundamentally selfish appetites from wreaking havoc. This is also an inadequate view of conscience. Emotions are associated with conscience, but conscience is not reducible to those emotions. Conscience may incite affective states such as regret or guilt, but these emotions are not what conscience is. Nor must the emotions associated with the activity of conscience necessarily be unpleasant or contrary to our truest and deepest desires.

Conscience also should not be confused with motive, whether that motive is an emotion or a belief. A judgment of conscience may eventually lead to a motivational state, and the belief that one ought not to violate one's conscience can be an important motive, but conscience is not primarily a motivational state. Conscience can help one to determine the proper reasons for acting, but it would be the reasons that motivate a rational moral agent, not conscience itself.

A Positive Account of Conscience

Conscience is a fundamental phenomenon of moral psychology operative in all persons. It is not constituted by or directed to any particular normative system or theoretical framework or set of principles. Conscience is not what makes one person a preference-maximizing utilitarian and another a neo-Aristotelian (even though one ought conscientiously to decide which perspective, if either, is true). Conscience supervenes upon all normative systems. Conscience is an aspect of moral psychology that comes into play when moral agents deliberate about particular cases.

Conscience as a Conjunction of Will and Judgment

All moral deliberation by moral agents involves a conjunction of will and judgment that we commonly call "'conscience.'" As a conjunction of will and judgment, conscience, like the Roman god Janus, has two faces. One face is turned toward its origin; the other is turned toward moral acts. The first face of conscience is an act of will: an assent to the truth that one should act morally. The other face of conscience is turned towards moral action: an assessment that what one has done or might be contemplating doing is contrary to one's fundamental moral commitments about what is right and what is wrong.

The first face of conscience is rooted in a fundamental commitment to morality.[7] As such, it is almost impossible to suggest anything more important to the moral life than conscience. That we should have fundamental moral commitments and that we ought to act in accordance with these commitments (that is, that we should act conscientiously), seem to be the sorts of precepts that come to us intuitively, by *synderesis*. If one rejects these premises, it would seem that there is no point in discussing ethics at all.

The second face of conscience is turned towards specific moral acts. This aspect of conscience is neither knowledge, nor a faculty of knowing, nor a conative (motivational) force moving a person towards good and away from evil. The activity of conscience is a meta-judgment that arises in particular moral deliberations. It is a judgment that a proposed act (or an act one has already accomplished) would violate one's fundamental moral commitments, including, importantly, the fundamental moral commitment to act with understanding.

Conscience as an act of will

Conscience, in its *willing* face, arises from a fundamental commitment or intention to be moral. It unifies the cognitive, conative, and emotional aspects of the moral life through a commitment to integrity or moral wholeness. It is a commitment to have and to uphold deep, self-identifying moral beliefs; a commitment to discern the moral features of particular cases as best one can, and to reason morally to the best of one's ability; a commitment to emotional balance in one's moral decision-making, to being neither too hard nor too soft; a commitment to making decisions according to the best of one's moral ability and acting upon what one discerns to be the morally right course of action. Conscience arises from this meta-moral commitment to morality itself, exercised (and experienced) in particular cases.

This very fundamental nature gives conscience its primacy in deliberation about particular acts. "Thus," says Hamlet, "conscience doth make cowards of us all."[8] Conscientious living is not easy. Following conscience means following through on this fundamental commitment to be moral. To lack this fundamental commitment to moral integrity is to be less than a full moral agent.

Conscience as an act of judgment

Conscience, in its *judging* face, concerns deliberation and decision-making regarding particular moral acts. The judgments of conscience are judgments that what one has done or one is contemplating doing are in violation of the fundamental commitment to be moral. As such, conscience is the most fundamental of all moral duties—the duty to unite one's powers of reason, emotion, and will into an integrated moral whole based upon one's most fundamental moral principles and identity.

An individual person's conscience "establishes a felt need or disposition to act in accordance with knowledge or belief, giving him a sense of personal integrity when he does the best he can, and a corresponding sense of inner failure, frustration, or guilt when, through some fault of his own, he fails to do so."[9] The exercise of conscience by an individual is thus often accompanied by emotions such as satisfaction or guilt. Sometimes it is these emotions that trigger the judgment. But the act of conscience itself is a meta-moral judgment, not an emotion.

In summary, conscience begins in the intuitive, self-evident understanding that a moral agent should be committed to morality itself; that a moral agent should have fundamental moral positions; that a moral agent ought to decide and act according to the agent's best judgment regarding the good and the right after having gathered the proper information; and that a moral agent ought to obey the moral rules that accompany the agent's fundamental moral commitments. Conscience is a coin with two faces. Conscience as an act of will consists in assenting to these fundamental propositions concerning all one's actions and to having and holding foundational moral positions. Conscience as an act of judgment is exercised in particular cases by ascertaining whether a course of action about which one is deliberating, either prospectively or retrospectively, would violate these commitments.

The Communal Aspects of Conscience

The moral community has a responsibility for the formation of good conscience. Other moral agents play important roles in nurturing: (a) the ability to discern the basic moral truths through *synderesis*, (b) the commitment to being moral, (c) the commitment to informing conscience appropriately, and the ability to discern the knowledge needed for conscientious decision-making, and (d) the ability to judge whether what is being contemplated is consistent with the agent's fundamental moral commitments. The first school for individual conscience formation is the family. Schools, churches, and communities all play important roles as well.

The community's role in conscience formation is ongoing throughout the life of a moral agent. Whole communities can become lax about conscience, making it difficult for individuals and institutions to exercise conscience properly.

Finally, while individual human beings and institutions will make their own decisions individually and will be held individually responsible for making those decisions conscientiously, consultation with others also plays a role in the formation of conscience about particular decisions. The Aristotelian dictum that one ought to seek the opinions of "the many and the wise" in deliberation and practical reasoning remains sound.[10] In particular, those whose consciences have already been formed in moral communities such as churches seem obliged to consult before making serious moral decisions in order to carry out the duty to inform conscience in particular cases.

Conscience and Moral Error

Akrasia

The concept of conscience illuminates the problem in moral psychology known as *akrasia*. The observation that human beings often do what they know to be wrong was first discussed extensively by Aristotle.[11] It also finds expression in the letters of St. Paul when he observes, "For I do not do the good that I want but the evil that I do not want" (Rom 15:19).

The activity of conscience is the recognition of the gap between a moral agent's knowledge of the good and the right, and the actual acts that the agent either has already undertaken or about which the agent is deliberating. It is a sad fact that such judgments do not lead moral agents universally to choose and to do the good and the right. If knowledge of the good and the right led moral agents infallibly to choose the good and the right, there would be no need for judgments of conscience because there would never be a gap between the agent's fundamental moral commitments and the agent's acts.

Moral agents may be led astray by a variety of mechanisms, e.g., the influence of other individuals or of the agent's own strong, conflicting beliefs or desires. What leads a moral agent ultimately to choose other than the good and the right, may be a stronger desire, or some competing, prior commitment, or another powerful belief, or the influences of other agents. The act of conscience itself, however, is the agent's judgment that a possible choice (or, in retrospect, a choice that has already been made) is something that violates the agent's fundamental moral commitments.

Conscience is thus not a faculty of judging right and wrong that is different from our usual ways of employing our faculties of reason, emotion, and will. Conscience arises from a commitment to engage in a "self-conscious activity, integrating reason, emotion, and will, in self-committed decisions about right and wrong, good and evil."[12]

How can an agent fail to act on the judgments of conscience? This is the puzzle of *akrasia*. The explanations are many and varied. For example, to acknowledge the primacy of conscience but to reason that a particular conscientious judgment does not apply in a particular case, and so to act otherwise, might be an instance of "self-deception." To allow unbalanced emotions to overwhelm the balanced judgment of reason and emotion, leading the agent to act against a conscientious judgment, would be "incontinence." In general, choosing to do other than what conscientious judgment would prescribe is simply called "weakness of the will."

Erroneous Conscience

Conscience can also err in its judgments. Adolf Eichmann, for instance, apparently acted conscientiously. His conscience, by report, was troubled by the few exceptions he made for those Jews that he had allowed, solely because of their personal connections with him and his family, to avoid the concentration camps he honestly felt they justly deserved.[13] This suggests, rather obviously, that conscience is not an infallible moral guide.

Acknowledging the primacy of conscience does not imply a belief in the infallibility of conscience. Conscience can err through ignorance or misunderstanding.

Error can occur through faulty reasoning, emotional imbalance, or poor judgment. Agents can choose conscientiously and wrongly. Some such mistakes may be cognitive. A moral agent may have erred in understanding the facts of the case as they pertain to the moral decision. The agent may be ignorant of the facts or about the applicable moral rules. The agent's moral premises might be wrong. Or, the agent might have employed faulty moral reasoning, perhaps because strong emotions have clouded the ability to decide.

The notion of conscience assumes an obligation for correct formation of conscience on the part of the agent. This obligation finds juridical expression in the notion of due diligence. A moral agent is responsible for doing a certain amount of work to inform conscience, both with respect to the adoption of moral principles and with respect to accurate knowledge of the particulars necessary to decide a case correctly. One may therefore judge that certain moral agents are culpable for their poorly formed consciences while others are not. Presumably we can judge that Eichmann's conscience was poorly formed and that he was culpable for his actions. In other cases, however, this judgment will be much more difficult to make.

Despite the possibility of mistakes, over the centuries most moral philosophers have come to the conclusion that an erring conscience is binding.[14] This is quite logical. If conscience is derived from the fundamental moral commitment to choose the right and the good, then one is obligated to choose what one has determined to be the right and the good. One is only culpable in those cases in which one has failed to inform conscience properly, so that one's determination of the right and the good was culpably wrong.

Conscience and Moral Complicity

Central to many vexing cases about conscience is the relationship between an individual agent's judgments of conscience, and cooperation with others who have reached different conscientious conclusions or have ignored the dictates of conscience. Everyone agrees that one should not be a moral accomplice to evildoers. The bank guard who leaves the bank door open in order to facilitate a robbery by his best friend is an accomplice in the crime and has acted wrongly.

Nonetheless, some cooperation with evil is part of the human condition. Human beings need to cooperate with one another—this is part of human nature. Yet it is also part of human nature that human beings are morally and intellectually finite. All of us are thus involved in wrongdoing. As Chesterton once observed, original sin is the only theological doctrine for which we have empirical proof.[15] But how does one determine whether one is so closely involved in another's wrongdoing that one is complicit? Can a physician be held complicit in adultery if she continues to employ a nurses' aide that she knows is involved in an adulterous relationship? Does the fact that the physician is providing the income that the aide uses to rent the hotel room, buy the flowers, etc., make her complicit in that aide's wrongdoing? Under what conditions can one judge that an agent is an accomplice in the wrongdoing of others? When must one simply accept the fact that all of us are morally fallible?

Obviously, conscientious judgments are required to determine whether one is complicit in the wrongdoing of others, judgments that must be informed by the virtue of prudence or practical wisdom. While others have written on the general subject,[16] the natural law tradition has developed a very complex and subtle set of principles for navigating such uncertain and often uncharted waters.[17] The first judgment to be made is whether the agent shares in the intent of the one who is doing wrong. This is called "formal" cooperation, and a well-formed conscience always ought to judge that such cooperation is morally wrong.

There can be no hard and fast rules for determining whether an agent's "material" involvement in the wrongdoing of another, even when the agent does not share the evil intention, is immoral. One must consider issues such as the following:[18] (1) How necessary is the agent's cooperation to the carrying out of the act? Could it occur without the agent's cooperation? The more likely that it could occur without the agent's cooperation, the more justified is the agent's cooperation. (2) How proximate is the agent's action to the act, in space and time and in the causal chain? The further removed the action is, the more justified is the agent's cooperation. (3) Is the agent under any degree of duress to perform the act? Is someone compelling the act at gunpoint? Does failure to cooperate mean loss of livelihood and ability to provide for a family? The more duress the agent is under, the more justifiable is the agent's cooperation. (4) How likely is it that the agent's cooperation will become habitual? The less likely, the more justifiable. (5) Is there a significant potential for scandal? (Scandal is used here in the technical sense of leading others to believe that the agent providing the material cooperation actually approves of the act so that observers might thereby be led to think it morally permissible.) The less the potential for scandal, the more permissible the cooperation would be. (6) Does the agent have a special role that would be violated by this action? The less the agent has special role responsibilities that potentially would be contravened by the act, the more justifiable it is. (7) Does the agent have a proportionately important reason for the cooperation? That is, is there some morally important good that will come about because of the agent's indirect cooperation? If so, the agent has a better justification for cooperation.

Note, however, that the prudential judgment necessary to determine that cooperation is justified is itself a matter for conscience. Individuals will differ in these judgments, but all are required to make such judgments conscientiously.

Institutional Conscience

Ought the notion of conscience to be extended to institutions? Can institutions properly be said to have consciences?

Clearly, neither the faculty account nor the emotional account of conscience would support extending the notion of conscience to institutions. Institutions do not have minds or emotions. The individual members of institutions have minds and emotions, but their thoughts and feelings cannot be ascribed to the institution per se. One could provide a list of the various moral intuitions of the individual members of an institution, or describe the average net emotional state of the members of an institution, but these would not be the intuitions or emotions of the institution. Institutions do not have thoughts or feelings, but institutions *do* exercise moral agency. The purpose of human institutions is collective action. Action requires intention, deliberation, and choice. The practical reasoning of institutions has a moral character, because ethics, as Aristotle has observed, is about what to do, when what to do is up to us.[19] Institutions engage in such practical reasoning, make choices about what to do, and are held responsible for their actions.

The multiplicity of individual agents that constitute a human institution join together to act collectively as a single moral agent. It may seem peculiar to attribute moral agency to institutions rather than only to individual persons. But the purpose of human institutions is, in fact, moral agency. Human institutions make decisions and act. And since they exercise moral agency, everything essential to the notion of conscience can be ascribed to institutions.

Institutions have identities. They are not random collections of professionals or other individuals thrown together in a building without a common purpose and identity that transcends each of them. In organizations that qualify as moral agents, the identity of the organization is not exhausted by merely tallying up the identities of the individuals. Organizations have an identity that is much more than the sum of their constituent parts.

Human institutions come together for a common purpose. They set that purpose in writing in such documents as their articles of incorporation and their mission statements. These statements (at least implicitly but often explicitly) set forth the fundamental moral commitments of these institutions. In fact, the self-identifying fundamental moral commitments of institutions are often clearer than those of individual human agents, because mechanisms such as mission and value statements help to make them explicit.

Institutions deliberate. Before acting, they weigh options and examine arguments for and against certain choices. They often consult, both internally and externally, so that they may be informed by the opinions of the many and the wise. They ascertain the fit between the choices before them and the aims and purposes for which the institution was created. They are organized into boards, officers, committees, administrators, and employees precisely in order to deliberate.

Institutions make decisions. They have structures by which in certain contexts acts by individuals will count as acts by the organization, and both the members of the organization and the society at large acknowledge the validity of these structures.[20] They are organized to do so through procedures such as voting or the delegation of authority. They decide to make certain things, buy certain things, publish certain things, advocate certain things. These are concrete acts that, while they could be undertaken by individuals, are potently undertaken by institutions. Institutions act in the world and affect the world on the basis of choices they have made.

Institutions are held morally and legally responsible for the choices they make and the collective actions they undertake. They are responsible to various constituencies, such as members, shareholders, the public, and those affected by their decisions. They are worthy of praise or blame for those decisions.[21]

Legally, incorporated institutions are considered persons. This is not only to hold the institutions legally responsible for their actions, but a recognition of the moral agency that is a necessary condition for assigning responsibility.

Human institutions can thus be true moral agents. They have an identity that is greater than the sum of the identities of constituent members of the group. Almost all have explicit mission statements. Some have religious identities. They act intentionally. They make decisions for which they may receive praise or blame. They have recognized institutional structures by which the decisions of some (e.g., the Board of Trustees, the CEO, the Dean, etc.) count as the decisions of the institution. We can appropriately criticize any of these leaders for acting in their own best interests rather than the interests of the institution. They are authorized to make decisions on behalf of an institution that is greater than any one of them, and their decisions must not undermine the fundamental self-identifying commitments of the institution.

Moreover, if human institutions are properly considered moral agents, they must also be understood to have consciences. Institutional conscience, like the conscience of individuals, is Janus-faced. The conscience of an institution is rooted in the fact that it professes a set of fundamental moral commitments and it must act in accord with them. The conscience of an institution is exercised in making the moral judgment that a decision that it has made or is considering would violate those fundamental moral commitments. Human institutions such as churches, incorporated businesses, professional organizations, schools, hospitals, and others act intentionally as institutions. They receive praise or blame for the decisions they make. They reason about these decisions. They must sort through the emotional experiences of their individual members in making decisions. They must make moral judgments. In so doing, the institution, if it is to be a truly moral institution, should pursue its goals, decisions, and actions with a fundamental commitment to moral integrity.

Like individuals, institutions can fail conscientiously through faulty reasoning, misplaced emotions, or poor judgment. In so doing, a hospital would join the ranks of other human institutions struggling for integrity in the midst of all the ambiguity of the moral world. Institutions can also fail to act upon their own conscientious judgments, either through reasoning by expediency, or by being overwhelmed by emotions such as panic or greed, or by weakness of the will. This is how institutions become caught up in the web of evil in the world.

All this would imply that human institutions can be said to have consciences, not merely by analogy, but actually.[22] Whether institutions recognize this fact, or actually act conscientiously, does not matter. Conscience is a fundamental moral commitment on the part of a moral agent to moral integrity, involving a commitment to uphold fundamental moral precepts and moral identity and, based upon these fundamental moral commitments, to make use of reason, emotion, and will to arrive at proper moral judgments and to act on these judgments.

Four Loci of Conscientious Agency

Certain logical complexities come into play once one ascribes moral agency and conscience to human institutions. This is particularly true of certain very common types of institutions that are composed of professionals rendering service to individual citizens. In such complex institutions there are actually four loci of conscientious agency: the individual citizens, the professional members of the institution, the institution itself, and the society of which the citizens, professionals, and institution are members (particularly, but not exclusively, as mediated by government). Some of the most pressing moral problems of our day concern conflicts of conscience between and among these four loci of conscientious agency. I have called these "loci" because to say "levels" might inadvertently convey a hierarchical or lexical ordering without argument. Whether there is such a hierarchy is a question that must be explored. Most importantly, one needs to know how best to sort out conflicts among various agents at the same locus or between and among different loci. How can competing moral claims of conscience be resolved in such complex institutions?

Tolerance

The notion of tolerance evolved in the seventeenth-century Western world as a way of resolving competing claims of conscience between and among individual citizens and between the state and individual citizens.[23] Initially, these differences were differences in religious conviction. Soon, however, it was recognized that the ambit of conscience and the sphere of tolerance encompassed moral as well as religious convictions.

Tolerance is necessary because moral knowledge is imperfect. Even a moral realist will acknowledge that although one might approach certainty regarding moral questions, moral reasoning has no empirical method of verification. Accordingly, conscientious persons will disagree about a wide range of moral issues. My view of moral epistemology is one of modified moral realism tempered by epistemic moral humility.[24] On this view, a number of very general moral principles can be known with certainty (e.g., good is to be done and evil to be avoided). A good number of specific acts can be determined to be wrong with moral certainty (e.g., putting people in gas chambers to rid the world of "imperfect genes"). With respect to a wide range of other moral issues, however, there will be less certainty. Particularly, in applying moral principles and rules to particular cases, there will be less certainty. This is *not* to say that there are no correct answers to particular moral questions. The idea of modified moral realism is that there *are* correct answers to well-formed moral questions, but that the limits of human reason and good will force us to be humble about our ability to know the answers to all of these questions with certainty. Each of us must be prepared to admit that we may be mistaken in our moral views. The careful way to understand moral uncertainty, then, is that given the imperfections of human moral knowledge and reasoning, one must acknowledge that disagreements will be inevitable. Yet, because there *are* correct answers to these questions, it is worth arguing over them. In the end, it is this modified moral realism tempered by epistemic humility that is the true basis for tolerance.

On this account, conscientious persons can argue with each other about moral questions, and have good reasons for doing so. Respect for the dignity that comes with each one's status as a moral agent, in fact, demands that each one take the other's moral agency and moral responsibility seriously enough to offer challenges if one believes the other is mistaken. If the cause of disagreement is faulty reasoning, and one can show one's interlocutor that a particular moral position is inconsistent with his or her previously espoused, fundamental, self-identifying moral principles, one should be able to convince a conscientious person to have a change of moral position. If the facts turn out to be other than they first appeared to be to someone, he or she might be convinced to change a moral position by learning certain empirical facts. But if the differences are at the level of fundamental self-identifying moral principles, sincere persons may reach an impasse on a particular case. This is how the most serious conflicts of conscience arise.

Because such conflicts are inevitable, and because there may be no way to prove that any particular view is correct, while all reasonable moral agents acknowledge the importance of moral argument because of a shared understanding that there are correct answers to well-formed moral questions even if the human capacity to reach those answers is imperfect, one must be prepared to tolerate a wide range of views within the boundaries of what can be known with certainty and definitively prescribed or proscribed. Respect for conscience is thus at the root of the concept of tolerance.[25] Tolerance may be defined as mutual respect for the equality and dignity of moral agents in their varied conscientious beliefs.

Tolerance is not, in the narrow and negative terms of Mill, mere noninterference in the self-regarding actions of others. The set of all purely self-regarding actions is probably an empty set. Tolerance is a sign of respect for other persons with whom we are connected, not a consequence of our inherent disconnectedness. Nonetheless, people's fundamental self-identifying moral commitments differ, and the conscientious moral judgments based on them will also, of necessity, differ. These conscientious differences command deep respect. Conscience is at the heart of morality, concerned with the fundamental commitment to be moral and the commitment to judge one's own actions according to moral standards. If one is to show respect for other moral agents, one does so first and foremost through respect for their consciences.

Without conscience, no morality is possible. To have a conscience is to commit oneself, no matter what one's self-identifying moral commitments, to respect for the consciences of others. This is the basis for the concept of tolerance.

The Equivalence Thesis

Despite the differences in organizational levels of the various loci of moral agency and conscience that I have outlined, I would like to argue that there is no hierarchy of the respect due to the conscientious decisions of individual citizens, professional members of institutions, and the institutions themselves, and that a just society will grant equal respect to claims of conscience arising at all of the loci of conscientious agency.

While societies also constitute a locus of moral agency and

conscience, my purpose is to understand how a just society will organize and adjudicate claims of conscience, and so, in this discussion, I will consider the society to be the context of the organization of claims of conscience and not a distinct locus of agency and conscience. In fact, a central role for the state is to protect and promote respect for conscience (tolerance) with regard to the adjudication of conscientious moral differences between citizens, professionals, and institutions. One might say that this is one of the conscientious roles of a good and just state.

The equivalence thesis states that claims of conscience by individual citizens, by professional members of institutions, and by institutions, should be treated with equal regard. This means that a claim of conscience of a citizen vis-à-vis a professional and of a professional vis-à-vis a citizen, and of a citizen vis-à-vis an institution and of an institution vis-à-vis a citizen, and of a professional vis-à-vis an institution and of an institution vis-à-vis a professional, must all be granted an equal degree of tolerance.[26]

The equivalence derives from the fact that claims of conscience are based on the ability to act as a moral agent and to make conscientious decisions for which the agent is responsible. Citizens, professionals, and institutions all exercise moral agency in equal measure, and their claims of conscience must therefore be tolerated in equal measure. Since conscience is close to the heart of what morality is, and a just society will not want to force the moral agents that constitute it to alienate themselves from their deepest self-identifying beliefs and commitments, the widest possible berth for tolerance should be afforded to all moral agents. And since a just society treats moral agents equally, the same wide berth of tolerance should be afforded to all moral agents in that society.

One important asymmetry is that an institution might, like a society, constitute a context for adjudicating differing claims of conscience. An institution, *qua* institution, may not have taken a firm position on a particular issue, either because of uncertainty about the morality of the practice or the position, or because the issue does not concern the fundamental self-identifying moral commitments of the institution. In such a circumstance, the institution would be in the position of a society adjudicating differing claims of conscience between and among citizens and professionals who interact under its auspices. As such, the institution would be bound by the moral rules that determine whether a society is just and tolerant. Individual citizens and professionals would never be in the position of providing a context for the operation of conscience and tolerance, but would be limited to individual interactions between and among citizens, professionals, and institutions.

The Boundaries of Tolerance

While tolerance, considered as mutual respect for conscience, entails that moral agents be given a very wide berth in their moral decision making, tolerance does not entail absolute forbearance in the face of moral differences between apparently conscientious people. Tolerance must have, like any virtue, an Aristotelian mean.

An intolerant society is one that draws the space of tolerance for differences in conscience too narrowly. A society that places too many acts outside the boundaries of tolerance for conscientious differences in belief is a "repressive" society. Repressiveness, one should note, knows no allegiance to any particular political ideology.

By contrast, a licentious society is one that gives conscience far too wide a berth, a society in which "anything goes." The condition of the late Roman Empire is often presented as an example of this sort of society.

The ideal, although it may be difficult to define, is a society that gives conscience its proper berth of tolerance. Such a society is one we would plainly call tolerant.

For the purposes of this discussion, a "practice" will be taken to mean a policy of acting or of refraining from acting, based on fundamental religious beliefs or other deeply held, self-identifying moral beliefs. The fundamental bases on which a tolerant and just society might deny such a claim of conscience include considerations such as the following.

In general, the moral warrant for a society to compel a moral agent to act contrary to conscience is greater if:

1) the agent's practice is incontrovertibly considered immoral by all reasonable persons;

2) the practice at issue is not a serious matter related to fundamental moral commitments;

3) the agent's practice undermines or contradicts the principle of tolerance itself;

4) the agent's practice entails a substantial risk of serious illness, injury, or death for those who do not share the belief that is said to justify the practice;

5) the agent's practice is at odds with a task that is central to the agent's role as a citizen, or is at odds with the core mission of the profession or institution to which the agent voluntarily belongs and from which the agent is seeking conscientious relief;

6) no reasonable alternatives to accommodate the conscientious objection are available;

7) the demand for the agent to act contrary to conscience would constitute a compulsory refraining from a particular form of speech or motor action rather than the compulsory performance of a particular form of speech or motor action.

The principles are not intended as algorithmic rules, and their concrete application will require the exercise of practical wisdom. As Aristotle observes with respect to a subject like ethics, one's measure can only be as precise as the subject to which it is applied.[27] Nonetheless, the articulation of such a set of principles constitutes an advance in the ethical analysis of conscience cases because there are, at present, almost no relevant guidelines or principles.

While no single principle automatically trumps the others, the first comes closest to doing so. Obviously, societies legally prescribe and proscribe many practices that all agree could be conscientiously supported only by a malformed conscience, e.g., rape, murder, and theft. Societies can be wrong about these sorts of considerations, and acts of conscientious objection with a willingness to accept the legal consequences of civil disobedience would be required of a good moral agent under such abnormal circumstances as a genocidal society and state. The issues of most general concern, however—those that require wise judgment in a normal society that is striving toward true justice and tolerance—are those practices that are in the gray zone, considered immoral by many but not all the members of a society; those practices that many but not all members of a society might even want to declare illegal, but do not violate the laws of that society as currently constituted and about which there is no moral consensus. Under what circumstances can a society legally prescribe or proscribe practices of this more nebulous nature that make a claim for tolerance?

The first of these grounds for making such a judgment would be if the plea for tolerance were based on purported claims of conscience regarding a practice that undermines or contradicts the principle of tolerance itself. The judgment that an appeal to conscience actually undermines or contradicts the principle of tolerance itself will not always be easy to make, but many cases will be obvious. More specifically, if the practice at issue is denial of services based on antipathy toward a person's fixed characteristics (such as race or gender), or is based on a mere dislike or disagreement with a moral agent's deeply held, self-identifying beliefs and affiliations that are unrelated to the practice at issue, then the denial of services would be intolerant and ought not to be tolerated. By contrast, if the denial of services *were* to be related to the beliefs at stake in the conscientious disagreement, that denial of services, *ceteris paribus*, ought to be tolerated.

So, for example, the denial of a loan to someone because she explicitly proposed to use that money to start a new pornography company, if one conscientiously were to believe that pornography is immoral, and that the loan would materially enable this immoral activity, ought to be tolerated in a just and tolerant society. By contrast, for a bank to deny a loan to someone because he or she was African-American would be intolerant and could not be the basis for a claim of tolerance based on conscientious objection. It would seem unjust to ask for tolerance for an intolerant belief, such as racial or religious discrimination. A moral system that tolerated intolerance would seem internally inconsistent.

This, I think, establishes one firm boundary for tolerance. One need not tolerate intolerance.

The next ground for considering whether it would be just to override a plea for tolerance of an allegedly conscientious practice would be a determination that the practice entails a substantial and imminent risk of serious illness, injury, or death to the party that disagrees with the practice. This presents a reasonable ground for considering whether the practice can justifiably be tolerated. However, since conscience, as I argued above, is so fundamental to morality, the grounds for contravening someone's conscientious disagreement must be very strong. Therefore, it would seem, in general, that inconvenience, psychological distress, or mild symptoms for one party would not be sufficient grounds to compel the conscience of another. Rather, one would need to demonstrate a likely and imminent risk of actual serious illness or injury to the party that disagrees with the practice. This standard is that which must be met in order to breach confidentiality under the Tarasoff precedent in medical ethics.[28] Respect for conscience, I suggest, is at least as important as the maintenance of patient confidentiality.

Of course, mutual respect for conscience would require a respectful means of sorting out disagreements short of a refusal to provide a requested service.[29] One would need, as specified in consideration 6 above, to explore whether there are reasonable alternative ways of accommodating a request that violates the agent's conscientious objection to the requested practice. Conscience is a serious matter, and if there are reasonable alternatives available by which a clash of conscientious judgments about a particular morally controversial practice may be adjudicated short of compelling a moral agent to act contrary to conscience, these alternatives must be employed. For example, if a banker conscientiously objects to working on a loan to a corporation he or she conscientiously believes is engaging in an immoral practice, and other bankers in the same bank do not share the objection and the bank itself has no position on the matter, it would be far more reasonable and just to allow the alternative banker to process the loan than to compel the original banker to act contrary to conscience.

In addition, the reciprocity of respect for conscience that is the basis of tolerance also requires that disagreeing parties refrain from active interference with each other's exercise of conscience. Thus, one could attempt to persuade a fellow citizen that eating meat is immoral, but one ought not to prevent that person, by force, from eating meat.

A final rule of thumb is that substantially greater moral justification should be required to compel an agent to engage in a form of speech or to perform a motor action that violates that agent's conscientious beliefs than should be required to compel an agent to refrain from a form of speech or to refrain from performing a motor action that the agent conscientiously holds to be a duty. For example, less justification should be required to prohibit public high school teachers from proselytizing students even if they feel a conscientious obligation to do so, than should be required to compel public high teachers against their conscientious objections to hand out condoms to students as part of a public health effort to diminish the spread of sexually transmitted diseases. No one should object to a prohibition on teachers proselytizing their students. Far more moral justification should be required, however, to compel the performance of an action that an individual finds conscientiously objectionable.

It would therefore seem that tolerant societies would set a very high threshold for compelling the performance of a practice in violation of conscience. Conscientious refraining from actions, when such restraint does not risk illness, injury, or death, and does not constitute traditional tort claims such as battery, assault, or libel, would not seem to rise to the level of sufficient grounds for compelling conscience.

Case Example

How might some of these considerations work in practice? Let us suppose a general case of —

Two citizens:	q and r
Two professionals:	x and y
Two institutions:	A and B
A number of practices:	*services* P_{s1}, P_{s2}, P_{s3}
	refrainings P_{r1}, P_{r2}, P_{r3}

Consider the general case of citizen q demanding controversial service P_{s1} of professional x in a tolerant society.

Let this general case be illustrated by the following example: The tolerant society at issue consists of 50% traditional Northeastern Africans and the practice at issue (P_{s1}) is female circumcision (female genital mutilation), which is not illegal, is widely practiced, but is very controversial in the society. Institution A is Doctors Without Borders Hospital and institution B is Save Our Traditions Hospital. Doctors Without Borders is firmly opposed to female genital mutilation. As a matter of policy it does not perform the procedure in any country where it sets up relief hospitals. The Save Our Traditions Intertribal Association, which sponsors hospital B, actively promotes, and is certainly not opposed to, performing female circumcisions. Professionals x and y are both physicians with admitting privileges at both hospitals. Dr. x is conscientiously opposed to female genital mutilation. Dr. y is not, arguing that it is much better to perform this service in a hospital because it is safe, effective, and associated with many fewer immediate and later complications for women if it is performed by physicians than if it is left in the hands of traditional tribesmen. Citizen q shows up at Doctors Without Borders Hospital and is assigned to Dr. x and asks for circumcision for her ten-year-old daughter. When he refuses, she complains, stating that her daughter's life would be ruined without it, that she does not trust the safety of traditional tribesmen performing the procedure. When told that she could go to the Save Our Traditions Hospital to have it done, she complains that her rights are being infringed. The save Our Traditions Hospital is ten miles away and she must walk. She is a working mother and fears she might lose her job if she takes off another day of work.

Question 1: Ought the conscientious objection of Dr. x be overridden and should he be forced to perform the procedure?

Question 2: Ought the Doctors Without Borders Hospital be required to transfer the care of citizen q and her daughter to Dr. y who would be willing to perform the procedure at the Save Our Traditions Hospital?

It would seem that the answer to both questions is no.

A. From an international and intercultural perspective, the issue of female circumcision is not one that is clearly settled such that no reasonable person could be opposed to the practice.

B. By the equivalence thesis, the opposition of both Dr. x and the Doctors Without Borders Hospital to what they consider female genital mutilation deserves equal respect. Both are moral agents for whom opposition arises from deeply held, self-identifying moral commitments. Therefore, the conscientious objection to the procedure on the part of Doctors Without Borders Hospital deserves equivalent respect to the objection of Dr. x.

C. Opposing female circumcision does not undermine the basis of tolerance.

D. The demand of citizen q is for the performance of a motor act, which requires a very high degree of justification in order to compel another citizen to perform it contrary to conscience.

E. The Save Our Traditions Hospital presents a reasonable alternative to accommodate this clash of conscientious beliefs.

F. While those who are at risk can be identified, the significant inconvenience of requiring citizen q and her daughter to walk ten miles does not meet the threshold of a significant, imminent risk of grave injury so that the grounds for overriding conscientious objection to the performance of this motor act are not met.

Conclusion

Many more combinations and permutations and test cases could be proposed. What I have done is the following: defined conscience and attempted to show how it applies to institutions as equally as it does to individual moral agents; explained what tolerance means; mapped the various loci of moral agency involved in complex conflicts of conscience among individual citizens, professionals, institutions, and societies; proposed a thesis of equivalence with respect to the regard due to claims of conscience among all these loci of moral agency and conscience; and proposed a set of criteria by which a just and tolerant society might go about mediating competing claims of conscience. These considerations should prove useful in contemporary debates about conscience, particularly as they relate to institutions and morally controversial practices in a pluralistic society that claims to be tolerant.

ENDNOTES

1   The basic ideas of this account are drawn from Daniel P. Sulmasy, "What is Conscience and Why is Respect for it so Important?" *Theoretical Medicine and Bioethics* 29 (2008):135–149.

2   Joseph Butler, *Five Sermons Preached at the Rolls Chapel and a Dissertation upon the Nature of Virtue* (Indianapolis: Bobbs-Merrill, 1950), 37–38.

3 See J.F.M. Hunter, "Conscience," in *Conscience*, ed. John Donnelly and Leonard Lyons (New York: Alba House, 1973) , 55–84.

4 Timothy C. Potts, *Conscience in Medieval Philosophy* (New York: Cambridge University Press, 1980), 61.

5 Thomas Aquinas, *Summa Theologiae*, Blackfriars ed. (New York: McGraw-Hill, 1963), I-II, q. 64, a. 2.

6 John Stuart Mill, "On Liberty," in *John Stuart Mill: Three Essays* (New York: Oxford University Press, 1975), 5–141.

7 Peter Fuss, "Conscience," in *Conscience*, eds. Donnelly and Lyons.

8 William Shakespeare, *Hamlet*, III.i.83.

9 Fuss, "Conscience," 43.

10 Aristotle, *Topics*, in *The Complete Works of Aristotle*, vol. I, ed. Jonathan Barnes (Princeton: Princeton University Press, 1984), 100b21–24.

11 Aristotle, *Nicomachean Ethics*, trans. Terence Irwin (Indianapolis: Hackett, 1985), 1145b8 ff.

12 Sidney Callahan, *In Good Conscience: Reason and Emotion in Moral Discourse* (New York: Harper, 1991), 14.

13 Hannah Arendt, *Eichmann in Jerusalem* (New York: Viking, 1963), 122.

14 Aquinas, *Summa Theologiae*, I-II, q. 19, a. 5; Alan Donagan, *The Theory of Morality* (Chicago: University of Chicago Press, 1977), 131–42..

15 G.K. Chesterton, *Orthodoxy* (San Francisco: Ignatius Press, 1995), 19.

16 F.M. Kamm, "Responsibility and Collaboration," *Philosophy & Public Affairs* 28 (1999):169–204.

17 James F. Keenan and Thomas R. Kopfensteiner, "The Principle of Cooperation," *Health Progress* 76 (April 1995): 23–27; Germain Grisez, *The Way of the Lord Jesus*, vol. 3, *Difficult Moral Questions* (Quincy, IL: Franciscan Press, 1997).

18 Grisez, *Difficult Moral Questions*, 871–97.

19 See Aristotle, *Nicomachean Ethics*, 1112a31–32.

20 Peter A. French, "Collective Responsibility and the Practice of Medicine," *Journal of Medicine and Philosophy* 7 (1982): 65–85.

21 Michael D. Smith, "The Virtuous Organization," *Journal of Medicine and Philosophy* 7 (1982): 35–42.

22 Thomas A. Nairn, "Institutional Conscience Revisited," *New Theology Review* 14 (May 2001): 39–49.

23 John Locke, *A Letter Concerning Toleration*, ed. James H. Tully (Indianapolis: Hackett, 1983).

24 See Sulmasy, "What Is Conscience and Why Is Respect for it so Important?"

25 Daniel P. Sulmasy, "Institutional Conscience and Moral Pluralism in Health Care," *New Theology Review* 10 (Nov. 1997): 5–12.

26 For the purposes of this essay I am assuming that institutions are free associations, i.e., that no citizen or professional is required to be a member of the institution and that no citizen is compelled to make use of its services, and that these are the only relevant relationships. Reality is considerably more complex. For example, some professionals belong to institutions consisting of other professionals such as practice groups and professional organizations and some institutions are state-sponsored. While the principles articulated here could be extended to encompass these other potential loci of moral agency and the potential complexities introduced by the idea of overlapping or sharing of moral agency, the simple model described here is complex enough to warrant limiting the discussion for clarity of exposition of the basic ideas. Further, the most pressing cases of the day arise in the basic model discussed in this essay, so that little of practical value will be lost through this simplification.

27 Aristotle, *Nicomachean Ethics*, 1094b.

28 Daniel P. Sulmasy, "On Warning Families about Genetic Risk: the Ghost of Tarasoff," *American Journal of Medicine* 109 (2000): 738–739.

29 Morten Magelssen, "When Should Conscientious Objection Be Accepted?" *Journal of Medical Ethics* 38 (2012): 18–21.

Chapter Four
Conscience and Its Enemies
Robert P. George

Introduction

Over the past few years, we have become all too aware of the threats to conscience rights in various domains, especially those having to do with issues pertaining to the sanctity of human life and to sexual morality, marriage, and the family. These specific threats reflect and manifest attitudes and ideologies that are now deeply entrenched in the intellectual world and in the elite sector of the culture more generally. President Barack Obama, Secretary of Health and Human Services Kathleen Sebelius, and many other federal and state officials are advancing and supporting policies trampling conscience rights, such as the notorious Department of Health and Human Services ("HHS") contraception and abortion drug mandate, because they have deeply absorbed me-generation dogmas that make nonsense of the very idea of conscience rights. Secretary Sebelius and her closest collaborators, especially the Planned Parenthood Federation of America, insist that opponents of the HHS mandate oppose both women's health and science itself.

There is rich irony here: over the past two years, neither HHS nor the White House has responded substantively to the flood of evidence submitted by experts demonstrating the lack of scientific support for the medical, demographic, or economic claims associated with the HHS mandate. This practice—refusing to grapple with the relevant evidence while using the mantle of "science" to silence or marginalize objectors— is commonly used by enemies of conscience. This chapter will analyze an important precursor to current incarnations of this practice: the 2008 report of the American College of Obstetricians and Gynecologists recommending the denial of meaningful conscience protection to medical professionals on the grounds of a non-scientific, ideologically dictated preference for widely available abortion.

Personal Opinions and Ideology, not "Science"—ACOG's "Limits of Conscientious Refusal in Reproductive Medicine"

On September 11, 2008, the President's Council on Bioethics heard testimony by Anne Lyerly, M.D., chair of the Committee on Ethics of the American College of Obstetricians and Gynecologists (ACOG). Dr. Lyerly appeared in connection with the Council's review of her committee's Opinion (No. 385) entitled "Limits of Conscientious Refusal in Reproductive Medicine." That Opinion proposes that physicians in the field of women's health be *required as a matter of ethical duty* to refer patients for abortions and sometimes even to perform abortions themselves.

I found the ACOG Ethics Committee's opinion shocking and, indeed frightening, not only in its lack of regard—bordering on contempt, really—for the sincere claims of conscience of Catholic, Evangelical Protestant, Orthodox Jewish, and other pro-life physicians and health care workers, but also in its treatment of feticide—the deliberate destruction of a child in the womb—as if it were a matter of health care, rather than what it typically is, namely, a decision based upon *non-medical* considerations (such as whether a woman or her husband or boyfriend happens to want a child). On the understanding of medicine implicit in the report, the ends of medicine are fundamentally not about the preservation and restoration of health considered as an objective reality and human good, but rather about satisfying the personal preferences or lifestyle desires of people who come to physicians requesting surgeries or other services, quite irrespective of whether these services are in any meaningful sense medically indicated.

Let's say that a woman conceives a child and is unhappy about it. Is she sick? Does she need an abortion for the sake of her health? Not on any reasonable understanding or definition of health, even if we mean mental health. Pregnancy is not a disease. It is a natural process. In the normal case, a pregnant woman is not sick. Nor in the overwhelming majority of cases does pregnancy pose a threat to a woman's health. This is clear enough, but to make it still clearer let's imagine that a woman who is initially unhappy to be pregnant changes her mind. On reflection, she's content to be pregnant and happy to have a baby on the way. Did she suddenly shift from being sick, and in need of "health care" in the form of an abortion, to being well? Now let's consider that a couple of months later, she changes her mind again. It turns out, let us suppose, that the baby is a girl, and she really wants a boy. So she is once again unhappy about the pregnancy and she reverts to wanting an abortion. Did knowledge of the baby's sex transform her from being a healthy pregnant woman to being sick? The question answers itself.

Now let us consider the ACOG Committee report. What jumped off the page at me when I first read it is that it is an exercise in moral philosophy—bad moral philosophy, but lay that aside for now—not medicine. It proposes a definition of conscience, something that cannot be supplied by science or medicine, then proposes to instruct its readers on "the limits of conscientious refusals, describing how claims of conscience should be weighed in the context of other values critical to the ethical provision of health care." Again, knowledge of these limits and values, as well as knowledge of what should count as the ethical provision of health care, are not and cannot possibly be the product of scientific inquiry for medicine as such. The proposed instruction offered by those responsible for the ACOG Committee report represents a philosophical and ethical opinion—*their* philosophical and ethical opinion.

The report goes on to "outline options for public policy," and to propose "recommendations that maximize accommodation of the individual's religious and moral beliefs while avoiding imposition of these beliefs on others or interfering with the safe, timely, and financially feasible access to reproductive health care that all women deserve."

Yet again notice that every concept in play here—the putative balancing, the judgment as to what constitutes an "imposition" of personal beliefs on others, the view of what constitutes health care or reproductive health care, the judgment about what is deserved—is philosophical, not scientific or, strictly speaking, medical.

To the extent that they are "medical" judgments even loosely speaking, they reflect a concept of medicine informed, structured, and shaped by philosophical and ethical judgments—bad ones, by the way, such as the implicit judgment that pregnancy, when unwanted, is in effect a disease.

Those responsible for the report purport to be speaking *as* physicians and medical professionals. The special authority the report is supposed to have derives from their standing and expertise *as physicians and medical professionals*, yet at every point that matters, the judgments offered reflect their philosophical, ethical, and political judgments, not any expertise they have by virtue of their training and experience in science and medicine. At the meeting of the President's Council, the chairman, Dr. Edmund Pellegrino, asked me to offer a formal comment on Dr. Lyerly's presentation of her committee's report, and I was happy for the opportunity to call her and her colleagues out on their attempt to use their special authority as physicians to force fellow physicians to practice medicine in accord with the contestable and contested philosophical, ethical, and political judgments of the members of the committee Dr. Lyerly chaired.

And make no mistake about it: at every key point in the report, their judgments are contestable and contested. Indeed, they are contested by the very people on whose consciences they seek to impose—the people whom they would, if their report were adopted and made binding, force into line with their philosophical and ethical judgments *or drive out of their fields of medical practice*. And they are contested, of course, by many others. And in each of these contests a resolution one way or the other *cannot be determined by scientific methods*; rather, the debate is *philosophical, ethical, or political*. And once this comes to light, what is evident is that the committee report represents a sheer power play on behalf of pro-abortion individuals who happen to have acquired power in their professional association. This is not about medicine. It is about ideology. It is about politics and political power.

Lay aside for the moment the question of *whose* philosophical and political judgments are right and whose are wrong. My point so far has only been that the report is laced with, and dependent at every turn upon, philosophical and political judgments. I have not offered a critique of those judgments, although anyone who cares to do so can find plenty of criticisms of them in my work.[1] But lay *that* aside for now, too.

The key thing to see is that the issues in dispute *are* philosophical *and can only be resolved by philosophical reflection and debate.* They cannot be resolved by science or by methods of scientific inquiry. As I have observed, the committee report reflects and promotes a particular moral view and vision, and particular understandings of health and medicine, shaped in every contested dimension and in every dimension relevant to the report's subject matter, by that moral view and vision.

The report, in other words, in its driving assumptions, reasoning, and conclusions, is not morally neutral. Its analysis and recommendations for action do not proceed from a basis of moral neutrality. It represents a partisan position among the possible positions debated or adopted by people of goodwill in the medical profession and in society generally. Indeed, for me, the partisanship of the report is its most striking feature.

Its greatest irony is the report's stated worry about physicians' allegedly imposing their beliefs on patients by, for example, declining to perform or refer for abortions—or at least declining to perform abortions or provide other services in emergency situations, and declining to refer for these procedures. The assumption here, of course, is the philosophical one that abortion, even elective abortion, is "health care," and that deliberately killing babies in their mother's wombs is morally acceptable and even a woman's right.

But lay *that* aside for now, too. The truth is that the physician who refuses to perform abortions or the pharmacist who declines to dispense abortifacient drugs coerces no one. He or she simply refuses to participate in the destruction of human life—the life of the child *in utero*. He is not "imposing" anything on anyone, just as a sports shop owner who refuses to stock hollow point "cop killer" bullets, even if he may legally sell them, is not imposing anything on anyone.

By contrast, those responsible for the report and its recommendations evidently *would use coercion* to force physicians and pharmacists, who have the temerity to dissent from the philosophical and ethical views of those who happen to have acquired power in the American College of Obstetricians and Gynecologists, either to get in line or to go out of business.

If their advice were followed, and if they had their way, their field of medical practice would be cleansed of pro-life physicians whose convictions required them to refrain from performing or referring for abortions. Faithful Catholics, Evangelicals and other Protestants, and many observant Jews and Muslims, would be excluded from or forced out of obstetrics and gynecology. The entire field would be composed of people who could be relied on either to agree with, or at a minimum go along with, the moral and political convictions of the report's authors. So, in truth, *who in this debate is guilty of intolerance? Who is favoring coercion? Who is trampling on freedom? Who is imposing their values?* These questions, too, answer themselves.

It will not do, in my opinion, to say that what is being proposed here for imposition on dissenters is not a morality, but merely good medical practice, for it is not science or medicine that is shaping the report's understanding of what counts as good medical practice. It is, rather, a moral opinion doing the shaping. The opinion that abortion is good medicine is a philosophical, ethical, and political opinion; it is a judgment *brought to* medicine, *not a judgment derived from it.* It reflects a view that abortion is morally legitimate and no violation of the rights of the child who is killed, as well as the view that medicine is rightly concerned to facilitate people's lifestyle choices even when they are neither sick nor in danger of being injured, and even when the "medical" procedure involves the taking of innocent human life.

Whether an elective abortion or, to take another example, an *in vitro* fertilization procedure or what have you, counts as health care, as opposed to a patient's desired outcome or personal choice, cannot be established or resolved by the methods of science or by any morally or ethically neutral form of inquiry or reasoning. One's view of the matter will reflect one's moral and ethical convictions either way.

So the report's constant use of the language of "health" and "reproductive health" in describing or referring to the key issues giving rise to conflicts of conscience is *at best* question- begging. No, that is too kind. The report's use of this language amounts to a form of rhetorical manipulation. The question at issue in abortion is not "reproductive health" or health of any kind, precisely because direct abortions are not procedures designed to make sick people healthy or to protect them against disease or injury. Again, pregnancy is not a disease. The goal of direct abortions is to cause the death of a child because a woman believes that her life will be better without the child's existing than it would be with the child's existing. In itself, a direct (or elective) abortion—deliberately bringing about the death of a child *in utero*—does nothing to advance maternal health. (One notable exception: sometimes the death of the child is an unavoidable side effect of a procedure—such as the removal of a cancerous womb—that is designed to combat a grave threat to the mother's life or health. Such cases do not qualify as direct abortions.) That is why it is wrong to depict elective abortion as health care.

There is yet another irony worth noting. The report, in defending its proposal to compel physicians at least to refer for procedures that many physicians believe are immoral, unjust, and even homicidal, states that such referrals "need not be conceptualized as a repudiation or compromise of one's own values, but instead can be seen as an acknowledgement of both the widespread and thoughtful disagreement among physicians and society at large and the moral sincerity of others with whom one disagrees."

Suddenly it's the case that the underlying issues at stake, such as abortion, are matters of widespread and thoughtful disagreement. I myself agree with that. And it becomes clear from the report that we should show respect for the moral sincerity of those with whom we disagree. But it seems to me that it follows from these counsels that thoughtful and sincere people need not agree that abortion, for example, is morally innocent or acceptable, or that there is a "right" to abortion, or that the provision of abortion is part of good health care or is health care at all, at least in the case of elective abortions.

But then what could possibly justify the exercise of coercion to compel thoughtful, morally sincere physicians who believe that abortion is a homicidal injustice, either to perform the procedure or make a referral for it, or else leave the practice of medicine?

The report's "my way or the highway" view of the thing is anything but an acknowledgement of the widespread and thoughtful disagreement among physicians and society at large and the moral sincerity of those with whom one disagrees. Indeed, it is a repudiation of it.

Conclusion: Abortion and Conscience—The Obama Administration Adopts the ACOG Strategy

Needless to say, the enemies of conscience in the American College of Obstetricians and Gynecologists, and elsewhere in the medical establishment, now have powerful friends in the highest realms of government. It has become all too clear that these friends share the desire to eradicate conscience protection for pro-life physicians and other health care workers and pharmacists. The Obama administration has formally abrogated the conscience protection regulations promulgated by the Bush administration in 2008. These regulations were long- overdue rules needed for the effective implementation and enforcement of conscience-protective federal laws that have been formally in place since the 1970s. They included definitions of key terms in the existing legislation (although the term "abortion" itself has not been formally defined, thus leaving open the question, for example, whether the administration of an abortifacient pill to prevent the implantation of the early embryo counts as an "abortion"). Still, the Bush regulations strengthened conscience protections for pro-life medical professionals and medical students in a variety of ways. For example, they very clearly prohibited any form of discrimination against practitioners and medical students who refused to undergo training for abortions, or to perform abortions, or to refer for abortions. Moreover, they proscribed discrimination in credentialing or licensing on grounds related to the refusal to be involved in the practice of abortion.

I suspect that the Obama administration's goal in abrogating conscience protection regulations is to establish a policy very much in line with the ACOG Ethics Committee's proposed "ethics" rules on conscientious refusal in "reproductive" medicine. In addition, I think we can expect the Obama administration to permit professional associations and accrediting and certification bodies to discriminate against pro-life individuals and institutions.

Of course, none of this is a surprise. President Obama's fervent support for abortion is a matter of public record extending over his entire political career. To my knowledge, he has never supported a restriction on abortion or opposed an effort to expand its availability. He famously said that if one of his daughters "made a mistake," he would not want to see her "punished" with a baby.[2] He usually does not claim even to be "personally opposed" to abortion, as most so-called "pro-choice" politicians claim to be. He opposed legislation prohibiting partial-birth abortions (a procedure in which the infant is killed after he or she is partially delivered outside the mother's body) and even fought against laws to protect children born alive after an unsuccessful attempt at abortion. As President, he has revoked the Mexico City Policy, which prohibited the government funding of organizations that perform or promote abortions overseas, and he has promised to fight over the long term for repeal of the Hyde Amendment, which forbids the federal funding of abortions in the United States. During his first presidential campaign, he promised to give priority to enacting the provisions of the so-called Freedom of Choice Act, which would, in the words of the abortion lobby, overturn hundreds of state and federal anti-abortion laws, such as parental notification requirements for minors seeking abortions and informed consent laws requiring women contemplating abortions to be informed of the facts of fetal development and the physical and emotional risks of abortion. And, of course, President Obama has attempted to impose on religious employers as well as everybody else a requirement of providing health care coverage not only for contraceptives and sterilization, but for abortion-inducing drugs such as Ella.

And so it falls to us to resist, and to do so not only for the sake of defending the lives of our most vulnerable brothers and sisters—children in the womb—but also in defense of what James Madison called "the sacred rights of conscience." Today, many of those who would sanction and support the taking of human life by abortion or in embryo-destructive research have also made themselves the enemies of conscience. We, who are the friends of life, must also be the friends of conscience. Indeed, we must be conscience's best friends. For many of us, standing up for conscience means defending the principles of our faith. For all of us, standing up for conscience means defending principles on which our nation was founded.

ENDNOTES

1   See, for example, Robert P. George and Christopher Tollefsen, *Embryo: A Defense of Human Life,* 2nd edition (Princeton: Witherspoon Institute, 2011); and Patrick Lee and Robert P. George, "The Wrong of Abortion," in Andrew I. Cohen and Christopher Wellman (eds.), *Contemporary Debates in Applied Ethics* (Oxford, UK: Wiley-Blackwell, 2005).

2   President Obama made the remark at a Town Hall meeting in Johnstown, Pennsylvania on March 29, 2008. So there can be no doubt that I am treating him completely fairly, I will provide the quotation in its full context. "When it comes specifically to HIV/AIDS, the most important prevention is education, which should include—which should include abstinence education and teaching the children—teaching children, you know, that sex is not something casual. But it should also include—it should also include other, you know, information about contraception because, look, I've got two daughters. 9 years old and 6 years old. I am going to teach them first of all about values and morals. But if they make a mistake, I don't want them punished with a baby. I don't want them punished with an STD at the age of 16. You know, so it doesn't make sense to not give them information." http://blogs.cbn.com/thebrodyfile/archive/2008/03/31/obama-says-he-doesnt-want-his-daughters-punished-with-a.aspx

Chapter Five

Institutional Ministries and the Church's Temporal Mission

Gerard V. Bradley

The term "institutional ministry" most literally suggests an evangelical mega-church, or perhaps Roman Catholicism or the Church of Jesus Christ of Latter-day Saints: established (small "e"), well-organized religious bodies possessed of a refined corporate legal structure, all very professional. But this chapter is not about worshiping communities and their intramural activities, however "institutionalized" they might be. The "ministries" considered here are not even distinguished by their engaging in the religious activities of prayer, liturgy, or catechesis.

The "ministries" with which we are concerned perform "good works." They do "social outreach." "Institutional ministries" are extramural activities of religious bodies, what comes after (if you will) prayer and worship. They are connected to churches, synagogues, mosques and the like—of them, but distinct and different from them. "Institutional ministries" have to do with the health-care institutions, social services, and some of the educational initiatives of religious bodies. "Institutional ministries" include religiously defined hospitals, nursing homes and hospices, counseling centers, group homes (for recovering addicts, the mentally or physically challenged, the homeless, and the juvenile delinquent). Think of Catholic Charities or Long Island Jewish Hospital. Think, too, of religious colleges and universities, such as Baylor, Brigham Young, and Thomas Aquinas.

Think, too, for that matter, of the institutions that come to mind when one reviews the monumental American debate in 2011–12 over the Health and Human Services "contraception" mandate, which failed to exempt religious institutions other than worshipping congregations.

Think also of Prison Fellowship and the Salvation Army, religious social service ministries that are independent of any particular church and swing free of any confession's doctrine. These outfits are "social outreach" all the way down. Each one's religious identity is nonetheless so sharply defined, and so suffuses its operations, that these groups, and others like them, count here as "institutional ministries."

This conception of "institutional ministries" captures the most common (if not the most literal) uses of the term. When we think of "institutional ministries" we most naturally think of Catholic Social Services or some evangelical church's relief efforts in Haiti, Sudan, or Somalia. This conception preserves the distinction between those religious activities (such as the inculcation of religious doctrine and the performance of liturgy) that have no secular counterpart, and those that do. The former might be well described as "inherently" or, better, "distinctively" religious activities. The latter include those services (such as medical care and adoption arrangements) that non-religious persons in secular settings can and very often do perform. Preserving this distinction is important especially because the constitutional law of many jurisdictions treats the promulgation of doctrine, worship, and devotional activities as "essentially" religious activity that lies beyond the legitimate reach of the state. The basic idea is that the truth of such theological matters is beyond the competence of the state to judge. What churches do in church is "private." When churches arrange for adoptions, though, many jurisdictions consider them to be engaged in "public" services, subject to state regulation. This paper concerns the principles of that regulation. More exactly, it is about the value of institutional ministries, one indispensable fount of those principles.

I propose to look at "institutional ministries" from the perspective of the political common good. By that term I mean nothing recondite or idiosyncratic. In line with a venerable tradition of thinking about it, what I mean by "political common good" (and cognate expressions) is the whole set of conditions in any politically organized community by which persons therein, as well as their communities (especially such natural communities as the family) may flourish.

But note well: the common good is not identical to the viewpoint of the state. The state's jurisdiction is not coterminous with the political common good. Besides natural limits that stop its authority short of the bounds of the whole political common good, positive law (particularly but not only constitutions) typically prescribes further limits on the state's authority over the common good. In fact, everybody has some sort of duty to care for the political common good. Non-state organizations (including institutional ministries) have such duties too.

This view nevertheless includes that of the state, whose role in caring for the common good is large, important, and indispensable. But that role is limited, and far from exclusive. The extraordinary volume of activity to promote the common good characteristic of the modern state might seem to suggest that public authority has some sort of exclusive license. It might suggest that non-state actors, including institutional ministries, exercise delegated public authority when they run schools or provide foster care. The state's portfolio is expansive, and can include authority to coordinate everyone's activities insofar as they affect the common good. Still, that does not mean that institutional ministries, for example, lack a natural right to occupy public space and to work unimpeded for the common good.

This chapter is not theological. It is not sectarian. Nothing in this analysis depends upon the truth of any theological proposition or divine revelation, or upon the validity of the pronouncements of any human religious authority. Religion and belief, nonetheless, do enter into the analysis. The existence of beliefs based on revelation and religious authority, as well their meaning for, and place in, the deliberations and choices of believers, is relevant to understanding institutional ministries and how they contribute to the common good.

This chapter is not about constitutional law or judicial doctrine. It is not offered as an interpretation of any extant constitution. Some of the claims defended here conflict with prevailing interpretations of the First Amendment (for example, the Establishment Clause doctrine that the state must not "endorse" religion), and of Article 8 of the European Convention of Human Rights (which has been read to protect the "privacy" of an adulterous church organist from dismissal by his parish on grounds of the scandal given).

This is not an analysis of rhetoric. This chapter is not devoted to finding the argument that will work in the Princeton faculty lounge, or that will appeal to a Senate committee, or that will win the perennial swing vote of Justice Anthony Kennedy. In this chapter I try to make sound arguments for conclusions that are true. Truth is parent to rhetoric and, one hopes, not very far removed from today's "winning" arguments.

What Institutional Ministries Do

One procedure by which to evaluate institutional ministries is to identify the ways in which these entities constitute opportunities for those involved in them to flourish. To do that we must figure out what it is, exactly, that institutional ministries do. This is not a question about patient treatment plans or about school curricula. It is more basic than that. It is about elementary act analysis. Once we unpack what institutional ministries do, their distinctive values for the people involved will become apparent. This "micro" value is not a matter of so many private satisfactions: the political common good has to do with those conditions, including the institutional composition of society, by which people are enabled to perfect themselves. If it turns out to be the case that institutional ministries teem with pathways to perfection, then their flourishing is important to the common good.

What do institutional ministries do? What is special about them? How are they different from, on the one hand, any other non-profit (but not religious) hospital or social service provider? How is Catholic Charities' mentor program different from that of Big Brothers and Big Sisters? Are they not all doing "good works" selflessly, and there is an end to it? What does it matter to the political common good that one mentor simply wants to serve humanity, and the other wants to serve humanity with some religious idea(s) thrown in?

On the other hand: how are institutional ministries different from secular counterparts wherein religious believers ply their trades? What's the specific institutional twist? If public authority does right by a Catholic nurse working in Cook County Hospital, what more is to be done when she moves over to Saint Vincent's Hospital? After all, religious individuals often see their work as somehow referred to God, or for the glory of God, or as a form of harmony with God, or as doing God's work "in the world." Some believers see transcendent meaning in almost everything they do. If such folks are treated right, how is the view from the common good altered by the presence of an institutional ministry, inhabited by these same sorts of people? Sound answers to these questions depend upon, first, delineating the singular richness—the complex, multi-layered meaning and value—of the acts whereby a religious person serves the poor, for example, against a baseline supplied by the non-religious servant. Then we can consider how the "institutionalization" of such a "ministry" is different from a secular outfit dedicated to feeding the hungry.

To get the first comparison aloft let us take the case of a passerby who gives twenty dollars to a man standing on the street corner. The recipient holds a cardboard sign that reads: "Have family. Need food. Please help." What is going on? Well, the cash transfer could be selfishly motivated. Perhaps the giver has no need of the money. He is filthy rich. Maybe he is lonely and feeling a tad guilty about being a spendthrift. He wants to "feel good about himself" again. He gives alms to gain some emotional or psychological benefit for himself, and to rationalize a lifestyle that is, on the whole, selfishly irresponsible.

But our giver might be acting on genuine charitable impulses. To the extent that he acts intentionally, he would surely mean to fulfill an urgent human need. Hence, Reason 1 for the almsgiving: promoting the health or at least relieving the hunger of the recipient's family. Reason 2 follows closely. It is the intent to promote their well-being as a family, to help keep them all together by alleviating one disintegrative pressure. Perhaps our donor acts also out of deep convictions about human solidarity. Maybe he intends to establish a certain bond by giving alms. Thus Reason 3 is comprised of human solidarity, an attenuated form of friendship.

Maybe our almsgiver is not an entirely secular-minded person. Though not a subscriber to any particular faith and scarcely "religious" in any conventional sense, he might see some wider significance to what he does. He cannot help thinking that good works exemplify something so noble in human character that their value somehow transcends time and space. He entertains the notion that almsgiving establishes a connection to some greater-than-human reality or force or Being. So, Reason 4—the promotion of a proto-religious belief, "natural" in more ways than one, but foreign to any revelation or positive religious system.

Reason 4 is a bridge to our comparator, a fully convinced Christian who hands over the twenty dollars. This character might also be acting selfishly. He might even be acting selfishly in a distinctly "Christian" manner. Perhaps he intends by his almsgiving to burnish his own reputation. Our donor could be seeking recognition among his Christian friends as a "good Christian."

This street-corner giver need not be a nascent Pharisee. Let us suppose that he is not. Indeed, one of the characteristic drives of institutional ministries is to foster the doing of good deeds for the right reasons. On this supposition, our giver's generous act includes all four of the aforementioned reasons: need, family, friendship, and a connection to the bigger scheme of things. But now there is much more to it. Peculiar to this Christian's act would be the more theologically informed spiritual well-being of the charitable giver. In Matthew 19, the rich young man asked Jesus: "Teacher, what good must I do to gain eternal life?" Jesus replied: "If you wish to be perfect, go, sell what you have and give it to the poor." Peter Maurin, co- founder with Dorothy Day of the Catholic Worker movement and a man of extraordinary vision, will serve as an exemplar. Maurin once famously said to a Bowery bum: "You give me the chance to practice Christian charity. You are an ambassador of Christ. Thank you."

Call these additional features of the twenty-dollar donation Reasons 5 and 6. Reason 5 is the fulfillment of a specifically religious duty. Reason 6 is about how revealed truth enlivens charity for the charitable. They are two different ways in which giving acquires an intelligible supernatural meaning and purpose. Reason 5 counts more negatively: it is what one does to avoid divine sanction or displeasure. Reason 6 represents the more positive acquisition of a religious virtue.

There is a distinctively Christian reciprocity to this exchange, too: the receiver might also encounter Christ. Peter Maurin saw the face of Christ in the beggar. But the beggar might encounter Christ in the almsgiver, who strives to be the image of Jesus. Another way of expressing this opportunity is to say that the giver might come to look upon the recipient as Christ would, to see this person as Jesus sees him or her. This is Reason 7: communicating with others what one holds to be true about God, namely, that He sent His only begotten Son to save humankind, that we are all His brothers and sisters. Reason 7 has value akin to that of proselytizing, or sharing what one believes for the purpose of attracting others to those beliefs.

The exchange is not just a mutual encounter with Christ. For the giver it may also be an opportunity to cooperate with Jesus in building the Kingdom of Heaven. This Reason 8 is, to be sure, dependent upon revelation for its intelligibility.[1] The basic idea is similar to, yet distinct, from Reason 5 (satisfying a duty) and Reason 7 (which is to cast, as it were, the face of Christ upon the other). Reason 8 introduces the specific possibility of acting not as servant or as a reflection but as a collaborator of Jesus. By so choosing to act, one seizes the opportunity to realize one more religious value.

So far considered, the religious act of charity is much richer than its secular counterpart. The religious giver participates in deeper and more diverse ways in human goods than does his unbelieving counterpart. Opportunities such as the street-corner meeting plainly constitute a chance for the persons involved to perfect themselves. This is not to make a virtue out of our beggar's situation, but the needy of one sort or another will always be with us. So far considered, public authority plainly ought to encourage this manner of meeting human needs.

But our almsgiver might encounter only a few beggars a day. Perhaps he wonders: what of the masses that never come my way? Is there some way to help more of them more of the time? After investigating the possibilities he might judge it expedient to band together with other generous souls and establish a Saint Vincent de Paul pantry. That goes reasonably well. But soon our donor wonders anew: we give fish to the hungry to eat. Is there a way to help them even more, by teaching them to fish?

Our band of givers may now decide to organize "The Apostles' Food Co-op" [AFC], in which the needy become "partners," working in the storeroom in return for food and wages. To do this, however, our organizers need to pool available resources, open a bank account, establish a governing structure (to coordinate their now more complex undertaking), acquire space, train personnel. They soon discover that to do these things, they have to incorporate. Then they have to seek government recognition as a non-profit, tax-exempt entity. They need a lawyer and an accountant and a fundraiser. Before long, our band of brothers is an institutional ministry.

The point of structuring my narrative this way is not that most institutional ministries grow organically out of one-on-one street encounters or the like, although some do. The point is that the mission or the common good supported by, for example, the AFC is to be understood in terms of Reasons 1–8. All its workers' activities can, and in some way typically do, share in those reasons for action. Even the accountant who never meets a hungry person participates in this rich complex of goods. True, he carries on day after day balancing the books, much as he would if he worked at Goldman Sachs. But at Goldman he would just be pulling in a paycheck. (If he is more conscientious than that, he would likely worry that his firm was fleecing people who could scarcely afford to be fleeced.) At AFC it is different. He relishes the number-crunching and does it better for less pay than at Goldman. He does so because he knows that he is part of a complex and sublime good.

Valuing AFC and similar undertakings is thus mostly accomplished by replaying in your mind steps 1–8 of the simple street encounter. The AFC is a better vehicle for meeting needs than a secular counterpart because it provides an opportunity for people to realize eight benefits, rather than three or four.

Institutional ministries include but also go beyond the properly religious meanings that propelled our Christian giver (Reasons 5–8). They do so in three important ways. One of those ways has already been suggested. Reason 9 is that the corporate structure of the AFC permits the communication of those eight reasons or values throughout the entire organization. Institutional ministries connect the accountant, the lawyer, and the stock-boy to the beggar on the street corner. These back-office helpers gain access to valuable opportunities for human flourishing that would otherwise—that is, when acting alone or in a non-religious organization—be unavailable to them.

That face-to-face street-corner encounter is fleeting and exceptional.. The conscientious Christian, moreover, shuns attention, lest he be tempted to preen. But the ideal of invisible almsgiving is neither possible nor desirable in the case of the AFC. It cannot raise funds or attract the attention of needy "partners" without making itself, and its Christian mission, conspicuous. There is another reason—a specifically Christian reason—why the institutional ministry should not be a secret Santa. AFC is supposed to be a billboard for Christianity. The institutional ministry consciously seeks to evidence or instantiate the meaning of Christianity. By the attractiveness of its work it seeks to testify to the truth of Christian faith. This Reason 10 is unique to institutional ministries. Let us call it "witness" value.

Because of this "witness" value, institutional ministries are (or at least should be) supremely concerned with the integrity of their activities, with the perspicuity of their "witness." Doing business as, say, "Catholic Charities" means acting in the name of the Church. It means that the faith of that Church suffuses the entire enterprise. When it acts it is the Church acting. Catholic Charities may no more engage in acts contrary to Catholic faith than may the Church. This imperative is perhaps a characteristic of, more than it is a reason for, an institutional ministry's action. Let us call it Reason 11 anyway.

Now we see clearly the nature and scope of the injury done to an institutional ministry by an employee's *false* witness. Whenever a member's conduct is reasonably judged by those in charge to be contrary to that set of purposes, then that person frustrates the corporate collaboration. The miscreant treats others involved in the work unfairly. In effect if not by design, such false witness undermines the whole project and deprives others of the opportunity to do as they have covenanted to do, to perfect themselves in the singularly rich way that joining an institutional ministry allows.

Ministries Meet the State

Most of the values catalogued since we left behind our secular giver have had to do with revealed truths or other aspects of positive religion, one might object. But the constitutions of many western democracies, most notably that of the United States, make the state "neutral" about such matters. Someone objecting along these lines might then conclude that the values of institutional ministries here identified are not really visible to public authorities. This objector could say too that beyond Reasons 1–3, all that this paper has adduced is a cluster of what might be called "private" goods. Reasons 5–8 at least would be just the quirky personal motivations of those involved in them.

In response: it is true that the American Constitution (among others) stipulates that the truth about putatively revealed propositions is beyond the state's competence. But the American state (like the others) does not need to affirm any such forbidden truth to affirm the values here denominated 1–11. For one thing, even on the assumption that the truth of revealed propositions is beyond the scope of political society, those charged with the care of its common good can, and should, recognize the truths of natural religion, including the truth that a divine entity created what there is and sustains it in being. America's political leaders regularly recognized these truths until recently. It is reasonable for those charged with such care (as it is reasonable for everybody else) to further expect that such an entity would communicate somehow with humankind. It is thus reasonable to hold, on philosophical grounds, that genuine revelation is not only possible but likely.

In fact, the root of religious liberty in our constitutional tradition is the natural truth about religion. This is seen in the *Memorial and Remonstrance* composed by James Madison during a 1785 Virginia controversy over tax support of Protestant clergy. He quoted the 1776 Virginia Declaration of Rights, which served as the preamble to the state's constitution: "Religion or the duty which we owe to our Creator and the manner of discharging it, can be directed only by reason and conviction, not by force or violence."[2] No doubt these natural truths can be and, in some cases, have been obscured and negated by the putative truths of some revealed religions (which counsel coercion, pressure, and subordination in the cause of faith). But they are true nonetheless.

Even public authorities that are bound not to affirm revealed truths may, and should, recognize that there is such a thing as revelation, that believers characteristically act on reasons supplied by revelation, and that their access to opportunities to act freely and in concert on those reasons are critical to their flourishing as fully human persons seeking to know and to live in harmony with whatever divine entity or being there is. Those with care for the common good, including those who hold public authority, ought to safeguard such opportunities.

A familiar example from established canons of constitutional law might help make this point clearer. Public authorities in America may not constitutionally affirm the validity of Eucharistic consecration, the inspiration of the Torah, or the efficacy of the Mormon baptism of ancestors. America's public authorities in fact do not affirm the truth of those practices as what God really teaches or as the genuine divine revelation to the exclusion (full or partial) of other putative revelations. Public authorities may scarcely even understand what these superficially eccentric behaviors and beliefs amount to. But public authorities nonetheless recognize and promote worship, which is a generic term for different ways that people give to God the thanks, remembrance, and adoration that is due to God.

Someone might object that, though there is a decent argument for valuing highly Christian and, even more specifically, Catholic institutional ministries, the argument establishes nothing about the value of institutional ministries as such. And surely, this objector might continue, the American Constitution forbids any government preference or favor toward a particular religion, including Christianity.

In reply: I have used a Catholic Christian example (AFC) partly because it is the religious tradition I know best. I use it also because the vast majority of America's institutional ministries are, in fact, Christian. But the soundness of the whole analysis above does not depend upon the truth of Christian revelation. The significance and value of institutional ministries (Reasons 9–11) can be affirmed apart from affirming the truth of any ministry's distinctive theological claims (see further my reply to the first objection).

Besides, nothing in this part of my argument depends for its soundness on the false assumption that all religions carry on institutional ministries in roughly similar proportions. Nothing in any constitutional norm of equal respect for different religions requires that we should pretend otherwise. Nothing in any such constitutional norm should inhibit public authority's favor for those institutional ministries that do exist, even though (in America at least) they are preponderantly Christian. For any surface appearance of unequal treatment arises, not from government discrimination, but rather from the theologies and institutional choices of the religions.

Religious entities that eschew ritual suffer no untoward

discrimination insofar as the law of religious freedom protects "worship." Religions that do not proselytize are not victimized by constitutional provisions privileging missionary activity. Faith communities that do not have health care ministries due to their distinctive metaphysics (e.g. Christian Science, in which disease is an illusion) or dualistic theologies (in which human suffering is insignificant) are not "unequal" to the Catholic Church, which maintains over six hundred hospitals and clinics in the United States alone.

The Good That Ministries Do

Public authorities should promote the religious life of the people because religion is a complex, important opportunity for persons to flourish. That flourishing is self-justifying. One need not go on to justify promoting religion by identifying its contribution to non-religious benefits. We have already undertaken an accounting of these ministries' value. Now we turn from that "micro" evaluation to a "macro" accounting. By "macro" I mean that view from the common good concerned with the benefits of institutional ministries, not so much for those within the firm (such as AFC), but for society at large. By and large these values are unrelated to religion or to religious liberty.

There are at least nine distinct "macro" values to institutional ministries. These are different ways in which promoting institutional ministries serves the political common good. I have arranged them in groups of three. The first cohort is more practical than the others. The second is about basic institutions in political society. These are the most important "macro" values. They are regime defining; "constitutional" with at least a small "c." The last group concerns more specifically cultural values, albeit with sizable collateral political benefits.

Practical Goods

Value 1. In its 1970 *Walz* v. *Tax Commission of City of New York* decision, the United States Supreme Court considered the constitutionality of property tax exemptions for churches.[3] An issue arose about this long-standing practice because the Court had recently minted a novel view of the First Amendment, namely, that the Establishment Clause forbade any government encouragement, aid, or support of religion. The underlying norm here was extraordinary: "neutrality" between religion and what the Court called "non-religion."

The *Walz* case was not precisely about institutional ministries. It was about tax exemptions for churches. But the Court's labored effort to save these breaks from invalidation by its audacious "neutrality" norm drove the justices to consider the social value of churches. And that led them to the "good works" that churches often perform. The *Walz* Court was led, that is, to consider institutional ministries.

In the course of a lengthy concurring opinion, Justice William Brennan said that each such group (here, effectively referring to institutional ministries) "contributes to the diversity of association, viewpoint, and enterprise essential to a vigorous, pluralistic society."[4] But this observation cannot be a terminal point in any discussion of value, for not all "diversity" and "pluralism" benefit political society. Lack of consensus about basic matters of justice and about fundamental human rights, for example, injures the common good and makes its practical realization that much harder.

Brennan's jejune thought needs to be completed. Completed, it could go something like this: the common good is served by the existence and ready availability of diverse sources of satisfying basic human needs (e.g., health care, nutrition), and of pursuing, in cooperation with others, opportunities for human flourishing. Justice requires that these needs be met. Justice also requires that adequate avenues for the pursuit of perfection be made available. Organizations that offer both are obviously consistent with justice and are great social amenities, too. Institutional ministries fit this profile nicely.

Society is enriched and the common good is promoted by the existence of a healthy competitive pluralism among institutional ministries, because the competition is likely to lead to improvements in services, and to ever more creative integrations of services with the reflexive benefits to those associated with the ministries. Besides, diversity here forestalls any perception that public authority is cozy with any one or two religious groups.

Value 2. Both Brennan and Justice John Marshall Harlan (in his separate concurring opinion) identified in *Walz* a further benefit of institutional ministries. Brennan said that these organizations "bear burdens that would otherwise either have to be met by general taxation, or be left undone, to the general detriment of the community."[5] Harlan opined that the services "*might* otherwise have to be assumed by government."[6] Interestingly, the majority opinion by Chief Justice Burger eschewed the conclusion but not the premise. Never denying the claims of Brennan and Harlan about the breadth of state authority, Burger found it "unnecessary" to justify tax exemption based on "the social welfare services or 'good works' that some churches perform."[7]

This thought of Brennan and Harlan also needs to be completed. The thought is that the state saves money by encouraging institutional ministries. No doubt it does. But so far expressed, the thought does not conclude with a net benefit for the common good. All that these two justices have spied is government off-loading of some cost. But government outsourcing is a net social benefit only on the assumption that, basically, government and the common good are coterminous. Then one could say that the government managed to privatize some cost it would otherwise have to bear, just as if some private philanthropists bought a B-2 bomber for the Air Force.

The "good works" performed by religious entities are likely to be more efficient than the performance of the same by public authority itself. It is very likely that institutional ministries will consistently attract competent personnel who will work harder for less (recall our AFC accountant, the refugee from Goldman Sachs). There is no necessity here. But as a matter of common sense and experience, why should we not expect that capable people will fly to institutional ministries when they can? What they give up in salary and perhaps in benefits is paid back to them by access to Reasons 4–8.

Value 3. State-delivered services, being relentlessly secular, cannot in any conscious or consistent way engage a recipient's dependence upon a greater-than-human source of meaning and value. What if, however, some services depend on or are greatly enhanced precisely by such feelings of powerlessness that emerge with religious consciousness? Empirical evidence from the annals of Alcoholics Anonymous (and spin-offs for gamblers and those addicted to pornography or sex) and from Prison Fellowship tell us that such feelings are invaluable aids for many people in trouble. Those in institutional ministries speak of "conversion" and the "power of God's grace," as well they should. Public authorities that are disabled by constitutional law from saying "amen" may and should nonetheless affirm the results. The common good is well served by helping people to get right by recourse to religious belief and experience, so long as they do so freely.

A synthesis along with a modest extension of the foregoing considerations might be illuminating here. Religious liberty is a mansion of many rooms. Perhaps the most obvious sense of it from the common-good viewpoint is to arrange things so that believers face fewer rather than more choices between doing what their religion requires (and avoiding that which is forbidden), and availing themselves of the ordinary possibilities on offer for professional, social, educational, and financial advancement. When we think of religious liberty, perhaps we most readily think of making it so that a young Muslim woman may choose to wear a headscarf and nonetheless attend public school, or that a young Muslim woman may choose not to wear a headscarf and still be a member of her family. Or we might think of Catholic pharmacists who wish to practice their profession while at the same time avoiding complicity in abortion, via Plan B.

One effective way to serve religious liberty in this focal sense is to promote institutional ministries. That much is apparent. The "macro" value to which I draw attention here is that set social structure, of which religious liberty is one linchpin, that keeps open society's opportunities for advancement to everybody, or to as many people as it is possible and just to do, regardless of their religion. A society that does so is simply better off than one that does not.

The United States is on the cusp of political and legal changes that would dramatically alter the landscape for institutional ministries and, in turn, the possibilities and thus the goals and aspirations of the rising generation. During the course of the debate in late 2009 and early 2010 about the comprehensive federal health-care reform, the very real possibility emerged that America's 685 (or so) Catholic hospitals would have to close, due to the impossibility of their carrying on without adequate conscience protection. Of course, many of those entities would (after a rough transition) re-emerge as non-sectarian hospitals. But not all of them would, and in any event the absence of conscience protection throughout the health-care system would make the choices of today's children and adolescents different. Any society in which whole segments of the population are effectively blocked from fruitful participation in whole sectors of the economy or certain professions is a society in distress.

In any event, the leading religious hospital trade group (the Catholic Health Association) supported the comprehensive health-care reform, even though America's bishops opposed the final bill. The pattern was similar for the later HHS "contraception" mandate, which basically required Catholic institutional ministries to provide insurance coverage for contraception, sterilization, and very early abortion (by means of the "week-after" pill) to all employees and their dependents. The bishops most strenuously opposed this unprecedented mandate. CHA supported it after the Administration announced a "compromise" on February 10, 2012. Later still, however, CHA announced its opposition.

Institutional Goods

The promotion of institutional ministries both presupposes and entails an authoritative endorsement of religion itself as good. This endorsement spawns two related but distinct and important social values.

Value 4. The *Walz* Court said (in the course of reconciling tax exemptions for churches with the Court's mangled interpretation of the Establishment Clause) that "certain entities [] exist in a harmonious relationship to the community at large, and foster its moral or mental improvement."[8] This statement is a faint echo of a long and distinguished tradition in American thought about the common good, political and legal practice, and constitutional law (until World War II), regarding the indispensable, beneficent influences of religion upon a free society. Washington's Farewell Address is perhaps the most famous among the countless such textual witnesses:

> Of all the dispositions and habits which lead to political prosperity, Religion and morality are indispensable supports. . . .
> And let us with caution indulge the supposition, that morality can be maintained without religion. Whatever may be

conceded to the influence of refined education on minds of peculiar structure, reason and experience both forbid us to expect that National morality can prevail in exclusion of religious principle.[9]

Plainly put and here paraphrasing the *Federalist* in terms that reverberate through the ages: a republican government presupposes a virtuous citizenry for its success. And religion is the essential source and support of virtue.

Value 5. Religion promotes an objective morality that is essential to the possibility of a genuine political common good. In the 1952 case of *Zorach* v. *Clauson* the Court affirmed that "[w]e are a religious people whose institutions presuppose a Supreme Being."[10] In the 1963 *Schempp* case, the Court invalidated devotional Bible reading in public schools. The majority opinion there nonetheless observed "that the Founding Fathers believed devotedly that there was a God and the unalienable rights of man were rooted in Him is clearly evidenced in their writings, from the Mayflower Compact to the Constitution itself."[11] Indeed they did, and the wider truth to which these texts point is that the political community's collective commitment to the existence of a greater-than-human source of meaning and value is a mainstay (perhaps an indispensable precondition) of belief in an objective morality that, in turn, makes a genuinely common good possible.

Value 6. Public authority's promotion of institutional ministries promotes the truth that not only the state, but the whole political common good, is limited and instrumental to persons' efforts to perfect themselves. Public authority's promotion of institutional ministries also exemplifies and further promotes subsidiarity, or a prescriptive systematic preference for devolution of functions and activities.

The combined effects of the preceding three values include the reinforcement by the state of an important cultural authority for which the state properly makes room in the public square. There is a zone of putative truths that transcend the state and that, precisely because they extend to public (if not yet unequivocally) political matters, potentially involve standards of criticism of what the state does. This is the nightmare of Hobbes and of every tyrant. Likewise there is a state recognition and validation of limits to what it may ask of citizens. It reinforces the notion, in other words, that the political community exists "under God"; that is, under divine judgment, according to standards of rectitude that neither the state not the people create or choose. It further promotes recognition (at least where the philosophical truth is concerned that religion involves a creator and sustainer of reality) of the dependence of the state's institutions, and of our rights, upon God.

Cultural Goods

Value 7. The flourishing of institutional ministries is valuable precisely because it evidences the productive integration of religious belief and commitment with the performance of worthwhile temporal services. It is not quite the lion lying down with the lamb, but against the backdrop of common rhetoric today about, first, the political divisiveness of religion and, second, the utter unintelligibility of it, it is something close to that unlikely reconciliation. This productive union contributes to understanding revealed religion as possessing an intelligibility to it, as opposed to an aesthetic (at best) or a descent into irrationality (at worst).

Value 8. Institutional ministries are a kind of mediating structure, occupants of public space but stemming from the more private realm and performing what might otherwise be performed by government (and which may today be widely regarded as indigenous government functions). As such they may serve as portals to civic engagement and community service for many who might otherwise be wary of doing so.

They certainly have in American history. Entire congregations of Catholic sisters came into being precisely with specific ministries in mind (chiefly, health care and education). Indeed, the whole history of Catholic parochial education and of Catholic charities in the United States is rooted in aversion to parallel public institutions that were more or less openly Protestant. And viewed over the span of a couple of generations, institutional ministries rooted in religious and, to a lesser extent, ethnic identity, have been engines of assimilation into the wider mainstream of American culture.

Today institutional ministries may be the only door to the public square through which some Muslim and Orthodox Jewish women may conscientiously walk. Many patients and potential nursing home residents may prefer—with good reason—going without needed care if it is only available in state-run facilities. Religious schools may be the only alternative to home-schooling for religiously scrupulous parents estranged from secular public schools.

Value 9. Institutional ministries can reduce, and have reduced, tensions among religions. Most obviously, wherever there are different religious traditions represented among ministries, and wherever a disaster brings scattered ministries together, there is common ground in the common work. Cardinal Gibbons said to his interfaith audience: "Though we differ in faith, thank God there is one platform on which we stand united, and that is the platform of charity and benevolence."[12] Institutional ministries are a form of self-disclosure, too, and the common service factor instigates an ecumenical and even interfaith dialogue. The collaboration possible and common among the various ministries establishes a posture of sober cooperation despite the presence of theological disagreements.

These last three considerations weigh heavily against the common view that religion in the public sphere is irredeemably divisive and that the remedy is to privatize it. They contribute to a critical theological culture, and connect the more private manifestations of religion to public matters.

Conclusion

The Obama Administration's contraception, sterilization, and early abortion "mandate," issued in 2011 and taking effect in 2013, instigated the most searching consideration of Catholic institutional ministries' meaning and value in all of American history. The debate occurred within the Church and outside it.. The debate revealed that very many people, both without and within the Church, hold a frankly reductionistic understanding of these ministries.

These people view the Church's ministries as government contractors whose value lies entirely in the efficient performance of some secular function, such as feeding, healing, and teaching. To these eyes, the religious identity of the contractor provides no cognizable additional benefit to anyone. To these eyes faith is irrelevant to the business at hand. To these eyes the religious convictions of the contractors are just so many personal idiosyncrasies and private satisfactions, which are tolerable so long as they do not manifest themselves in any conspicuous way. To these eyes, religion is a potentially divisive force whose tumultuous effects upon public matters must always be monitored, and stymied. They view religious people as suspected proselytizers who must be watched carefully lest they interject their beliefs into the secular exchange—feeding, healing, teaching—for which the government has bargained. These eyes could stare down with aplomb the bishops' warning that the mandate might force the closure of all the Church's institutional ministries.

The bishops' conference and many other Catholics have stood tall during the argument over the HHS "contraception" mandate. Their central contention is not a defense or even an explanation, however, of the meaning and value of institutional ministries, viewed either with the eyes of faith or from the political common good. Their central defense is a broad-gauged argument about the American constitutional tradition of religious liberty. Their central claim has been that the mandate is simply un-American. They wanted a lawyer's and a historian's argument. They got in return claims about what equality for women requires. As President Obama said in early 2012 about keeping abortion legal, it is about "our daughters" having the same "opportunities as our sons."[13]

The mandate is indeed "un-American," in more ways than the bishops and their collaborators described. The net effects of their choice of defensive ground cannot yet be calculated. But it is at least worth noting, now, that the bishops could have left the constitutional lawyers' arguments to the constitutional lawyers. The bishops could then have seized a golden, and perhaps unrepeatable, opportunity to evangelize the American people, and to teach America's Catholics as only America's bishops can about what Jesus did and about what Jesus wants us to do.

ENDNOTES

1   See Second Vatican Council, *Gaudium et Spes*, "Pastoral Constitution on the Church in the Modern World" (1965), §§ 38–39.

2   James Madison, "Memorial and Remonstrance Against Religious

Assessments," June 1785, in Madison, *Writings*, ed. Jack N. Rakove (New York: Library of America, 1999), 30.

3 397 U.S. 664 (1970).

4 *Ibid.*, at 689 (Brennan, J., concurring).

5 *Ibid.*, at 687.

6 *Ibid.*, at 696 (Harlan, J., concurring).

7 *Ibid.*, at 674 (Burger, C.J., for the Court).

8 *Ibid.*, at 672.

9 George Washington, *Writings*, ed. John Rhodehamel (New York: Library of America, 1997), 971.

10 *Zorach* v. *Clauson*, 343 U.S. 306 (1952), at 313.

11 *Abington School District* v. *Schempp*, 374 U.S. 203 (1963), at 213.

12 James Cardinal Gibbons, "Message to the Parliament of Religions," in Walter Raleigh Houghton, ed., *Neely's History of the Parliament of Religions and Religious Congresses of the World's Columbian Exposition*, 4th ed. (Chicago: F. Tennyson Neely, 1893), 191.

13 Statement by the President on Roe v. Wade Anniversary, 22 January 2012, http://www.whitehouse.gov/the-press-office/2012/01/22/statement-president-roe-v-wade-anniversary.

Chapter Six
Competing "Rights" Claims: Defending Rights of Conscience in the Policy Arena
Richard M. Doerflinger

In the legislative arena, claims for a right of conscience—including claims based on religious belief—frequently run up against the argument that various competing rights neutralize or simply override conscience rights.

To be sure, important federal protections for conscience rights in the health-care field, especially though not exclusively regarding abortion, have been enacted into law in recent decades. These conscience rights measures include the Church amendment enacted in 1973 and subsequently expanded; the "abortion-neutral" and "religious tenets" clauses of the Civil Rights Restoration Act in 1988; the 1996 Coats/Snowe amendment protecting ob/gyn residency programs that do not provide abortion training; the Hyde/Weldon appropriations rider on abortion approved by Congress in 2004 and all subsequent years; and the conscience clauses allowing Catholic and other faith-based grantees to take part in PEPFAR (the President's Emergency Plan for AIDS Relief), which were included when the program was established in 2003 and reaffirmed with improvements when it was reauthorized in 2008.[1] It is noteworthy that none of these longstanding provisions has ever been shown to result in any adverse effects for people in need of health care. Yet today it is increasingly common to hear the charge that such laws are overly broad, and that they need to be reevaluated and weakened so that the demands of conscience are more fairly "balanced" against other values and imperatives.[2]

Some claims about countervailing values are simply ideological assertions by advocates who believe that certain values should be given more weight in American law than they have ever enjoyed. Some such claims are in tension with other claims made simultaneously by the same advocates. Some pose internal tensions of their own. Others are based on specific factual claims open to dispute. These include, for example, claims that particular drugs or procedures are "goods" contributing to human flourishing, on an individual or social level, or that these can only be provided properly if conscientiously objecting individuals or institutions cooperate, even at the risk of the latters' extinction. In each case, as I hope to show in what follows, the claims themselves are vulnerable to a first-level critique. They need not be accepted at face value before arguing that they are nonetheless trumped by freedom of conscience.

Abortion will be a primary, though not exclusive focus of my review due to the uniquely severe conflict between Catholic moral teaching and American law concerning abortion. Obviously, maintaining a right not to participate in abortion against one's conscience is important not only for Catholics but also for millions of other people in the United States. At the same time, if religious freedom is seen in Catholic teaching as the paramount human right, the right to life is the most *basic*, the condition for all other rights, and hence to be defended with maximum determination. Direct abortion is rejected in all circumstances as an attack on innocent human life, and deliberately acting to ensure that an abortion is performed is one of the very few kinds of actions by which Catholics can excommunicate themselves in canon law. Hence a law forcing health-care providers to help provide abortions attacks Catholic moral and social teaching and Catholic identity at its core, and its enforcement would essentially drive faithful Catholics out of the health care ministry in this country.

Yet our Supreme Court has declared a woman's freedom to choose abortion a constitutional right since *Roe* v. *Wade* in 1973. And today, supporters of legal abortion insist further that abortion is an ordinary part of the continuum of "reproductive health." They characterize strong protection for conscience regarding abortion (and often regarding other controverted areas of medicine) as a threat to other people's consciences, to public health, to women's lives, or to equality. Each of these claims will be discussed in turn.

Conscience Against Conscience?

Ironically, the most basic and most common charge against strong conscience protection regarding abortion and other procedures, is that it ignores a right of conscience—the patient's right to decide about a treatment that will affect his or her life in important ways. The decision about an abortion, for example, has been described by some justices on the U.S. Supreme Court as tantamount to "the right to define one's own concept of existence, of meaning, of the universe, and of the mystery of human life."[3] If two conscience rights are in conflict and only one can prevail, should it not be this exalted decision by the woman who wants an abortion?

Sometimes it is argued that this claim is especially strong when the conscientiously opposed provider of health care or social services is an institution. Surely, organizations or institutions lack a conscience, or have one only in a very attenuated sense. Therefore, runs the argument, if an institutional policy conflicts with the conscientious view of an individual, perhaps a view alleged to be religiously based, the latter should prevail.

This argument fails under current constitutional jurisprudence. Persons have a right of religious freedom when they gather collectively, not only when they act as separate individuals, and efforts to limit members' voluntary collective action in support of their beliefs could also infringe on other constitutionally protected values such as freedom of association.[4] In addition, the view that religious faith is primarily held by the individual, and is held by associations only in a secondary and attenuated sense, can itself be seen as a controverted theological statement. In Catholicism and some other Christian traditions, as well as in the Jewish tradition from which they developed, it is first and foremost the community, the "people of God" as a whole, that has a covenant with the Almighty; the individual receives that faith from the community, and participates in the covenant by being grafted onto that community. Catholics, in particular, refer to the Church as the Body of Christ; and at each Sunday Mass they pray for God's mercy and favor by asking: "Look not on our sins but on the *faith of your church*." The community is the standard against which individual faith is measured, as it is the community and not the individual whose belief God has guaranteed against serious error. To be sure, some Protestant denominations have a more individualistic belief about the nature of faith and conscience; but to make that belief into a binding legal norm would risk creating an un-constitutional establishment of religion.

More broadly, the scenario described here, in which a person seeks an abortion or other procedure, and a provider objects, is not a situation of consciences in conflict. A person's conscience can inform that per-son's decision as to which actions it is right for him or her to perform; it generally cannot determine for others what they must do, much less guarantee that external circumstances will cooperate with the person's desires as to when, how, and by whom this activity will be assisted. If a woman wants an abortion and a Catholic physician or hospital refuses in conscience to perform it, the woman's conscience has not been vio-lated—she simply needs to seek assistance elsewhere. Her project may be inconvenienced or delayed. But if the woman prevails and the provider is forced to take part in something the provider sees as unjust killing, or as violating the law of God in other ways, that provider has undermined at its core the reason for being involved in the health-care ministry in the first place. The provider's identity has been forsaken, now and in the future, and it is difficult to see how it can be regained.

In short, a conscientious objection to some activity is not trumped by a simple demand for assistance in that activity, no matter how sincere or intense the desire for that assistance may be. It is remarkable that many people, including lawmakers, are not clear on the difference be-tween interfering with a right to choose something and simply declining to support or promote it. The difference has long been clear in the Supreme Court's abortion jurisprudence dealing with the government's own obligations. A woman's "right" to an abortion is seen as a negative right, a "right to be let alone" by government in making a decision about whether to bear a child. This does not translate into a right to demand the assistance of the government in seeking or obtaining an abortion. On the contrary, as the Supreme Court has stated several times, the govern-ment is free to make "a value judgment favoring childbirth over abor-tion" and to implement this policy by providing funds, facilities and personnel for the former but not the latter.[5] There is no legal warrant for the government to deny religiously motivated individuals and organizations the freedom to make this same judgment.

Conscience Against Health?

The debate becomes more serious when it is claimed that the sought-after procedure is not simply elective but rather necessary to prevent the worsening of the patient's medical condition. The claim here could be stated on an individual basis in terms of the needs of one patient, or more broadly in terms of the public good. As one advocate has stated: "[T]he very reason for the licensing and regulation of the health professions is to *protect patients* and *advance public health*. The licensed individuals or entities have responsibilities that may sometimes be more important than their religious rights."[6]

The problem with this claim is that, by and large, conscientiously objecting physicians are refusing to perform the demanded procedures precisely because they see them as inimical to patients' well-being or best interests; in other words, the physician is practicing good medicine. Some critics, including some medical groups, claim that the defining standard should instead be the patient's best interests *as seen by the patient*. This, however, simply repeats the claim discussed above that desires trump conscience, and ends by reducing the medical professional to a vending machine.[7] By that standard, if a patient thinks that a particular procedure is good for her—amputating a healthy limb, or providing a lethal drug overdose, or performing genital mutilation, or trying to force ovulation at the age of 55 with drugs that raise the risk of ovarian cancer—no doctor or hospital could disagree.

At the other extreme, some claim that a health-care provider cannot cite a concern for patients' ultimate personal or psychological well-being as a standard; medicine is a science, and so one must judge by *objective scientific evidence* what will serve the patient's strictly physical well-being.[8] Yet most people making this claim simultaneously want to insist on making unwilling health professionals provide contraceptives and sterilizations, whose claim to objective medical benefit is precarious.[9]

To be sure, some secular feminist accounts posit that readily available contraception is essential to leading a meaningful and fulfilling life.

Some women have even said it is "a crucial part of what allows us to participate in this society."[10] But that is a sociological or even ideological statement, not a strictly scientific one, and it is open to question. Are mothers, or virgins, or women who plan their families without contraception or sterilization, not truly participating members of society?

Furthermore, from a scientific, biological perspective, contraception and sterilization do not cure a pathology but rather create one, whether temporarily or permanently. They take a healthy functioning system of the human body—even secular feminist accounts refer to it as the *reproductive* system – and cause it to malfunction. People may have very serious reasons why they personally want this to happen at any given time in their lives, but those reasons are not based on a commitment to the healthy functioning of biological systems. For that matter, prescription contraceptives pose their own potentially serious risks to life and health.[11] Evidence of some of these effects has recently grown.[12]

This attempt to mandate participation in contraceptive services, in the name of "science," becomes internally contradictory when the same advocates insist that health professionals must also provide fertility treatments such as *in vitro* fertilization (IVF) to which they have moral or religious objections. One cannot have it both ways, claiming that objectively both fertility and infertility are pathologies that scientifically-oriented health professionals are called upon to cure.

It is claimed that either condition may get in the way of personal plans for the future and overall well-being, if they are unwanted. But seeking to change a condition simply because it is unwanted is the very definition of an "elective" procedure, not a medically necessary procedure. There is no convincing argument for demanding that conscientiously opposed medical professionals participate in such procedures, unless the goal of medicine is simply to serve other people's wishes generally.

A particularly intense argument against respecting the consciences of both physicians and pharmacists arises in connection with so-called "emergency contraception" (EC), which can reduce the chances of pregnancy if taken up to 72 hours after unprotected intercourse or contraceptive failure. The desire to avoid an unexpected pregnancy may be especially strong here, even creating a sense of entitlement. For example, if a woman took precautions to prevent conception, but those malfunctioned, she may feel strongly that it is only fair to be assured ready access to a means for correcting this failure. Planned Parenthood has even encouraged women to see EC as a time machine for undoing their decisions about sexual activity during this time, distributing postcards with a picture of a rumpled bed and the caption: "You have 72 hours to erase last night."[13]

This promise that EC can "erase" the past is not only false but cruel. Uncommitted sex might easily have dire emotional and psychological after-effects, or lead to a variety of sexually transmitted diseases, some of which are life-threatening and none of which is prevented in any way by EC. But even the sense of an entitlement to sex without any chance of pregnancy is, at best, unrealistic: every contraceptive has a theoretical failure rate, and a much higher real-life failure rate.[14]

This situation does become truly harrowing in a case of rape, when the woman herself was in no way responsible for the risk of pregnancy and she has come to an emergency room hoping to minimize the consequences of this assault. Does her claimed right to such treatment override the right of conscience of, say, a Catholic hospital?

Assessing this question requires us to understand some facts.

First, the Catholic Church's objection in this case is not to contraception, since the prevention of pregnancy from rape is not forbidden by Catholic teaching but is seen as part of a woman's legitimate right of self-defense against an act of violence.[15] If conception (that is, fertilization) can no longer be prevented, however, Catholic morality forbids dispensing a drug whose only purpose would be to prevent the implantation (or otherwise interfere with the survival) of what Catholics and many others recognize as a newly conceived human being. Some drugs proposed for "emergency contraception" are thought to include such a post-fertilization effect among their modes of action. In fact, the latest drug to be approved by the Food and Drug Administration as an "emergency contraceptive," ulipristal acetate or HRP 2000 (trade name "Ella"), is a close analogue to the "abortion pill" mifepristone (commonly known as RU-486) which can induce an abortion weeks after implantation.[16] So the question is whether a Catholic hospital may do ovulation testing to help determine whether the drug, in a given case, may act as a contraceptive (by preventing fertilization) or could act (if it acts at all) only as an abortifacient—and *then* decline to provide it in the latter case.

Second, it now seems that the overall effectiveness of EC in preventing pregnancy has been exaggerated.[17] A fertile woman's chance of conceiving from one act of intercourse is never higher than about 33% on the most fertile day of her cycle; her chance of conceiving from such an act occurring randomly in the cycle may be 8%, but more recent studies suggest it may be closer to 3%.[18] It is often thought this figure is still lower in a case of rape, though this has been disputed.[19] During over three-quarters of the woman's cycle her chance of conceiving is almost zero. Thus, without testing for where a woman who was sexually assaulted may be in her cycle, one can estimate that if EC is 80% effective, it may reduce the chance of pregnancy from, say, 5% to 1%.

Third, if we do not know where a woman is in her reproductive cycle, we also do not know how such a drug could or would work. The anti-implantation or abortifacient effect would be very unlikely at some times, and may be the only possible way for the drug to prevent (or, in the case of Ella, to disrupt) an implanted pregnancy at other times. So if a Catholic hospital is barred from doing any test to determine which of these situations exists, it must be willing to give the drug even if it will in fact operate as an abortifacient in that case, which would violate the hospital's moral and religious convictions. To reduce the chance of pregnancy by single-digit percentage points, the hospital must be willing to violate its conscience in 100% of cases.[20] This scenario may also pose a serious dilemma of conscience for the woman herself, who may want protection from pregnancy but object to a procedure that would destroy her newly conceived embryonic child. "Ignorance is bliss" is not a convincing policy for a profession that is striving to be "evidence-based."

In practice, this dilemma is being taken out of the emergency room by the FDA's policy of making EC readily available "over the counter" for all adults (whether male or female) without a prescription — a policy that the FDA has also sought to extend to minors under twelve years old.[21] This places the dilemma more squarely on the shoulders of individual pharmacists, some of whom have a conscientious objection to providing drugs that can act as abortifacients.[22] But at least a conscientiously opposed pharmacist can generally point out that other pharmacists and pharmacies are available—and that no pharmacy stocks every drug that patients may request, not even every life-saving medication.[23]

Conscience Against Life?

In recent years the most serious attack on conscience rights, particularly regarding abortion, has been the claim that respect for such rights endangers women's lives. It is said that laws protecting conscience must have an "emergency" exception for cases when a woman's life-threatening medical condition demands an abortion. State and federal laws ensuring patients' access to "emergency" medical treatment in times of crisis are cited here, and attempts are made to have these laws explicitly override conscience laws.[24]

To be sure, even this claim is sometimes made in bad faith and in service to a much broader agenda. For example, the American Civil Liberties Union says an exception must be made for all "life-saving" and "health-saving" abortions, and a suit against the federal Hyde/Weldon conscience amendment by the California attorney general argued that the state should be able to require all "medically necessary" abortions.[25] These advocates surely know that both "health" and "medically necessary" are terms of art in the abortion context, and are defined by federal courts in line with the Supreme Court's reference in its *Doe* v. *Bolton* decision to include a woman's social, emotional, financial and familial "well-being"—a standard difficult to distinguish from simple abortion on demand.[26]

Ironically, supporters of this standard for the legality of abortion have argued that it is not completely vacuous, because the decision must still be between "a woman and her physician"—with the physician determining that the woman's well-being is indeed at stake. But if each physician has the freedom to agree or disagree that the abortion is necessary, the debate on conscience rights would seem to be over, and the health care provider's decision wins. In the end, what these supporters really seem to mean is that a physician's personal and medical judgment is unreviewable by others only when it is *in favor of* performing an abortion.

However, physicians and lawmakers will argue that there are rare circumstances—severe eclampsia, pulmonary hypertension, etc.—in which a women's life may be saved only through abortion. When one case of severe pulmonary hypertension occurred in a pregnant woman in a Catholic hospital in Phoenix, for example, the hospital reportedly decided that terminating the pregnancy was the only course it could follow to save the woman's life. It claimed that under the circumstances this procedure was not a direct abortion forbidden by Catholic teaching. The local Catholic bishop studied this claim, consulted other experts, and concluded that it was a direct abortion and could not morally be performed. The hospital refused to accept the bishop's judgment on Church teaching, and said it would do the same thing again in similar circumstances. Ultimately the bishop felt he had no recourse but to remove the hospital's status as an official Catholic institution. Although the hospital continues to operate, and to be a member of a Catholic health system, the ACLU has urged the federal government to prevent bishops from making such judgments as to which institutions are Catholic in the future—basically inviting the government to engage in a constitutionally problematic "entanglement with religion."[27]

The implication here is that if a hospital does follow Catholic teaching as interpreted and applied by the bishop, it should be penalized by the government for violating "emergency services" laws and possibly other laws. Since Catholic teaching forbids direct abortion in all circumstances, this could become the wedge that essentially renders illegal the faithful provision of health care to women in the Catholic tradition. So this claim deserves especially serious scrutiny.

The ACLU's central claim is that, if the law protects conscience rights on abortion even in difficult medical circumstances, this "would allow a hospital to *turn away a pregnant woman* experiencing a life-threatening complication without further regard for her health or well-being."[28] What can be said in response?

The first difficulty with this claim is that the Hyde/Weldon amendment and other federal laws have already protected conscience rights on abortion in all circumstances for many years, with some laws in effect since 1973. Also, the great majority of states have similar laws with no "emergency" exception.[29] In all this time, no one has documented a case in which any of these laws led a health-care provider to "turn away" a pregnant woman, or prevented a woman from obtaining emergency treatment needed to save her life. So the allegedly "dangerous" law has actually been in place for many years, with no documented adverse consequences.

Second, it is true that since 1986, a federal law has *forbidden* emergency rooms to turn away patients in medical emergencies, and required them to provide treatment to stabilize the medical condition of such patients—specifically including pregnant women. But this law, the Emergency Medical Treatment and Active Labor Act (EMTALA), does not require in any case that *abortion* be the stabilizing treatment. In fact, "emergency medical condition" is defined by law as a condition that may jeopardize "the health of the individual (or, with respect to a pregnant woman, the health of the woman *or her unborn child*)," and the goal of stabilizing treatment is to prevent deterioration of the health of both mother and child.[30]

Third, as the Obama administration recently reaffirmed when issuing a regulation on enforcement of federal conscience laws, there is no conflict between those laws and EMTALA. The administration wrote that the two bodies of law operate "side by side." EMTALA requires care for the pregnant woman and her unborn child, without second-guessing health-care providers' judgments as to what treatment is most appropriate; the conscience laws ensure that health-care providers who care for pregnant women and their children will not be penalized or otherwise discriminated against by governmental bodies because the treatments they provide are treatments other than abortions.[31]

Fourth, Catholic health facilities, whose ethical code forbids *all* direct abortions, have been shown in various studies to provide the most effective medical care in the country. A recent study of 255 health systems found: "Catholic and other church-owned systems are significantly more likely to provide higher quality performance and efficiency to the communities served than investor-owned systems. Catholic health systems are also significantly more likely to provide higher quality performance to the communities served than secular not-for-profit health systems."[32] Moreover, no Catholic hospital has been found to violate EMTALA because of its ethical policy on respect for human life before as well as after birth. If new restrictions on these providers' civil rights force Catholic facilities, physicians and nurses to leave the health care system—or to violate the ethical code that grounds their commitment to optimum care for all—these restrictions would undermine women's access to life-affirming health care, thus endangering many women's lives. Such new restrictions could also pose serious problems for the vast majority of all hospitals that do not generally provide abortions. These facilities are likely to have many medical professionals on their staff who decline involvement in abortions, since most practicing ob/gyns—86% in one recent survey—do not perform them.[33]

Fifth, genuine treatments are increasingly available for the conditions ordinarily identified as necessitating "therapeutic" abortion. The concept of the "abortion needed to save the mother's life" was always questionable; today it is even more so.[34] For example, in one recent study on treatment for pulmonary hypertension, the condition at issue in the Phoenix hospital case, a medical team was able to help nine women in a row—and their ten unborn children—survive pregnancy and live birth.[35] In these cases the treatment team had to find better ways to respond to the condition because the women themselves had absolutely refused an abortion. If these physicians had felt bound by law or ethics to see abortion as the only solution in these circumstances, and had not learned another way to respond, some of these women probably would have died.

In short, a woman experiencing heart failure or uncontrolled high blood pressure most likely needs circulatory or cardiac treatment, and an abortion may only exacerbate her condition. A woman hemorrhaging during pregnancy needs the hemorrhaging controlled. A hospital that finds itself at a loss regarding how to save a pregnant woman's life may well consider transferring her to a facility that is better equipped to diagnose and treat her condition—but this is already provided for in EMTALA. Sending a patient to a facility better equipped and trained to diagnose and treat high-risk cases is quite different from simply referring her for an abortion.

We also need to be aware that, in cases where treatment for a pregnant woman's life-endangering condition may also risk harm to the child, many physicians recommend an abortion before they will provide treatment—*not* because the abortion is the only or better way to meet the medical needs of the mother, but because otherwise the child may be born *alive* with some injury that could be attributed to the treatment, and the physician is seeking to avoid any legal liability for such harm. He risks no liability for recommending abortion, even if it has no chance of improving the mother's condition. This creates what an eminent maternal-fetal medicine expert calls "a tremendous imbalance" in pressures on physicians to recommend abortion over other treatments.[36] Government should not aggravate this imbalance by removing longstanding conscience protections from doctors who are able and willing to save both mother and child.

Sixth, while pro-life health care providers have a long history of respecting and saving women's lives, abortion providers have a well-documented history of taking the lives of *hundreds* of women since *Roe* v. *Wade* was decided in 1973. Most of these women probably assumed that because abortion is legal it is "safe." Almost all of them were perfectly healthy until they died at abortion providers' hands.[37] In the cases of women suffering pulmonary hypertension or another life-threatening condition, abortion itself is more dangerous than it is for other women.[38] Effective regulations that would help protect women from the dangers of legal abortion are often opposed by groups promoting abortion—often the same groups that claim they want to protect women's lives by punishing physicians who do *not* provide abortions.[39]

This controversy helps bring the "public health" argument against conscience rights into clearer focus. If, as studies report, religious nonprofit health-care institutions provide the best and most effective health care, especially for the poor and underserved, then it seems that any policy aimed at pushing them out of the health-care arena must meet the burden of showing how it could possibly save more lives than it places at risk. If we allow the "reproductive health-care" agenda to override our commitment to optimum health care generally, many patients—including many women—will find it more difficult to access basic health care that could save their lives.

Ironically, the oft-repeated argument of abortion advocates that the government should stay out of health-care professionals' medical decisions has been turned on its head in the debate on conscience rights.

They have long held that physicians who want to provide abortions—even the grotesque late-term procedure called partial-birth abortion (now banned by federal law and many state laws)—must be allowed full discretion to choose such procedures, even in the absence of evidence that they are medically necessary.[40] Now they say that physicians who choose to care for women and their unborn children without performing abortions must have their freedom suppressed, even in the absence of evidence that such coercion would help women. Their stance—that the government must respect the medical and ethical judgment only of medical personnel who wish to perform abortions—defies logic and fairness.

Sometimes the argument against conscience is intensified by the claim that in some cases, this institution may be the only provider available in the area to provide an abortion or other procedure. But that claim only raises three new questions. First, if this is the only provider in the area, how does driving it out of business serve the health of women or anyone else? Second, if those making this claim believe this particular service is essential for public health, why have none of them stepped forward to provide it? Are they not even more responsible for this gap in the provision of health care, since they have no reason not to ensure access to it except convenience and a desire for greater profits elsewhere? Third, especially if a woman is experiencing a complicated medical condition, does she really want her abortion performed by someone who ordinarily never performs abortions, opted out of abortion training on conscience grounds, and is involved now strictly under protest? Even some abortion advocates have acknowledged the weakness of this claim. In the words of Jill Robinson of the National Women's Health Center: "I don't want a doctor performing my abortion if he has moral reservations about it. Thanks but no thanks."[41]

Conscience Against Equality?

Finally, the claim is made that respect for religiously grounded conscientious objections may conflict with constitutional or statutory requirements concerning equal protection or nondiscrimination. The Christian fertility doctors in California who were sued for failing to provide artificial insemination to a lesbian woman (or, as the doctors claimed, to any unmarried person) provide a good example of the dispute. The California Supreme Court refused to find that the physicians' right to free exercise of religion exempted them from a state law prohibiting discrimination based on sexual orientation.[42] Ironically, this charge is a bit harder to bring against a health-care provider following Catholic teaching, which would refuse to provide artificial insemination, "surrogate" motherhood, or in vitro fertilization to anyone, regardless of marital status or sexual orientation. Catholic reproductive medicine is aimed simply at helping a man's or woman's reproductive system to function normally again.

Any refusal to provide abortions has been called a form of sex discrimination, on the basis that pregnancy and the interruption of pregnancy are realities peculiar to women.[43] This claim has not fared well in U.S. courts, which seem to understand that opposition to abortion is based on something else altogether. When the U.S. Supreme Court upheld bans on public funding of abortion in health programs that fund childbirth, it concluded: "Nor is it irrational that Congress has authorized federal reimbursement for medically necessary services generally, but not for certain medically necessary abortions. Abortion is inherently different from other medical procedures, because no other procedure involves the purposeful termination of a potential life."[44] (The court's only error here is the obscure phrase "potential life," since "evidence-based" policymaking would force us to admit, after review of any embryology textbook, that the human individual in the womb is *actually* alive until he or she is made actually dead by an abortion.) The Supreme Court has also dismissed the claim that opposition to abortion is based on animus against women.[45] While some state courts have invoked a state Equal Rights Amendment to invalidate bans on state funding of abortion, the Pennsylvania Supreme Court, in ruling otherwise, surely had common sense on its side when it said concisely that a ban on funding abortion is directed against abortion as a procedure, not against women as a class.[46] If the government itself may validly use its funding power to encourage childbirth over abortion, certainly individuals and institutions, including health-care providers, may have that same preference and act on it without interference or discrimination by the government.

It is true that federal statutory law such as the Pregnancy Discrimination Act of 1978 ("PDA," Public Law 95–555), amending Title VII of the Civil Rights Act, treats discrimination based on pregnancy as tantamount to discrimination based on sex. However, the statute itself excludes any mandate for abortion, except in cases of danger to the mother's life—an exception that has itself been challenged in court.[47] So the question remains whether refusal to provide other procedures such as IVF, contraception, or sterilization is discrimination based on "pregnancy," therefore based on sex.

One difficulty in trying to give an affirmative answer here lies in the fact that supporters of this sex-discrimination argument use the same argument to demand medical practices for producing *infertility* (contraception and sterilization) as they do to demand medical practices for producing *children* (new reproductive technologies). Fertility and infertility cannot both be pathologies. In no other branch of medicine could such a contradictory mandate be imposed. Contraception and sterilization themselves would seem to "discriminate against" pregnancy, while IVF implements a preference in its favor. The conclusion seems inescapable that preventing pregnancy is a lifestyle goal of some women, and achieving pregnancy is a lifestyle goal of other women (or of the same women at different times). Both decisions are generally based on something other than medical need—that is, they are "elective" procedures, the kind of procedure that in any other branch of medicine would never be *mandated* on all providers or expected of all women. Therefore it is arbitrary to claim that a conscientious objection to providing some of these procedures is grounded in an animus against women.

Some have tried to argue that the PDA requires pregnancy to be treated like any other disease or disability—some informally even call it the Pregnancy *Disability* Act. But that is not what the Act says. Such an interpretation would first of all make the Act's exclusion of abortion irrational. If pregnancy is a disability like any other, abortion would have to be seen as curing a disease or disability whenever it destroys a healthy pregnancy. That interpretation would also render irrational any attempt under the PDA to require services to maintain pregnancy and bring women through to live delivery, since that would be tantamount to requiring the provision of care designed artificially to prolong a disease or disability.

What the Act does say is that women affected by "pregnancy, child-birth, or related medical conditions" will be treated by employers like other employees *with a comparable ability or inability to work*. Thus *if* pregnancy makes a woman unable to work, she must be given the same benefits, including leave time, as if she were rendered unable to work by some other cause. This does not imply that pregnancy across the board must be treated as akin to a disease or disability that physicians have a mandate to prevent or "cure"; in fact, the primary purpose of the Act is the laudable one of maintaining health coverage and leave time for women who are already pregnant and wish to remain that way.

Another argument equates denial of contraceptives to women with denial of Viagra or other treatments for sexual dysfunction to men. If a physician provides the latter, it is claimed, he or she cannot discriminate by denying the former even on the basis of a religious objection.[48] But again, precisely from a medical and not a religious viewpoint, these situations are opposites: Viagra helps the reproductive system function, while contraceptives make it cease to function. It could be added that contraceptives do not enable anyone to have sexual relations as such, and that hormonal contraceptives can have the side-effect of interfering with female sex drive.[49]

A final observation regarding "equality" arguments. When some members of Congress tried to amend the Patient Protection and Affordable Care Act in a House committee, to ensure that the new Act would not require health-care providers to violate their moral or religious convictions, their effort drew criticism from two very different quarters. Secular liberals said a broad conscience clause would allow conservative Christian health care providers to deny all care to classes of people they dislike, such as homosexuals with AIDS. The National Right to Life Committee expressed a different concern: that such protection would allow some providers (especially secular utilitarians) to deny life-saving treatment to elderly and disabled patients whom they see as having a low "quality of life" and hence a life not worth living. The broad conscience clause was not accepted as part of the health care reform law. However, the National Right to Life Committee did manage to negotiate language into the final Act, amending a provision that allows a federal commission to rate medical treatments by their cost-effectiveness: the Secretary of

HHS may not use the commission's evidence or findings "in a manner that treats extending the life of an elderly, disabled, or terminally ill individual as of lower value than extending the life of an individual who is younger, nondisabled, or not terminally ill."[50]

After enactment of the Affordable Care Act, a bill was introduced to address the conscience problem posed by the new law's creation of mandatory benefits lists for "essential" and "preventive" health services for most health plans.[51] This bill references the provision quoted immediately above, ensuring that the conscience legislation will not protect decisions to withhold such treatment based upon a judgment about the value of different people's lives. This addresses the right-to-life concern, and may also alleviate concerns about providers choosing to withhold life-saving treatment from people with AIDS who have a homosexual orientation. The proposal distinguishes between conscientious objections to specific procedures, and animus against certain classes of people, and may therefore serve as a model for future legislative efforts.

Conclusion

Critics who invoke competing claims to trump or limit rights of conscience want to insist that the voice of conscience does not have the last word, that it exists in a larger world in which the common good must be served. They claim that when religious bodies leave their chapels and sanctuaries and participate in the provision of services to the public, they must set aside their convictions and play by the same rules as everyone else—by which they mean, rules established by those same critics.

But these competing claims must also be put to the test of the common good. For even the individual goods they stand for may be open to criticism as goods, or they may be served as well or better without attacking rights of conscience. Those claims are also not the last word, because they exist in a larger world in which the contributions of people of conscience are necessary for maintaining life-affirming health care and other essential services for all, especially for those who are most in need. Religiously based providers' freedom to care for the sick, without being marginalized or pushed out of the provision of public services, will be vitally important for the life and health of Americans of any faith or of none. This reality needs to be advanced more assertively in the public square, allowing Americans to make an informed decision about the kind of society and the kind of health-care system they want.

ENDNOTES

1 Citations and texts for the laws listed here and others can be found in USCCB Secretariat of Pro-Life Activities, "Current Federal Laws Protecting Conscience Rights" (February 2012), at http://www.usccb.org/issues-and-action/religious-liberty/conscience-protection/upload/Federal-Conscience-Laws.pdf .

2 For example: C. Grealis, "Religion in the Pharmacy: A Balanced Approach to Pharmacists' Right To Refuse To Provide Plan B," *The Georgetown Law Journal* 97 (2009): 1715–37, at 1717 ("pharmacists' right to object on conscience grounds must be balanced against the need for women to access Plan B"); National Health Law Program Standards of Care Project, *Health Care Refusals: Undermining Quality Care for Women* (National Health Law Program 2010) at 66 ("The authors of this report hope to initiate change in how policymakers, providers, and the public view ideologically or religiously based care denials and restrictions as violating the medical standards of care and jeopardizing patient and public health"), available at www.healthlaw.org/images/stories/Health_Care_Refusals_Undermining_Quality_Care_for_Women.pdf.

3 *Planned Parenthood* v. *Casey*, 505 U.S. 833, 851 (1992) (joint opinion of O'Connor, Kennedy, and Souter, JJ.).

4 For the U.S. Supreme Court's recognition of a freedom of expressive association for groups dedicated to a message or set of values, see *Hurley* v. *Irish-American Gay, Lesbian, and Bisexual Group of Boston*, 515 U.S. 557 (1995), and *Boy Scouts* v. *Dale*, 530 U.S. 640 (2000).

5 See, e.g. *Harris* v. *McRae*, 448 U.S. 297, 314 (1980), citing *Maher* v. *Roe*, 432 U.S. 464, 474 (1977).

6 Jill Robinson of the National Women's Health Center, in The Pew Forum on Religion and Public Life, "Dr. No? The Debate on Conscience in Health Care" (September 8, 2006), Event Transcript, at http://pewforum.org/Church-State-Law/Dr-No-The-Debate-on-Conscience-in-Health-Care.aspx.

7 For example, the ethics committee of one medical organization judges the validity of conscientious refusal partly by its impact on "well-being *as the*

patient perceives it"—which is in considerable tension with the committee's simultaneous insistence that physicians' decisions in such situations must be objectively "evidence-based." See Ethics Committee of the American College of Obstetricians and Gynecologists, "The Limits of Conscientious Refusal in Reproductive Medicine" (ACOG Ethics Committee Opinion No. 385), 110 *Obstetrics and Gynecology* 1203–8 (2007) at 1205.

8   It is actually somewhat misleading to call medicine a science, as it is an ethically grounded profession informed by science; and some of the most egregious and widely condemned violations of medical ethics throughout history have occurred when doctors forgot that their primary objective is to heal patients, not to use them as opportunities for gaining scientific knowledge. Moreover, almost all codes of medical ethics, beginning with the Hippocratic Oath, demand respect for patients' human dignity in ways that transcend purely physical survival or organic functioning.

9   In this regard, what the FDA's own medical advisors said 46 years ago remains true today: "The oral contraceptives present society with problems unique in the history of human therapeutics. Never will so many people have taken such potent drugs voluntarily over such a protracted period for an objective other than for control of disease." U.S. Food and Drug Administration, Advisory Committee on Obstetrics and Gynecology, *Report on the Oral Contraceptives* (1966), 1.

10   J. Robinson, The Pew Forum, note 6 *supra*.

11   Various contraceptives have been associated with increased risk of myocardial infarction, stroke, venous thromboembolism, and hypertension, as well as sexually transmitted diseases. R.A. Hatcher et al., *Contraceptive Technology,* 18th rev. ed. (New York: Ardent Media, 2004), at 404–410, 445.

12   For example, see U.S. Food and Drug Administration, "FDA Drug Safety Communication: Safety Review of possible increased risk of blood clots with birth control pills containing drospirenone" (May 31, 2011) (available at www.fda.gov/Drugs/DrugSafety/ucm257164.htm) (documenting the blood clot risk from a recent and widely advertised contraceptive commonly known as "Yaz"); R. Heffron, *et al.*, "Use of hormonal contraceptives and risk of HIV-1 transmission: a prospective cohort study," 12 *The Lancet Infectious Diseases* 19–26 (2012), available at www.thelancet.com/journals/laninf/article/PIIS1473–3099(11)70247–X/abstract (finding that women using hormonal contraceptives have an increased risk of contracting and transmitting HIV).

13   See Helen Alvaré, "Saying "Yes' Before Saying 'I Do': Premarital Sex and

Cohabitation as a Piece of the Divorce Puzzle," 18 *Notre Dame Journal of Law, Ethics & Public Policy* 7–87 (2004) at 52.

14   See, e.g., J. Trussell, "Contraceptive failure in the United States," 83 *Contraception* 397–404 (2011).

15   See U.S. Conference of Catholic Bishops, *Ethical and Religious Directives for Catholic Health Care Services* (5th ed., 2009), Directive 36: "A female who has been raped should be able to defend herself against a potential conception from the sexual assault. If, after appropriate testing, there is no evidence that conception has occurred already, she may be treated with medications that would prevent ovulation, sperm capacitation, or fertilization. It is not permissible, however, to initiate or to recommend treatments that have as their purpose or direct effect the removal, destruction, or interference with the implantation of a fertilized ovum," available at www.usccb.org/issues-and-action/human-life-and-dignity/health-care/upload/Ethical-Religious-Directives-Catholic-Health-Care-Services-fifth-edition-2009.pdf.

16   *See* A. Tarantal et al., "Effects of Two Antiprogestins on Early Pregnancy in the Long-Tailed Macaque (*Macaca fascicularis*)," *Contraception* 54 (1996): 107–115, at 114 ("studies with mifepristone and HRP 2000 have shown both antiprogestins to have roughly comparable activity in terminating pregnancy when administered during the early stages of gestation"); G. Bernagiano and H. von Hertzen, "Towards more effective emergency contraception?" *The Lancet* 375 (2010): 527–28. at 527 ("Ulipristal has similar biological effects to mifepristone, the antiprogestin used in medical abortion"); European Medicines Agency, *Evaluation of Medicines for Human Use: CHMP Assessment for Ellaone* (2009) at 8 ("Ulipristal acetate prevents progesterone from occupying its receptor, thus the gene transcription normally turned on by progesterone is blocked, and the proteins necessary to begin and maintain pregnancy are not synthesized") and 16 (in animal tests "ulipristal acetate is embryotoxic at low doses"). The European Medicines Agency report is available at www.ema.europa.eu/docs/en_GB/document_library/EPAR_-_Public_assessment_report/human/001027/WC500023673.pdf.

17   Population experts who promote ready access to the "Plan B" regimen found that enhancing access to the drug could not be shown to reduce unintended pregnancies or abortions in the target population in *any* of 23 studies designed to show such impact. Based on studies of the drug's efficacy when used as prescribed, the authors noted that "we can be 95% confident that it reduces pregnancy risk by more than 23%. But just how much more

remains poorly defined; the published efficacy figures calculated from currently available data on this regimen—on average, approximately 80%—may overstate actual efficacy, possibly quite substantially. Clearly, if the method is only weakly efficacious, it is unlikely to produce a major reduction in unintended pregnancy rates no matter how often women use it." E. Raymond et al., "Population Effect of Increased Access to Emergency Contraceptive Pills," *Obstetrics & Gynecology* 109 (2007): 181–8, at 187.

18 See A. Wilcox et al., "Likelihood of conception with a single act of intercourse: providing benchmark rates for assessment of post-coital contraceptives," *Contraception* 63 (2001): 211–215.

19 The conventional wisdom is that various factors, ranging from sexual dysfunction on the part of some rapists to the anovulatory effect of the trauma of rape on some women, reduces the likelihood of pregnancy further. However, one survey estimates as much as a 5% risk of pregnancy from rape involving women of reproductive age. See M. Holmes et al., "Rape-related pregnancy: Estimates and descriptive characteristics from a national sample of women," *American Journal of Obstetrics and Gynecology* 175 (1996): 320–325, available at http://www.sciencedirect.com/science/article/pii/S0002937896701412. I use this higher estimate in what follows.

20 For the administration of such a drug to be morally acceptable, "Catholic providers must have moral certitude that there will not be two victims affected by emergency contraception, the sexual assault victim of the unjust aggressor and an unborn child who has already been engendered… To administer emergency contraception when there is insufficient information as to its effect is not only morally illicit but medically unsound." E. Furton et al. (eds.), *Catholic Health Care Ethics: A Manual for Practitioners*, 2nd ed. (Philadelphia: National Catholic Bioethics Center, 2009). Requiring the Catholic provider to administer EC to each victim regardless of whether she has ovulated (or regardless of whether testing has been done to determine this) forces providers with this moral position to act irresponsibly toward the new human life that may be present, contrary to their consciences.

21 As of this writing, the proposed extension to young minors has not been accepted by the Obama administration. See R. Stein, "Obama administration refuses to relax Plan B restrictions," *The Washington Post*, 7 December 2011, at www.washingtonpost.com/national/health-science/obama-administration-refuses-to-relax-plan-b-restrictions/2011/12/07/gIQAF5HicO_print.html.

22 For a recent decision granting declaratory and injunctive relief to

pharmacists who raised such objections to an administrative rule requiring provision of "emergency contraception," see *Morr-Fitz* v. *Blagojevich*, No. 2005–CH-000495 (Ill. Cir. Ct., Sangamon County, April 5, 2011), available at http://media.aclj.org/pdf/judgerienziruling_20110405.pdf. The Appellate Court of Illinois, Fourth District, recently held that the state's Health Care Right of Conscience Act prohibits enforcement of the administrative rule. See *Morr-Fitz* v. *Quinn*, 2012 IL App (4th) 110398, available at http://www.state.il.us/court/opinions/AppellateCourt/2012/4thDistrict/4110398.pdf.

23   As Kevin Hasson of the Becket Fund observed in his 2006 debate with Jill Robinson, his medication for Parkinson's disease is not carried by every pharmacy and can be difficult to find in a rural area. "If I run out of it or lose it, and I don't get a prescription for it within about 24 hours, I'll go into convulsions. But not every pharmacist in the country is required to carry amantadine and carbidopa and levodopa, and I don't see why every pharmacist in the country should be required to carry Plan B either." The Pew Forum, note 6 *supra*.

24   For example, the main section dealing with abortion in the Patient Protection and Affordable Care Act of 2010 includes a provision stating: "Nothing in this Act shall be construed to relieve any health care provider from providing emergency services as required by State or Federal law, including section 1867 of the Social Security Act (popularly known as 'EMTALA')." Sec. 1303 (d). H.R. 358, the Protect Life Act, was introduced in the 112th Congress to bring this Act into conformity with policies on abortion funding and conscience rights that prevail in other federal programs; but when this bill sought to clarify that the provision on "emergency services" would remain "subject" to the Hyde/Weldon policy, protecting conscience rights on abortion in all cases, abortion advocates in the House vigorously opposed this proposal and offered amendments (unsuccessfully) to reverse it.

25   The ACLU's July 2010 and December 2010 letters, urging HHS to suppress health care based on Catholic teaching, are available at www.aclu.org/reproductive-freedom/aclu-sends-second-letter-asking-government-investigate-potential-denials-emerge. For the dismissal of the California law suit on ripeness grounds see *California* v. *United States*, 2008 WL 744840 (N.D. Cal. March 18, 2008).

26   "Whether, in the words of the Georgia statute, 'an abortion is necessary' is a professional judgment that the Georgia physician will be called upon to make routinely. We agree with the District Court… that the medical judgment may be exercised in the light of all factors—physical, emotional,

psychological, familial, and the woman's age — relevant to the wellbeing of the patient. All these factors may relate to health. This allows the attending physician the room he needs to make his best medical judgment." *Doe v. Bolton*, 410 U.S. 179, 192 (1973).

27 See the ACLU's December 2010 letter, at note 25 *supra*. More recently, the ACLU has sued the USCCB in a case allegedly involving a denial of proper medical care; see http://www.nytimes.com/2013/12/03/us/lawsuit-challenges-anti-abortion-policies-at-catholic-hospitals.html.

28 American Civil Liberties Union, "House Holds Hearing on Dangerous Abortion Legislation" (Feb. 9, 2011), at www.aclu.org/reproductive-freedom/house-holds-hearing-dangerous-abortion-legislation (emphasis added).

29 For federal laws see note 1 *supra*. For state laws see Protection of Conscience Project, "Protection of Conscience Laws United States: States and Territories," available at www.consciencelaws.org/laws/usa/law-usa-01.html. For an overview by a group that generally opposes such laws see Guttmacher Institute, *State Policies in Brief As of January 1, 2012: Refusing to Provide Health Services* (2012), available at www.guttmacher.org/state-center/spibs/spib_RPHS.pdf.

30 See 42 U.S.C. §1395dd (emphasis added).

31 On the relationship between conscience laws like Hyde/Weldon and other federal laws like EMTALA, the administration said: "The conscience laws and the other federal statues have operated side by side often for many decades. As repeals by implication are disfavored and laws are meant to be read in harmony, the Department fully intends to continue to *enforce all the laws it has been charged with administering*.... [E]ntities must continue to comply with their... EMTALA... obligations, *as well as* the *federal health care provider conscience protection statutes*." Department of Health and Human Services, "Regulation for the Enforcement of Federal Health Care Provider Conscience Protection Laws," 76 *Fed. Reg.* 9968–77 (Feb. 23, 2011), at 9973, 9974 (emphasis added).

32 David Foster, Ph.D., M.P.H., *Research Brief: Differences in Health System Quality Performance by Ownership* (Thomson Reuters, August 9, 2010), at www.100tophospitals.com/assets/100TOPSystemOwnership.pdf.

33 See D. Stulberg et al., "Abortion Provision Among Practicing Obstetrician–Gynecologists," *Obstetrics and Gynecology* 118 (2011): 609–614.

34 Recent congressional debate on a proposed federal conscience provision featured testimonials from four experts with a combined experience of 108 years in obstetrics and gynecology, maternal and child health, and

emergency medicine, stating that they had never seen a case in which abortion was needed to save a mother's life or in which a conscientious objection to abortion led to a denial of needed care. See remarks of Rep. Burgess on the Protect Life Act, H.R. 358, citing letters from Drs. Byron C. Calhoun, John Thorp, Edward J. Read, and Steve Calvin, *Cong. Record*, October 13, 2011, at H6896–7. Writes one physician who has performed abortions for decades: "The idea of abortion to save the mother's life is something that people cling to because it sounds noble and pure—but medically speaking, it probably doesn't exist." D. Sloan, M.D. and P. Hartz, *Choice: A Doctor's Experience with the Abortion Dilemma* (New York: International Publishers, 2nd ed, 2002) at 46. Even half a century ago, when medical science was far less developed, the medical director of the Planned Parenthood Federation of America said that "medically speaking, that is, from the point of view of diseases of the various systems, cardiac, genitourinary, and so on, it is hardly ever necessary today to consider the life of a mother as threatened by a pregnancy." M. Calderone, "Illegal Abortion as a Public Health Problem," *American Journal of Public Health* 50 (1960): 948–954, at 948–9.

35 D. Kiely et al., "Improved survival in pregnancy and pulmonary hypertension using a multiprofessional approach," *BJOG: An International Journal of Obstetrics & Gynecology* 117 (2010): 565–574; for other studies see notes 13–20 of this article, as well as N. Austriaco, "Abortion in a Case of Pulmonary Arterial Hypertension," *National Catholic Bioethics Quarterly* 11 (2011): 503–518, at 506 n. 11.

36 T. Goodwin, "Medicalizing Abortion Decisions," *First Things*, March 1996, pp. 33–36 at 35–6; www.firstthings.com/article/2007/10/003–medicalizing-abortion-decisions-15.

37 See Centers for Disease Control and Prevention, *Abortion Surveillance—United States, 2007* (Feb. 25, 2011), p. 36, Table 25 (showing 452 women's deaths from abortion since abortion was legalized in 1973, 383 of which are from legal abortions); available at www.cdc.gov/mmwr/pdf/ss/ss6001.pdf. For a discussion of why these statistics may be a significant understatement see David Reardon, Ph.D., "The Cover-Up: Why U.S. Abortion Mortality Statistics Are Meaningless" (2000), at http://after-abortion.org/2000/the-cover-up-why-u-s-abortion-mortality-statistics-are-meaningless/.

38 It has been noted that while expert opinion still tends to recommend abortion as safer than delivery for women with pulmonary arterial hypertension, "pregnancy interruptions in patients with PAH are also associated with an

elevated risk of maternal death." Joseph G. Parambil and Michael D. Mc-Goon, "Pregnancy and pulmonary hypertension," chapter 6 in Celia Oakley and Carole E. Warnes, *Heart Disease in Pregnancy*, 2nd ed. (Malden, MA: Blackwell Publishing 2007), 73.

39 See: Melinda Henneberger, "Kermit Gosnell's Pro-Choice Enablers (Is This What an Industry That Self-Regulates Looks Like?)," *Politics Daily*, January 23, 2011, at www.politicsdaily.com/2011/01/23/kermit-gosnells-pro-choice-enablers-how-clinics-become-death-t/; William Saletan, "The Back Alley: How the Politics of Abortion Protects Bad Clinics," *Slate*, February 16–25, 2011 (Eight-part series), at www.slate.com/articles/news_and_politics/the_back_alley.html.

40 It is now known that ACOG's 1997 statement on dilation and extraction (the procedure used in partial-birth abortions) initially said only that its own medical experts could find no circumstance in which this procedure is necessary for a woman's life or health. At the urging of then-White House staffer Elena Kagan, the final statement added that despite this lack of evidence, the procedure nevertheless "may be the best or most appropriate procedure in a particular circumstance to save the life or preserve the health of a woman." The U.S. Supreme Court quoted this sentence when it overturned Nebraska's ban on partial-birth abortion. See http://cnsnews.com/news/article/elena-kagan-helped-edit-statement-medical-association-defeat-partial-birth-abortion-ban.

41 See J. Robinson, The Pew Forum, note 6 *supra*.

42 *North Coast Women's Care Medical Group v. Superior Court*, 44 Cal.4th 1145 (Cal. 2008).

43 For example, see Center for Reproductive Rights News Release, "Sex Discrimination Continues in Florida After Court Refuses to Overturn Ban on Medicaid Funded Abortions," September 3, 2003, at http://reproductiverights.org/en/press-room/sex-discrimination-continues-in-florida-after-court-refuses-to-overturn-ban-on-medicaid-f.

44 *Harris* v. *McRae*, note 5 *supra*, at 325 (footnotes omitted).

45 "Whatever one thinks of abortion, it cannot be denied that there are common and respectable reasons for opposing it, other than hatred of, or condescension toward (or indeed any view at all concerning), women as a class—as is evident from the fact that men and women are on both sides of the issue…" *Bray* v. *Alexandria*, 506 U.S. 263, 270 (1993).

46 *Fischer* v. *Dept. of Public Welfare*, 502 A.2d 114, 125 (Pa. 1985).

47 The PDA's mandate for covering abortions in cases of danger to the mother's life was challenged by the National Conference of Catholic

Bishops, but a U.S. district court found the case not ripe for adjudication as no federal official had taken steps to impose this requirement on the bishops' conference. See *National Conference of Catholic Bishops* v. *Bell*, 490 F. Supp. 734 (D.D.C. 1980), *aff'd*, 653 F.2d 535 (D.C. Cir. 1981). This situation has not changed over three decades later.

48 This comparison was often cited after the federal Center for Medicaid Services interpreted the law in 1998 to require provision of drugs like Viagra in Medicaid whenever a physician deemed it "medically necessary" in treating male sexual dysfunction. See www.cms.gov/smdl/downloads/smd103098.pdf. The Center for Reproductive Rights has even claimed that a policy of funding Viagra but not abortions in Medicaid makes women "second class citizens." See note 43 *supra*. However, a number of states no longer fund Viagra in Medicaid; some cited the Medicaid law's restrictions on drugs open to widespread abuse, after discovering that the drugs were being provided to men without erectile dysfunction and even to sex offenders. Note that according to the government's 1998 letter cited above, drugs to *promote* fertility in women were excluded from the Medicaid requirement; this disparity in policy has stirred no comparable protest.

49 See "Hormonal Contraceptives Associated With Higher Risk of Female Sexual Dysfunction, Study Finds," Science Daily, May 4, 2010, at www.sciencedaily.com/releases/2010/05/100504074841.htm.

50 See 42 U.S.C. § 1320e-1(c)(1).

51 112th Congress, the Respect for Rights of Conscience Act (H.R. 1179). See Cardinal Daniel N. DiNardo, Letter to House of Representatives on H.R. 1179 (April 6, 2011), http://www.usccb.org/issues-and-action/religious-liberty/conscience-protection/upload/DiNardo-Letter-Apr-6–2011–HR1179.pdf.

Chapter Seven
Discrimination in Discrimination: Confronting Half-Truths in Anti-Discrimination Laws that Threaten Institutional Religious Freedom
Anthony R. Picarello, Jr.

That a lie which is half a truth is ever the blackest of lies;
That a lie which is all a lie may be met and fought with outright—
But a lie which is part a truth is a harder matter to fight.
—Alfred Lord Tennyson, *The Grandmother,* St. 8.

Addressing the question of "legislative opportunities" in the area of protecting the religious freedom of institutions is a tall order. The term "opportunities" suggests the possibility of real upside potential, in an area that is inherently about avoiding enormous downside potential, namely, the infringement of religious liberty.

For this reason, I am not going to characterize as "opportunities" the fact that there are bills to eliminate or mitigate the various legislative and regulatory threats to institutional religious liberty now before us. These are not opportunities at all; they are urgent necessities that merely bring us up to baseline. In an important sense, the news is bad in this area, and we need to be candid with each other about that fact.

Characterization aside, it would be of limited interest simply to detail the religious freedom risks and corresponding remedies. That would amount to little more than a snapshot of our legislative agenda for religious freedom at this particular moment in time. That may be valuable and interesting, but more suited to an audience of grassroots activists who need simply to understand what they need to mobilize against in the very next battle.

What I would like to do instead is reflect on the legislative landscape of the last few years in order to see if there are trends that also represent openings—true "opportunities"—actually to gain some ground in the area of institutional religious freedom. And here, I think the news is good, because there is at least one legislative trend that would allow us to play offense rather than just defense. That trend is what I would call the discrimination half-truth: antidiscrimination laws that define "discrimination" over-broadly, in order to prohibit not only conduct that is actually morally repugnant, but officially disfavored religious exercise as well.

This tactic is clever and often effective in attacking religious exercise. It disguises the intention to target religious exercise, helping the law both to pass the legislature and to survive constitutional scrutiny. It harnesses the legitimate moral outrage against the actual unjust discrimination covered by the definition, serving both as an engine to drive passage of the prohibition on religious exercise (which could not pass standing alone) and as a deterrent against attempts to carve that religious exercise out of the definition. It divides to conquer: in a Church community that should be united both against unjust discrimination and in support of religious liberty, these laws tend to pit people and groups against each other who tend to be focused more on one value than the other.

But this tactic also presents a genuine opportunity to advance the cause of religious freedom. Because the tactic involves a certain measure of deceit, it is possible to go on offense by exposing that fact, requiring proponents to rebut the claim that they are attempting to smuggle religious discrimination into the law. It also provides an occasion for Church leaders to teach in the public square—to highlight and explain the value of the religious exercise that would be infringed, and to affirm that portion of the law that would forbid actual unjust discrimination.

In situations where these counter-measures succeed, we would end up better off than where we started; we would do more than just avoid losing ground. Our opponents would lose credibility, we would reach more people with the truth, and fewer people would subscribe to the half-truth that our opponents had urged at the outset. This is, in other words, a genuine opportunity on the legislative front.

But these half-truths, by their nature, are not obvious and will take some work to expose and exploit. In other words, going on offense will require developing a corresponding tactic on our side.

So my hope is to begin that development by describing two steps. The first is to identify this particular pattern of attack against religious freedom with sufficient clarity that we can recognize it when it is deployed, and persuade reasonable skeptics that a particular proposed law represents an example of the pattern. Having diagnosed the disease, the second step is to begin developing possible cures. I will discuss the strengths and weaknesses of one possibility in particular: proposing alternative legislative definitions that expressly reinforce the distinctions that the half-true definitions attempt to blur or collapse.

I have entitled this chapter "Discrimination in Discrimination" because the phrase bears at least two meanings, one that summarizes the problem, and one the solution. The basic problem is the surreptitious embedding of religious discrimination within legislative definitions of prohibited discrimination; and the basic solution is to cast a more discriminating eye on those definitions of discrimination, in order to sort the wheat from the chaff.

Identifying the Target: Laws or Regulations That Define "Discrimination" to Include Institutional Religious Exercise

I propose to identify the category of laws and regulations that we might target on offense in two ways, first by providing a series of examples, and second, by contrasting them with categories of laws that bear some (but not all) of the same features.

Examples of Laws or Regulations Involving "Discrimination In Discrimination"

There are at least three categories of antidiscrimination laws whose definitions of "discrimination" are typically broad or malleable enough both to forbid actual, unjust discrimination and to threaten the religious liberty of institutions: (1) religious discrimination; (2) sex discrimination; and (3) sexual orientation discrimination. Each of these is discussed in turn below, including examples of how the definition of discrimination has recently been applied over-broadly to threaten religious liberty.

Religious Discrimination

Title VII of the Civil Rights Act of 1964 generally forbids discrimination in employment based on, among other things, "religion."[1] The statute's definition of "religion" starts out broadly, "includ[ing] all aspects of religious observance and practice, as well as belief."[2] Impermissible discrimination occurs when religion thus defined is even "a motivating factor for any employment practice, even though other factors also motivated the practice."[3] Discrimination also includes the failure to accommodate an employee's religion, unless the employer "is unable to reasonably accommodate" the employee's "religious observance or practice without undue hardship on the conduct of the employer's business."[4] Many other state and local laws forbid discrimination based on "religion" in similar terms,[5] adding to the scope of those covered (especially employers with fewer than 15 employees),[6] and in some cases, the scope of the protection where it applies.[7]

This breadth is a good thing in some important respects. For example, the law forbids Ford Motor Company (or Sears, or Microsoft) from posting signs that Catholics (or Jews, or Muslims) need not apply, or from following such a policy of unjust discrimination less explicitly. In fact, in one respect, Title VII's definition of religious discrimination is not broad enough, because it has been construed to impose only a negligible burden on employers to accommodate religion in the private workplace.[8]

But the general breadth of this prohibition on religious discrimination would be a disaster for religious freedom if applied to religious employers. The resulting absurdities are amusing to consider, but also illustrate important principles. Take the example of a Reform Jewish synagogue that is searching for a new rabbi and a new janitor. On its face, Title VII's broad prohibition on religious discrimination would forbid the synagogue from denying the rabbi position to an applicant because he is Orthodox or Conservative Jewish, or indeed, even because he is a Christian or a Muslim. Similarly, the synagogue would be forbidden from denying the janitor position to an applicant because he is a Jew for Jesus, or if he holds the religious belief that Judaism is evil or a sham.

Fortunately, these problems were foreseen in Congress, and the statute does guard against them—but, importantly, not as a definitional matter. Title VII contains two overlapping exemptions from the general prohibition on religious discrimination: one is limited to religious educational institutions,[9] and another covers religious educational institutions and "a religious corporation, association . . . or society."[10] This would allow the synagogue in our example to take religion into consideration in hiring for both positions, the rabbi and the janitor alike.

And in the case of the rabbi, the U.S. Constitution provides an additional layer of protection. Beginning as early as 1972, the federal appellate courts have consistently held that the religion clauses of the First Amendment forbid the application of employment laws, such as Title VII, to the employment relationship between a religious institution and its ministers.[11] So even if there were no statutory exemption to Title VII's ban on religious discrimination, there would still be a constitutional one in a case where an employee fills a role that is unmistakably that of a religious minister.

In light of this, one may be tempted to conclude that there is no problem, or more precisely, that there was a problem, but it has already been solved. Yes, there is an overbroad definition of discrimination that is half-true and half an infringement on institutional religious freedom; adequate solutions have been applied, however, and not only by the legislature, but the courts as well.

But these two solutions have always been partial, and while they may have held strong in the past, they are now subject to increasingly frequent attacks designed either to narrow them or to eliminate them altogether. And in all cases, these newer attacks trace back conceptually to the fact that these two solutions are not applied to the root cause of the problem, which is the over-broad definition of "religion discrimination."

More precisely, these solutions do not challenge the implicit premise of the definition that all religion-based distinctions in employment, whether made by a Catholic diocese or by Ford or Sears or

Microsoft, are equally morally repugnant. Instead, the solutions appear to accept that premise and attempt only to stave off its enforcement against religious institutions on pragmatic or other grounds. It is a much weaker position to argue that employment practices that *even we admit* amount to "discrimination" should nonetheless be permitted, than to argue that the employment practices are not "discrimination" at all. And as a result, institutional religious freedom is gradually losing ground. This is happening on various fronts.

Current threat: charitable choice

The debate over "charitable choice" or the "faith-based initiative"— government funding of faith-based social service providers on equal terms with secular ones—illustrates the problem well. Beginning in the Bush administration, but continuing through the Obama administration, the refrain of opponents of equal treatment for religious institutions has been the same: government should not "subsidize religious discrimination."[12] We recently heard the same mantra from a coalition supporting a bill to reauthorize the federal Substance Abuse and Mental Health Services Administration ("SAMHSA") Act that would have required faith-based organizations to waive their statutory exemption under Title VII in order to participate in the program as a provider.[13] And when the Colorado legislature proposed a bill placing a similar condition on its social service funds, advocates explained that the bill "starts with a simple premise: taxpayer funds should not be used for religious discrimination."[14]

Arguments of this type are predicated on the idea that the religious distinctions that religious social service providers make in their employment practices are simply evil, no different than the "religious discrimination" forbidden to secular employers. Perhaps a religiously diverse society might tolerate such invidious discrimination at the margins of the private sector—especially if that tolerance was the political price for passing a general ban on such discrimination—but to have the government subsidize it is simply out of the question. Correspondingly, if those faith-based employment practices were recognized as innocent and even necessary to maintain the religious character of the organization—as not "discrimination" at all—the specter of government support would lose its rhetorical force. Thus, the conceptual problem lies in lumping what should be forbidden as unjust discrimination, together with what should be protected as religious freedom, in a single category of "religious discrimination."

But even apart from situations involving government funding, the two protections of institutional religious freedom — statutory and constitutional — that would help our hypothetical Reform synagogue, have been under sustained attack and may well be narrowed or even eliminated.

Current threat:
Title VII's statutory exemption for religious employers

Two recent federal appellate decisions under Title VII's statutory exemption for religious employers from the general prohibition of "religious discrimination" have underscored the fact that it does not cover all self-described religious employers, and they suggest that its scope may narrow after a long period of presumed breadth. In both cases, the employer was found to qualify for the exemption by a divided vote of a three-judge panel. But the various rationales for determining the scope of the exemption raise serious concerns for the future of protecting institutional religious freedom against an overbroad charge of "religious discrimination," whether under Title VII or more broadly.

In *Spencer* v. *World Vision,*[15] a three-judge panel of the Ninth Circuit divided three ways on the applicable test for assessing whether a religious employer falls within the exemption, and two of those judges found World Vision to satisfy their respective tests. In *Leboon v. Lancaster Jewish Comm'y Ctr. Ass'n,*[16] the majority of a Third Circuit panel adopted a multi-factored test, which the particular employer was found to satisfy, but which was rejected not only by the dissent, but later by all three of the *Spencer* judges. More to the point here, even amid this doctrinal fragmentation, three of the five opinions in these cases emphasized the evils of prohibited "religious discrimination" and linked them to the need to construe narrowly the scope of the religious exemption from that prohibition.[17]

Current threat: The "ministerial exception" to Title VII and other employment laws

The "ministerial exception" under the First Amendment was also put at risk, and for similar reasons. Although the federal Courts of Appeal have been unanimous since 1972 in adopting some form of ministerial exception, they are divided on various aspects of its scope. And until 2012, the U.S. Supreme Court had never taken up the question of its scope, or even its existence. In March 2011, the Court granted *certiorari* in *Hosanna-Tabor Evangelical Lutheran Church and School* v. *EEOC,* in which a panel of the Sixth Circuit had found a teacher at a Lutheran school *not* to be a "minister" for purposes of the exception.

There were various important issues at stake in the case, but for present purposes, the key question was whether the exception would survive to a degree that it would remain helpful in counteracting the overbreadth of the definition of "religious discrimination."[18] To the surprise of many, the Department of Justice took the position that the "ministerial exception" simply did not exist—that the religion clauses added nothing to the protection afforded by the First Amendment's protection of freedom of expressive association, and in turn, that religious institutions had the same constitutional protection of their choice of minister as labor unions or the Boy Scouts had in the selection of their leaders. To the relief of many, the Supreme Court not only rejected this argument, but did so in resounding terms:in a 9–0 opinion that reaffirmed the existence of the ministerial exception, the Court found for the religious defendant in the particular case, and characterized the Justice Department's position in denying the existence of the exception altogether as "untenable" and "remarkable."[19]

This is of course good news, but it is also further evidence of the phenomenon I would highlight. As the various plaintiff-side briefs consistently reflected, the impulse to narrow or eliminate the ministerial exception was driven precisely by the concern that evil discrimination would go unpunished if the exception were to exist and to have meaningful effect. Because the exception does not run to the definition of "discrimination," the exception may readily be characterized as an evasion of the good prohibition on that "discrimination," rather than a protection of the good of religious freedom. And that will make the future battles over the scope of the ministerial exception that much more challenging.[20]

Sex Discrimination

Laws prohibiting sex discrimination, like those prohibiting religious discrimination, are usually defined broadly and malleably and serve the important moral purpose of forbidding some unjust discrimination.[21] Both prohibitions have also been in force for about the same time, and both exist at the federal, state, and local levels. But with some notable exceptions, sex discrimination prohibitions generally have not conflicted with institutional religious liberty. When there is a conflict, however, there is no statutory exception that allows religious institutions to engage in sex discrimination, only the constitutional exception which is limited in application to "ministerial" employees.[22]

Recent developments threaten to change this generally peaceful coexistence. And once again, the change would come in the form of expanding the definition of "sex discrimination" so that it includes not only unjust discrimination rightly prohibited, but wholly foreseeable and likely intended burdens on the religious commitments of institutions.

Most notoriously, the federal Equal Employment Opportunity Commission (EEOC) has recently construed discrimination "on the basis of sex" or "because of sex" within the meaning of Title VII to include the decision of Belmont Abbey College to remove coverage of contraceptive drugs from its employee health insurance policy. According to the EEOC:

> By denying prescription contraceptive drugs, [the College] is discriminating based on gender because only females take oral prescription contraceptives. By denying coverage, men are not affected, only women.[23]

In light of the College's strong commitment to the teaching of the Catholic Church on contraception, the impact of this decision on institutional religious liberty is obvious.[24] But the implications of this rationale would extend much further, effectively imposing on all employers covered by Title VII, religious and secular alike, a mandate to provide contraceptive drug coverage. And most importantly for present purposes, this mandate would be accomplished by an overbroad interpretation of the meaning of "sex discrimination."[25] Although this interpretation has not generally fared well in court,[26] the theory behind it crops up frequently in legislative and regulatory contexts and has some proponents in the legal academy,[27] and therefore raises a significant concern for the future.

Sexual Orientation Discrimination.

Laws prohibiting discrimination based on "sexual orientation" are of more recent vintage than those based on religion and sex. Also, unlike the latter, there is no federal law generally forbidding "sexual orientation" discrimination in employment (or any other context); all the laws in force exist at the state and municipal level. Moreover, the question of the scope of the definition of "sexual orientation discrimination," including its impact on religious liberty, has been at the forefront of debate from the outset.

As a consequence, like religious discrimination, but unlike sex discrimination, laws against sexual orientation discrimination almost always include a statutory exception for religious institutional employers.[28] In fact, those exceptions are typically modeled on, or even incorporate by reference, existing exceptions for religious institutions against claims of religious discrimination. Accordingly, these exceptions bear the same limitations as in the religious discrimination context: (1) failure to address the fundamental, conceptual problem that the statutory definition of discrimination still lumps together, as equally evil, core religious exercise and actual unjust discrimination; and (2) vulnerability to gradual judicial narrowing, as signaled in *Spencer* and *Leboon*, in part because the religious exercise protected by the exception is still considered morally problematic "discrimination."

The impact of the statutory definition of "sexual orientation," however, has not been ignored—it varies meaningfully among jurisdictions, and in ways that are relevant for present purposes. The definition contained in the recurrently proposed federal Employment

Non-Discrimination Act (ENDA), and close variants, is perhaps the most common: "The term 'sexual orientation' means homosexuality, heterosexuality, or bisexuality."[29] Use of the ambiguous terms ending in "-ity" blurs the key distinction between sexual inclination and sexual conduct, which is critical in the context of Catholic moral teaching in this area.[30] Indeed, this distinction tracks closely (but not entirely) the distinction between core institutional religious commitments that must be protected, and unjust discrimination that may be forbidden.[31]

By contrast, some state legislatures were willing to address this distinction, rather than simply leave it to the courts to decide. Some distinguished status and conduct indirectly, by excluding from the definition of "sexual orientation" any illegal conduct.[32] But this exclusion was effective only where anti-sodomy laws remained on the books and valid, which ended instantly and nationwide in 2003 with the U.S. Supreme Court's decision in *Lawrence* v. *Texas*.[33] And alas, the District of Columbia has also taken up the status/conduct distinction, but in order intentionally to *include* conduct as protected "orientation."[34]

It is under the rubric of "sexual orientation discrimination" that we have seen perhaps the most aggressive exploitation of the bundling together of unjust discrimination and religious exercise in one category.[35] Even with exemptions for religious institutional employers so common in these laws, the exempted conduct is considered to be evil "discrimination" just as fully as what is otherwise prohibited,[36] and is tolerated only because the exemption was probably politically necessary for the law to pass at all. Statutory exemptions can withstand this kind of pressure only for so long, so the long-term strategy should be to relieve the pressure and to work toward establishing clearly in the law and the culture that distinctions based on sexual conduct are not "discrimination" at all.

Distinct Categories of Laws or Regulations with Some Similar Features

Having provided some examples of laws that embed "discrimination in discrimination," I would further clarify the category by contrasting it briefly with related, but importantly distinct, categories of problematic laws that appear on the current landscape: (1) laws that pit overbroad liberty/autonomy interests, rather than equality/antidiscrimination interests, against institutional religious liberty; (2) laws that bundle together and treat alike, even explicitly, conduct that should be prohibited and conduct that should be protected, other than unjust discrimination and religious liberty; and (3) laws that that smuggle or conceal the harms they would cause.

Laws asserting overbroad liberty interests

Though they are the focus of this chapter, antidiscrimination laws are certainly not the only kind that threaten institutional religious liberty. Another major category consists of laws that assert an overbroad liberty, rather than equality, interest as superior to the claim of religious liberty. Typical of these are laws that would require religious employers to provide insurance coverage for—or require religious medical providers actually to provide—contraception, abortion, sterilization, or other morally illicit "medical services."[37] These laws do not rely on an overbroad concept of "discrimination" to do their work, but instead on a claim of entitlement to "access" services—not merely the negative liberty interest in government non-interference, but the positive liberty interest in government (and even private-sector) facilitation. Thus, opponents of such laws are not characterized as discriminators and bigots, but instead as enemies of freedom and choice.

Laws that bundle the commendable and intolerable

Frequently, legislators will attach a provision that is morally unacceptable to the Catholic Church to a law that is otherwise morally desirable to the Church. The antidiscrimination laws discussed above combine such things surreptitiously, where the desirable is a ban on some form of unjust discrimination, and the unacceptable is the threat to religious liberty. But this same general approach is often pursued more explicitly, and with respect to a wider range of competing values. For example, in mid-2009, Congress considered an immigration bill called the Uniting American Families Act (UAFA), which would have genuinely promoted the uniting of migrant families—a core value in the Church's advocacy on immigration—but would have defined those families to include same-sex couples—rendering the bill impossible for the bishops to support.[38] Even when religious liberty is not at stake, laws like this are especially damaging to the Church, because they threaten to divide it, particularly by tempting some within it to take a proportionalist approach—to urge acceptance of the morally unacceptable provision in order to secure the "greater good" accomplished by the morally desirable provisions.[39]

Laws that conceal the intolerable

Laws that threaten foundational values rarely do so explicitly or directly, but out of plain sight, presumably to minimize negative political consequences. This chapter focuses on concealed threats to religious liberty within antidiscrimination laws, but threats to other core commitments are smuggled into laws in other policy contexts as well. Most notorious of these is the concealment of abortion funding and inadequate conscience protection in federal health-care reform legislation.[40]

To the extent that these three categories of laws differ from laws representing "discrimination in discrimination," they help define that target category more clearly by contrast; to the extent that they share particular features with the target category, they provide a store of experience that may help in formulating tactics for responding to those features.

Developing Tactics for Going on the Offensive

The preceding section was dedicated to identifying with some precision a category of laws that present a genuine opportunity for progress in the protection of institutional religious liberty. That category consists of antidiscrimination laws that define forbidden "discrimination" so broadly that it includes both unjust discrimination (which should be prohibited) and institutional religious exercise (which should not). That is, the definitions of "discrimination" are half-true, and the remainder that is false effectuates discrimination against religious institutions.

This section will proceed in two parts. The first will explain why this particular category of laws bears special promise. The second will propose initially, for discussion and further development, one possible tactic for realizing that promise, namely, proposing amendments to legislative definitions of "discrimination" that exclude the religious exercise they would otherwise forbid.

Laws Involving "Discrimination In Discrimination" Represent an Especially Desirable Target for Going on the Offensive

Opposing overbroad definitions of discrimination offers the prospect of real progress in the area of institutional religious liberty, for several reasons.

First, the core religious liberty problem presented by this group of laws—defining the good of institutional religious liberty as the evil of unjust discrimination—has remained largely unaddressed for years. The difficulty in finding a solution to this definitional problem is probably one reason why it has not been addressed. Another reason may be the ready availability of the crutches of the statutory and ministerial exceptions, which have helped religious institutions avoid liability in particular cases without addressing the conceptual problem at their root. But for whatever reason, we have not yet begun to fight on this issue—and once we do begin, we can expect progress.

Second, the upside potential of successfully tackling this problem is huge. To be sure, this is because the downside potential of continuing to be deemed an evil "discriminator," particularly in a society increasingly intolerant of anything labeled "discrimination," is also huge. But the point remains.

Third, religious institutions would break out of the defensive posture to which they have become accustomed in this area. No longer would they accept the premise that their conduct is discrimination, and argue from that deficit that the discrimination is nonetheless permissible. Furthermore, by calling attention to the threats to religious exercise lurking in overbroad definitions of discrimination, we would put our opponents in a defensive posture, calling on them to justify those threats (and their concealment).

Fourth, religious communities might be more effectively inoculated against the division that might otherwise be sown within them by laws that bundle together competing values, which different segments of the community, rightly or wrongly, weigh differently.

Confronting the Half-True Definition of "Discrimination" Directly by Proposing a Legislative Amendment

What remains is the question of particular tactics. In general, the focus should be on narrowing the definition of "discrimination" in some way, so that it no longer encompasses the religious exercise of institutions. But with what precise language? Executive agencies and courts may offer some limited avenue for refining such a definition, but the tactic with the greatest impact might lie in modifying the statutory language of the definition through the legislature. Such amendments might take the following general form:

> "Discrimination on the basis of [religion, sex, sexual orientation, etc.] does not include [general category of religious exercise formerly captured by the definition]."[41]

Legislative amendments to longstanding statutory definitions of discrimination will be difficult to pass, especially at the federal level. On the other hand, passage of an amendment may not be the only way to make progress; rejection may have its benefits as well. Particularly, rejection of an amendment to carve out some category of religious exercise from a broader category of activity otherwise deemed "discriminatory" could be cited as evidence of hostility to that religious exercise—whether in a re-election campaign or a constitutional challenge under the Free Exercise Clause.[42]

There may be more hope of amending the definition of "sexual orientation discrimination," because it is never of particularly long standing in the states or localities where it has passed, and it has not passed at all at the federal level. On the other hand, an amendment that expressly excludes from the definition of "discrimination" adverse employment action based on moral or religious disapproval of same-sex sexual conduct would meet strong resistance from the gay-rights community.[43] On still another hand, if such an amendment were to pass, it would not represent a complete solution to the religious freedom problems with such a law, as certain inclination-based distinctions would have to be excluded in some contexts as well.[44]

In any event, these are merely introductory considerations to start a conversation—which I would welcome—on the precise form that a legislative amendment to a half-true definition of "discrimination" might take.

ENDNOTES

1 42 U.S.C. § 2000e-2(a).

2 *Id.* § 2000e(j).

3 *Id.* § 2000e-2(m).

4 *Id.* § 2000e(j)

5 *See e.g.* A.R.S. § 41–1461 and A.R.S. § 41–1463; V.T.C.A., Labor Code § 21.108.

6 42 U.S.C. § 2000e(j).

7 *See e.g.* Neb. Rev. Stat. §48–1104 (1): ("It shall be an unlawful employment practice for an employer: (1) To fail or refuse to hire, to discharge, or to harass any individual, or otherwise to discriminate against any individual with respect to compensation, terms, conditions, or privileges of employment, because of such individual's race, color, religion, sex, disability, marital status, or national origin").

8 *See Trans World Airlines, Inc.* v. *Hardison,* 432 U.S. 63 (1977) (employers need not accommodate if it would impose more than a "*de minimis*" burden on the employer).

9 42 U.S.C. § 2000e-2(e) ("[I]t shall not be an unlawful employment practice for a school, college, university, or other educational institution or institution of learning to hire and employ employees of a particular religion if such school, college, university, or other educational institution or institution of learning is, in whole or in substantial part, owned, supported, controlled, or managed by a particular religion or by a particular religious corporation, association, or society, or if the curriculum of such school, college, university, or other educational institution or institution of learning is directed toward the propagation of a particular religion.").

10 *Id.* § 2000e-1(a) ("This subchapter shall not apply ... to a religious corporation, association, educational institution, or society with respect to the employment of individuals of a particular religion to perform work connected with the carrying on by such corporation, association, educational institution, or society of its activities.").

11 *See McClure* v. *Salvation Army,* 460 F.2d 553 (5th Cir. 1972). *See also*

Rweyemamu v. *Cote,* 520 F.3d 198 (2d Cir. 2008); *Hollins* v. *Methodist Healthcare, Inc.,* 474 F.3d 223 (6th Cir. 2007); *Tomic* v. *Catholic Diocese of Peoria,* 442 F.3d 1036 (7th Cir. 2006); *Petruska* v. *Gannon Univ.,* 462 F.3d 294 (3d Cir. 2006); *Elvig* v. *Calvin Presbyterian Church,* 375 F.3d 951 (9th Cir. 2004); *Bryce* v. *Episcopal Church in Diocese of Colo.,* 289 F.3d 648 (10th Cir. 2002); *Gellington* v. *Christian Methodist Episcopal Church, Inc.,* 203 F.3d 1299 (11th Cir. 2000); *EEOC* v. *Catholic Univ. of Am.,* 83 F.3d 455 (D.C. Cir. 1996); *Scharon* v. *St. Luke's Episcopal Presbyterian Hosp.,* 929 F.2d 360 (8th Cir. 1991); *Natal* v. *Christian & Missionary Alliance,* 878 F.2d 1575 (1st Cir. 1989); *Rayburn* v. *Gen. Conference of Seventh-day Adventists,* 772 F.2d 1164 (4th Cir. 1985).

12 *See, e.g.,* Adelle M. Banks, "Faith-based reform gets mixed reviews," *Religion News Service* (Nov. 17, 2010) (available at <http://www.christian-century.org/article/2010–11/obama-signs-order-reform-faith-based-office>) (quoting J. Brent Walker of Baptist Joint Committee, as saying, "It's simply wrong for the government to subsidize religious discrimination."); Anti-Defamation League, "The Faith-Based Initiative and 'Charitable Choice': Harmful to Religious Liberty and Civil Rights" *Religious Freedom Resources* (available at <http://www.adl.org/religious_freedom/resource_kit/faith_based_initiative.asp>) (last visited, May 31, 2011) ("'Charitable Choice' laws and the Faith-Based Initiative permit government-subsidized religious employment discrimination.").

13 *See* Letter from The Coalition Against Religious Discrimination (CARD) to Hon. Patrick Kennedy (May 21, 2010) (available at <http://www.aclu.org/files/assets/Coalition_Letter_to_Representative_Kennedy_on_SAMHSA_and_Charitable_Choice.pdf>)(describing "charitable choice" as "a highly controversial legislative scheme that authorizes government-funded religious discrimination in employment"). *See also* H.R. 5466, 111th Cong., 2d Sess. Section 501(m), at 23 (May 28, 2010) (providers excluded unless they agree "to refrain from considering religion or any profession of faith when making any employment decision regarding an individual who is or will be assigned to carry out any portion of the activity … notwithstanding any other provision of Federal law, including any exemption otherwise applicable to a religious corporation, association, educational institution, or society."). This proposal elicited strong resistance from supporters of faith-based hiring and ultimately stalled. See Letter from Representatives of Various Faith-Based Service Providers to Sen. Harry Reid (Aug. 25, 2010) (available at <http://www.worldvision.org/resources.nsf/main/religious-hiring-rights/$file/RHR-letter.pdf>). *See also*

Stephanie Strom, "Religion-Based Groups Protest Restrictions in Bill," *The New York Times* (Aug. 25, 2010) (available at <http://www.nytimes.com/2010/08/26/us/26religion.html>).

14 Anti-Defamation League, "ADL Supports House Bill 1080 to Restore Colorado's Ban on Religious Discrimination" (Jan. 30, 2008) (available at <http://regions.adl.org/mountain-states/news/adl-supports-house-bill-1080.html>).

15 619 F.3d 1109 (9th Cir. 2010).

16 503 F.3d 217 (3d Cir. 2007).

17 *Spencer,* 619 F.3d at 1127 (Kleinfeld, J., concurring) (emphasizing that Title VII was "intended to free us from the curse of discrimination in hiring by … 'religion,'" and warning that a generous religious exemption would authorize such discrimination too widely, particularly in hospitals); *Spencer,* 619 F.3d at 1150 (Berzon, J., dissenting) (emphasizing that "Title VII's prohibition on religious discrimination aims to protect the religious freedom of employees" as among the reasons why religious exemption should be construed narrowly, and warning against "a society in which employers could self-declare as religious enclaves from which dissenters can be excluded"); *Leboon*, 503 F.3d at 235 (Rendell, J., dissenting) (criticizing "the majority's analysis and ultimate ruling" for various reasons, but "worst of all, [because they] sanction discriminatory employment decisions that go far beyond those Congress intended to exempt from Title VII."). Though not expressly cited in these opinions, the inclination to construe these exceptions narrowly is also closely related to the general rule of construction that civil rights laws, such as Title VII, should be construed broadly.

18 Although the ministerial exception does trump claims of religious discrimination, most courts have held it to preclude discrimination claims on other bases as well, including race and sex. *See EEOC v. Roman Catholic Diocese of Raleigh, N.C.,* 213 F.3d 795, 801 (4th Cir. 2000) (describing the ministerial exception as "robust where it applies"). *Hosanna-Tabor,* for example, involved a claim of disability discrimination under the Americans with Disabilities Act (ADA).

19 132 S.Ct. 694, 706 (2012). Later in the opinion, the Court characterized another aspect of the government's position, which also tended to narrow dramatically the scope of the ministerial exception, as "extreme." *Id.* at 709.

20 Some of the immediate reactions to the Supreme Court's decision prefigure these future battles over the scope of the ministerial exception. *See, e.g.* Rob Boston, "Exceptional Power: Supreme Court Says 'Ministerial

Exception' Trumps Civil Rights Laws When Religious Organizations Hire Clergy," *Church & State* (Mar. 2012); Marci A. Hamilton, "In *Hosanna-Tabor Evangelical Lutheran Church and School v. EEOC*, the Supreme Court Embraces a Narrow Ministerial Exception to Federal Anti-Discrimination Laws," *Verdict* (Jan. 12, 2012).

21 For example, pursuant to the Pregnancy Discrimination Act (PDA), Title VII's definition of sex discrimination specifically prevents an employer from firing a woman because she is pregnant. *See* 42 U.S.C. § 2000e(k) (expressly including within definition of sex discrimination employment decisions "because of or on the basis of pregnancy, childbirth, or related medical conditions"). Of course, even this generally salutary protection can become a religious freedom problem, as when a religious school feels obliged to discipline a teacher who becomes pregnant out of wedlock. *See, e.g.,* NYCLU Press Release, "Catholic School Cannot Discriminate Against Unwed Pregnant Teacher, EEOC Rules" (Oct. 11, 2006) (reporting EEOC ruling against Catholic school) (available at <http://www.nyclu.org/news/catholic-school-cannot-discriminate-against-unwed-pregnant-teacher-eeoc-rules>); Péralte C. Paul, "Religious school will pay to settle pregnancy discrimination suits," *Atlanta Journal-Constitution* (Mar. 26, 2010) (settling EEOC actions against Baptist schools) (available at <http://www.ajc.com/news/dekalb/religious-school-will-pay-407766.html>). *See also Cline v. Catholic Diocese of Toledo,* 206 F.3d 651 (6th Cir. 2000) ("[c]ourts have made clear that if the school's purported 'discrimination' is based on a policy of preventing nonmarital sexual activity which emanates from the religious and moral precepts of the school, and if that policy is applied equally to its male and female employees, then the school has not discriminated based on pregnancy in violation of Title VII."). Apart from the PDA's specific inclusion of pregnancy, "sex discrimination" is essentially undefined under Title VII. *See* 42 U.S.C. § 2000e(k).

22 In unusual cases, a sex discrimination case against a religious institution may implicate First Amendment protections apart from the "ministerial exception." *See, e.g., Curay-Cramer v. Ursuline Academy of Wilmington, DE,* 450 F.3d 130 (3d Cir. 2006) (rejecting Title VII sex discrimination claim on the basis that it would require the court to compare the relative severity of alleged violations of religious doctrine by teachers).

23 Determination of Reuben Daniels, District Director, EEOC Charlotte District Office (July 30, 2009).

24 *See* North Carolina Family Policy Council, "Becket Fund Defends Belmont Abbey" (Oct. 12, 2009) ("As a Roman Catholic institution, Belmont Abbey

College is not able to and will not offer nor subsidize medical services that contradict the clear teaching of the Catholic Church") (quoting Dr. William Thierfelder, president of Belmont Abbey) (available at <http://ncfamily.org/stories/091012s1.html>).

25 Notably, this is only one of several legislative and regulatory attempts to mandate contraceptive drug coverage. In about half the states, beginning with New York and California, insurers who provide any prescription drug coverage at all must include contraceptive drugs within that coverage. The recent federal health care reform law mandates coverage of "preventive services," which Planned Parenthood and its allies have argued must include contraceptive services. Arguably, laws like these are greater threats, at least by volume, to institutional (and even individual) religious liberty than the administrative interpretation of Title VII discussed above. But this paper focuses on the latter nonetheless, because it represents an example of the broader phenomenon of expanding definitions of "discrimination" as a means to threaten institutional religious liberty.

26 *Compare In re Union Pac. R.R. Empl't Practices Lit.*, 479 F.3d 936, 942 (8th Cir. 2007), *with Cooley* v. *Daimler Chrysler Corp.*, 281 F. Supp. 2d (E.D. Mo. 2003).

27 *See, e.g.,* Sylvia A. Law, "Sex Discrimination and Insurance for Contraception," Washington Law Review 73 (1998): 363; Lisa A. Hayden, "Gender Discrimination within the Reproductive Health Care System: Viagra v. Birth Control," Journal of Law & Health 13 (1998–99): 171.

28 One notable exception is the District of Columbia, which does not provide a statutory exception for religious employers to its prohibition on sexual orientation discrimination.

29 H.R.1397, 112th Cong., 1st Sess., at § 3(a)(9) (Apr. 6, 2011). *See* Dayna Shah, Associate General Counsel, GAO, "Sexual Orientation-Based Employment Discrimination: States' Experience with Statutory Prohibitions," GAO-02–878R, at 4 (July 9, 2002) (available at <http://www.gao.gov/new.items/d02878r.pdf>) (Table 1 listing definitions of "sexual orientation discrimination" in state law as of 2002). *See also* Dayna Shah, Managing Associate General Counsel, GAO, "Sexual Orientation and Gender Identity Employment Discrimination: Overview of State Statutes and Complaint Data," GAO-10–135R (Oct. 9, 2009) (available at <http://www.gao.gov/new.items/d10135r.pdf>) (updating 2002 letter).

30 In sum, all same-sex sexual conduct is morally illicit, "intrinsically disordered" and "in no case to be approved of"; by contrast, some distinctions based on inclination apart from conduct may be licit, while others represent

"unjust discrimination." *See* Congregation of the Doctrine of the Faith, *Some Considerations Concerning the Response to Legislative Proposals on the Non-discrimination of Homosexual Persons* ("1992 CDF"), Nos. 1, 7, 11, 12 (July 23, 1992); *The Catechism of the Catholic Church,* Nos. 2357–59.

31 *Id.*

32 *See, e.g.,* R.I. Gen. Laws § 28–5–6(13); HRS § 378–1.

33 539 U.S. 558 (2003).

34 *See* D.C. Code § 2–1401.02(28) (defining "sexual orientation" to include "Male or female homosexuality, heterosexuality and bisexuality, by preference *or practice*.") (emphasis added).

35 *See, e.g.*, Marc D. Stern, *Same-Sex Marriage and the Churches, in* SAME-SEX MARRIAGE AND RELIGIOUS LIBERTY: EMERGING CONFLICTS 1, 1–57 (Douglas Laycock, Anthony R. Picarello, Jr., & Robin Fretwell Wilson eds., 2008).

36 *Cf. Christian Legal Society* v. *Martinez,* 561 U.S. ___, 130 S. Ct. 2971 (2010) (rejecting Free Speech Clause defenses to exclusion from public university facilities based on government concern to avoid "sexual orientation" and "religious" discrimination).

37 *See supra* note 23. *See also* Richard Doerflinger, "Competing 'Rights' Claims: Defending Rights of Conscience in the Policy Arena," Chapter Six of this book.

38 *See* USCCB News Release, "Bishops Support Family Reunification Senate Bill, Not Able to Support Similar House Legislation" (available at <http://www.usccb.org/comm/archives/2009/09–122.shtml>).

39 It has been suggested that this is what occurred in the intra-Church debate over federal health care reform. *See, e.g.,* Statement by Francis Cardinal George, OMI, President, USCCB, "The Cost is Too High; the Loss is Too Great" (Mar. 15, 2010) (available at <http://www.usccb.org/comm/archives/2010/10–043.shtml>) ("[T]he leaders of the Catholic Health Association . . . believe . . . that the defects that they do recognize can be corrected after the passage of the final bill. The bishops, however, judge that the flaws are so fundamental that they vitiate the good that the bill intends to promote.").

40 *See* Anthony Picarello and Michael Moses, USCCB Office of General Counsel, "Legal Analysis of the Provisions of the Patient Protection and Affordable Care Act and Corresponding Executive Order Regarding Abortion Funding and Conscience Protection" (Mar. 25, 2010) (available at <http://www.usccb.org/ogc/Healthcare-EO-Memo.pdf>).

41 It bears emphasis that the religious exercise to be excluded should be cast in general enough terms that it may not be characterized as a denominational preference.

42 This single fact would probably not suffice alone to support a Free Exercise Clause challenge, whether as a "religious gerrymander" or otherwise as evincing enough religion-based animus to fail the requirement of "neutrality." *See Church of Lukumi Babalu Aye v. City of Hialeah,* 508 U.S. 520 (1993). But this refusal, paired with other exceptions in the statute made for non-religious reasons, might well suffice to trigger heightened scrutiny. *See Fraternal Order of Police, Newark Lodge No. 12 v. City of Newark,* 170 F.3d 359 (3d Cir. 1999).

43 The U.S. Supreme Court has recently rejected the status / conduct distinction in *dicta*, rendering the gay rights community all the less likely to accede to it. *See Christian Legal Society v. Martinez,* 130 S. Ct. 2971, 2990 (2010).

44 *See, e.g.,* 1992 CDF, No. 11. Even if the amendment provided all necessary exclusions on its face, there is still the question whether civil courts would apply these exclusions faithfully, or otherwise well enough that the error rate would be tolerable.

Chapter Eight

Institutional Conscience: From Free Exercise to Freedom of Association and Church Autonomy

Michael P. Moreland

Introduction

The very use of the term "conscience" is an indication that things have already gone badly. As John Finnis notes, one rarely invokes *conscience* when deciding merely *what to do*: "when you are considering what to do, here and now, the question simply is 'What is the right thing to do?' There is no separate question 'What do I in conscience think is the right thing to do?' or 'What does my conscience tell me to do?'"[1] When an individual or institution makes a legal claim on behalf of conscience, it is usually because his (or her, or its) moral judgment has come to a view at odds with what the political order is demanding. The widespread use of claims of conscience should give us pause, and it indicates a certain form of political failure. Such failure is of at least two kinds: (1) to persuade lawmakers to enact (or not to enact) some policy into law (for example, a requirement that all hospitals perform a particular procedure), and (2) to persuade lawmakers to accommodate religious views (for example, exempting religious hospitals from the requirement to perform a particular procedure to which the hospital has an objection). Going to the courts to pursue a judicial remedy is a second-best option, one to be pursued when individuals or institutions face the prospect of being coerced into doing something that violates their conscience.

This chapter assesses the constitutional arguments employed by advocates of institutional conscience in courts of law.[2] Before the Supreme Court's decision in *Hosanna-Tabor* v. *EEOC*[3] in 2012 and in the wake of *Employment Division* v. *Smith*[4] (and regardless of one's views about whether *Smith* was correctly decided),[5] one was tempted to say that the prospects for successful litigation looked bleak and leave it at that.[6] So long as a law is "neutral" and "generally applicable," there is, *Smith* holds, no constitutional right to a religious exemption under the Free Exercise Clause. Developments post-*Smith,* however, indicate that a more secure basis for institutional conscience may yet be found in the constitutional categories of freedom of association and church autonomy. I will briefly summarize the familiar background to the law of free exercise exemptions in the first part below before moving in the second part to a consideration of institutional forms of liberty, namely, freedom of association and church autonomy.

The Diminishing Role of Free Exercise

The conventional story of the recent history of free exercise claims is that from the time of the Supreme Court's decision in *Sherbert* v. *Verner*[7] until *Employment Division* v. *Smith*, such claims were subject to strict scrutiny.[8] That is, a sincere religious believer claiming that a law imposed a substantial burden on the practice of his or her religion was entitled to an exemption unless the government could show that the law was narrowly tailored to advance a compelling government interest.[9] In practice, such claims were rarely successful, and the strict scrutiny applied was "strict in theory but futile in fact." An Air Force officer claiming an exemption to wear a yarmulke[10] and a challenge to the location of a road next to a Native American burial ground[11] are just two examples of the many unsuccessful claims during that period. In fact, the only successful claims were either in cases similar to *Sherbert* insofar as they involved individually assessed claims for a government benefit,[12] or in a challenge to a mandatory school attendance requirement brought by the Old Order Amish in *Wisconsin* v. *Yoder*.[13]

Employment Division v. *Smith* was the Supreme Court's effort to bring some predictability and coherence to the entire field. In *Smith*, the Court characterized its free exercise cases as "consistently [holding] that the right of free exercise does not relieve an individual of the obligation to comply with a valid and neutral law of general applicability on the ground that the law proscribes (or prescribes) conduct that his religion prescribes (or proscribes)."[14] But notwithstanding *Smith*'s holding that there is no right of constitutional exemption from a neutral law that is generally applicable, later cases, most notably *Church of the Lukumi Babalu Aye* v. *City of Hialeah*,[15] demonstrate that there can be failures of "neutrality" or "general applicability" where religion is singled out for discriminatory treatment or is not treated on an equal basis with similar secular activities. As summarized by Douglas Laycock: "*Smith* changed free exercise from a substantive liberty—a rebuttable guarantee of freedom to act within the domain of religiously motivated behavior—to a comparative right, in which the constitutionally required treatment of religious practices depends on the treatment of some comparable set of secular practices."[16]

Catholic Charities v. *Superior Court* is a prominent post-*Smith* example of a claim by a religious institution, rather than an individual, for an exemption from a statutory requirement.[17] California, along with several other states, has enacted a statute that requires all employers who provide prescription drug coverage as part of their employee health benefit plan to include coverage for prescription contraceptives.[18] The California statute contained an exemption for religious employers, but was drawn so narrowly that religious social service agencies, colleges and universities, and health care facilities were, for the most part, unable to avail themselves of the exemption. The California exemption was limited only to institutions that have the primary purpose of inculcating religious belief, primarily serve and employ members of that religious faith, and fall under the IRS provisions for "churches, their integrated auxiliaries, and conventions or associations of churches," or "the exclusively religious activities of any religious order."[19] Catholic Charities and other Catholic social service agencies, Catholic health-care institutions, and Catholic colleges and universities do not, generally, consider their missions to be primarily the inculcation of religious doctrine nor do they primarily serve or employ Catholics. None of these institutions, then, is eligible for the statutory exemption.

A First Amendment challenge to the California statute and, later, a challenge to a similar New York statute[20] were rejected in the state courts. The U.S. Supreme Court denied *certiorari* in both cases.[21] The state opinions concluded that these cases presented a straightforward question under *Smith*: the contraceptive mandate statutes were neutral and generally applicable, but even if they were not, they could survive strict scrutiny analysis because of the state's compelling interest in enforcing a putative gender-discrimination law.

Courts resolve most claims of institutional conscience just as they resolve claims of individual conscience: both face the obstacles to free exercise claims imposed by *Smith* with a small *Lukumi*-based exception where claimants can establish a failure of neutrality or general applicability. There are at least three respects, though, in which the current doctrine is particularly muddled: the distinction between individual and institutional claims of conscience, the proper scope of religious exemptions, and the significance of the context-dependent and varying substantive areas in which these cases arise.

First, should religious institutions be viewed differently from individuals in free exercise cases, and, if so, why?[22] Justice Janice Rogers Brown's dissent in the California *Catholic Charities* case suggests—but little more—that institutional claims for free exercise should be analyzed differently from claims by an individual free exercise claimant.[23] Similarly, in his work on institutional theories of rights, Roderick Hills argues that the usual individual anti-coercion account of constitutional rights is inadequate and needs to be complemented by an account of the rights of so-called private governments, including churches.[24] As I will discuss below, the Supreme Court's decisions in *Boy Scouts* v. *Dale*[25] and *Hurley* v. *Irish-American Gay, Lesbian and Bisexual Group of Boston*[26] have expanded the scope of the right of freedom of association just as the Court has contracted the reach of the Free Exercise Clause, leading Richard Garnett to argue that "the Supreme Court's 'expressive association' and similar cases . . . suggest that the First Amendment's Free Speech Clause, if not the Religion Clauses, protects the ability of private, mediating associations to generate, inculcate, and propose competing norms and claims, and thereby to play a space-creating, authority-dividing role in civil society."[27]

Garnett goes on to point out, however, that "it is not clear . . . that there actually is, in American constitutional law, a commitment to—or even room for—the *libertas ecclesiae* principle, richly understood."[28] To be sure, there is a recognition of church autonomy in a narrow range of cases—church property dispute cases, ministerial employment cases, and doctrinal disputes that are brought to civil courts.[29] But, as Garnett argues, "these and other constitutional values and doctrines do not, in fact, evidence a robust, underlying commitment in our law to the *libertas ecclesiae* principle. Instead, it could well be that we are living off the capital of this idea—that is, we enjoy, embrace, and depend upon its free-dom-enabling effects—without a real appreciation for or even a memory of what it is, implies, and presumes."[30] We will return at length to argu-ments for institutional freedom in the next part of this chapter.

The second question is how to assess the proper *scope* of exemptions for religious institutions in cases of institutional conscience. As we noted above, the California contraceptive mandate statute's religious exemption did not cover the full range of institutions that religious claimants wanted it to cover. But would the state be better off giving no exemption at all? Is the state better off not granting any exemption in these statutes so that the state has a cleaner, more straightforward *Smith* argument as to neu-trality and general applicability, rather than trying to forge an exemption that leaves out larger entities, such as Catholic hospitals and social serv-ice agencies? Or does a partial exemption raise the prospect of a religious gerrymander, such as the exemption for kosher slaughterhouses in *Lukumi* that left Santeria outside the scope of the exemption?[31]

Finally, in thinking about institutional conscience and religious free-dom, we should attend carefully to the particular facts giving rise to con-science claims. In recent years, Catholic hospitals have faced the issue of whether to administer Plan B contraception to sexual assault victims in emergency rooms,[32] and Catholic social service agencies have been required not to discriminate based on sexual orientation in the placement of children for adoption with same-sex couples.[33] Theological principles of cooperation might sometimes permit compliance—reluctantly—with such requirements.[34] For example, Catholic hospitals have sometimes complied with the legally mandated administration of Plan B contracep-tion in emergency rooms, and Catholic institutions have in many in-stances agreed to provide same-sex partner benefits or prescription contraceptive benefits.[35] Several of the statutes in the conscience cases considered above provide an alternative to following the requirement, even if a difficult one to pursue. In the contraceptive mandate statutes, for example, an employer is generally not required to provide prescription drug coverage in the first place, but, if an employer *does* provide a prescription drug benefit, then it must include prescription contraceptives in the plan.[36]

Freedom of Association and Church Autonomy

I propose that framing claims of institutional conscience as asserting a right of freedom of association or church autonomy might be a more promising avenue for preserving institutional conscience than reliance on free exercise exemptions. Association and autonomy claims are primarily about the *internal ordering* of groups and may not be reducible to claims of *conscience*. The potential problem of reducing the protections for religious freedom in the First Amendment to conscience, and ignoring the role of church autonomy, was pointed out by Douglas Laycock 30 years ago. "One of the most common errors in free exercise analysis is to try to fit all free exercise claims into the conscientious objector category and reject the ones that do not fit," he wrote. "Under this approach, every free exercise claim requires an elaborate judicial inquiry into the conscience or doctrines of the claimant. If he is not compelled by religion to engage in the disputed conduct, he is not entitled to free exercise protection."[37] As Laycock suggested then, church autonomy (and, I would now add, freedom of association) has been, until quite recently, an underexplored aspect of authentic religious freedom.

Freedom of Association

Freedom of association cases alternate between basing associational rights in either a tenuous and derivative account of individual rights, or in an inchoate account of group autonomy.[38] Consider the following cases involving a variety of forms of association:

Should a state political party be able to close its primary and limit primary voters to registered members of the party, or should states be able to impose a "blanket primary" method of selecting party nominees that is open to all registered voters, thereby (arguably) leading to the nomination of more moderate candidates for the general election? In *California Democratic Party* v. *Jones*,[39] the Supreme Court held that freedom of association protects the right of political parties to limit their primaries to registered members of the party.

Should the Boy Scouts be able to exclude homosexual men from serving as scoutmasters, notwithstanding a state anti-discrimination statute that prohibits discrimination in public accommodations based on sexual orientation? In *Boy Scouts* v. *Dale*,[40] the Supreme Court held that the Boy Scouts were protected by freedom of association in their right to exclude the homosexual scoutmaster.

May the government limit the political campaign spending of non-profit groups? In *Citizens United* v. *FEC*, the Supreme Court held that First Amendment protections for freedom of speech extended to corporate election-related speech.[41]

May a state require a small group engaging in advocacy on a local government issue to disclose the names and addresses of anyone contributing more than $20 and to register as an "issue committee" under state law? The U.S. Court of Appeals for the Tenth Circuit held in *Sampson* v. *Buescher*[42] that freedom of association protected the group from being required by the state of Colorado to register and to disclose its contributors on account of the burden to freedom of association posed by the registration and disclosure requirements.

The three leading recent cases on the freedom of association—*Roberts* v. *United States Jaycees*,[43] *Hurley* v. *Irish-American Gay, Lesbian, and Bisexual Group of Boston*,[44] and *Boy Scouts* v. *Dale*[45]—all concern groups that sought to invoke associational rights against a state's claim that the group was engaged in unlawful discrimination.[46] In *Roberts* v. *United States Jaycees*, the Jaycees brought a challenge to a Minnesota statute that prohibited racial and gender discrimination.[47] The Jaycees limited their regular membership to men between 18 and 35, but the Minneapolis and St. Paul chapters had begun to admit women. When the national organization of the Jaycees threatened the local chapters with revocation of their charters, members of the local chapters filed charges with the Minnesota Department of Human Rights, and the national organization brought suit against the state of Minnesota seeking an injunction against enforcement of the Minnesota Human Rights Act.

Writing for the Court, Justice Brennan began by delineating the scope of the freedom of association. One aspect of the right to association, he argued, "conclude[s] that choices to enter into and maintain certain intimate human relationships must be secured against undue intrusion by the State because of the role of such relationships in safeguarding . . . individual freedom."[48] As such, the freedom of association "receives protection as a fundamental element of personal liberty."[49] A second aspect of the freedom of association, wrote Justice Brennan, is for "the purpose of engaging in those activities protected by the First Amendment—speech, assembly, petition for the redress of grievances, and the exercise of religion."[50] In this sense, freedom of association is "an indispensable means of preserving other individual liberties."[51] Justice Brennan went on to denote these as, respectively, the "intrinsic and instrumental features of constitutionally protected association."[52]

Note that for the *Roberts* Court, the freedom of association is derivative of individual freedom. Groups, as such, do not enjoy associational rights except insofar as the state's interference with a group jeopardizes some exercise of individual liberty. The Court suggests that it is (merely) because "[a]n *individual's* freedom to speak, to worship, and to petition the government for the redress of grievances could not be vigorously protected from interference by the State unless a correlative freedom to engage in *group* effort toward those ends were not also guaranteed" that the freedom of association is recognized.[53] Although "[t]here can be no clearer example of an intrusion into the internal structure or affairs of an association than a regulation that forces the group to accept members it does not desire,"[54] the Court nonetheless concluded that enforcement of the Minnesota anti-discrimination statute against the Jaycees was constitutionally permissible. The Court held that the state has a compelling interest in "eradicating discrimination against its female citizens," which justifies enforcement against the Jaycees.[55] Furthermore, the Court claimed there was no imposition on the expressive purpose of the Jaycees because the inclusion of female members did not compromise the message of the organization.[56]

The most important recent cases addressing the freedom of association have posed largely the same issue posed in *Roberts*, namely the attempted enforcement of anti-discrimination statutes against organizations that seek to exclude certain members or those bearing a particular message. The protection afforded freedom of association has, though, arguably expanded considerably since *Roberts*. In *Hurley* v. *Irish-American Gay, Lesbian, and Bisexual Group of Boston*, the Court considered a suit brought by GLIB, an Irish-American gay and lesbian group, that sought to march in a St. Patrick's Day parade in South Boston sponsored by the South Boston Allied War Veterans Council. GLIB brought constitutional claims and a claim under the Massachusetts public accommodations statute, which prohibited discrimination based on, among other grounds, sexual orientation. The Massachusetts Supreme Judicial Court affirmed a lower court's holding that the parade was a public accommodation and that there was no expressive purpose in the parade.[57]

The Supreme Court reversed. Writing for a unanimous Court, Justice Souter began by noting that "[i]f there were no reason for a group of people to march from here to there except to reach a destination, they could make the trip without expressing any message beyond the fact of the march itself."[58] But parades such as the South Boston St. Patrick's Day parade are a form of expression, argued Justice Souter, for "we use the word 'parade' to indicate marchers who are making some sort of collective point."[59] And even though the South Boston parade organizers liberally permitted groups to participate in the parade, "a private speaker does not forfeit constitutional protection simply by combining multifarious voices, or by failing to edit their themes to isolate an exact message as the exclusive subject matter of the speech."[60] Because "every participating unit affects the message conveyed by the private organizers," the Court argued, "the state courts' application of the statute produced an order essentially requiring petitioners to alter the expressive content of their parade."[61]

Hurley, then, marked a subtle but important shift in the Court's freedom of association jurisprudence away from framing associational rights in terms derivative of individual rights, and toward according rights to groups as such. Indeed, the Court's discussion of what is denoted by a "parade" signals the collective aspect of the activity. The purpose of gathering for a parade, rather than just walking from one point to another, is to engage in collective expression. The forced inclusion of a message with which the group disagrees risks altering the message of the *group* and does not merely risk abridging the free speech rights of the *individual* members.

The gesture in *Hurley* toward a thicker conception of associational rights became more pronounced in *Boy Scouts* v. *Dale*. James Dale was an assistant scoutmaster in New Jersey. While in college, Dale became active in gay and lesbian causes and was co-president of the Lesbian/Gay Alliance at Rutgers University. In response, the local Boy Scouts' council revoked Dale's adult membership in the Boy Scouts. Dale filed suit under a New Jersey public accommodation statute that, like the statutes in both *Roberts* and *Hurley*, prohibited discrimination on a number of grounds, including (under the New Jersey statute) sexual orientation. The New Jersey Supreme Court held that the Boy Scouts were a public accommodation within the meaning of the statute and that the organization's "large size, nonselectivity, inclusive rather than exclusive purpose, and practice of inviting or allowing nonmembers to attend meetings, establish that the organization is not sufficiently personal or private to warrant constitutional protection under the freedom of intimate association."[62] The New Jersey Supreme Court further held that forcibly reinstating Dale "does not compel the Boy Scouts to express any message."[63]

The Supreme Court again reversed the state court. Chief Justice Rehnquist began by referring to *Roberts* and noting that "[t]he forced inclusion of an unwanted person in a group infringes the group's freedom of expressive association if the presence of that person affects in a significant way the group's ability to advocate public or private viewpoints."[64] But the most remarkable aspect of Chief Justice Rehnquist's opinion is his insistence that the Court should broadly interpret what constitutes an "expressive association" and should defer to the organization in determining the purpose of expression and what would impair the group's ability to express itself. With the Boy Scouts' stated goals of inculcating values in their members, they are "indisputabl[y]" engaged in expressive activity.

As for any effort to review the content of the Scouts' message on sexual matters or the consistency with which the Scouts have spoken on such topics, the Court contended that "our cases reject this sort of inquiry; it is not the role of the courts to reject a group's expressed values because they disagree with those values or find them internally inconsistent."[65] And just as the Court held that it must defer to an organization's claims about "the nature of its expression," so it "must also give deference to an association's view of what would impair its expression."[66] In an effort to bring together the unanimous holding of the Court in *Hurley* with his argument for the Boy Scouts' associational rights in *Dale*, Chief Justice Rehnquist concluded:

> Here, we have found that the Boy Scouts believes that homosexual conduct is inconsistent with the values it seeks to instill in its youth members; it will not "promote homosexual conduct as a legitimate form of behavior." As the presence of GLIB in Boston's St. Patrick's Day parade would have interfered with the parade organizers' choice not to propound a particular point of view, the presence of Dale as an assistant scoutmaster would just as surely interfere with the Boy Scouts' choice not to propound a point of view contrary to its beliefs.[67]

As to the question of whether forced inclusion of Dale would then compromise the Boy Scouts' message, the Court sharply disagreed with the New Jersey Supreme Court's view that such a step would not significantly affect the Scouts' ability to disseminate their message. The Court held that a group does not have to gather for the purpose of expression in order nonetheless to receive First Amendment protection.[68] Furthermore, internal disagreement or a failure to place an elaborate and uniform message at the center of the organization's purpose—both of which were arguably true of the Boy Scouts—does not undermine the protection for expressive association: "The fact that the organization does not trumpet its views from the housetops, or that it tolerates dissent within its ranks, does not mean that its views receive no First Amendment protection."[69]

The important difference of framing the right to association as a group right rather than an aggregated individual right is spelled out by John Garvey in *What Are Freedoms For?*[70] The *Roberts* Court roughly reflects what Garvey terms the "individualist" view: "[G]roup action has value because it is an aggregate of valued individual actions. . . . People form groups in order to advance their own interests more effectively."[71] The alternative to such individualism, as suggested by *Hurley,* emphasizes the potential for genuine *group* action. Surveying examples drawn from family life and team sports, Garvey concludes:

> What distinguishes these cases from the individualist view is that in each of them members see in the group a good more important than their own self-interest. In each case the good is interpersonal, a kind that can only be enjoyed by a group: victory for the team, love, peace, grace. Love, for example, is a relation between persons. It cannot be divided (like a baked Alaska) into separate shares and handed around for individual enjoyment.[72]

As summarized by Russell Hittinger, "[i]n the case of a real group-person, common action is an intrinsic aspect of the common end or purpose. . . . Achievement of a mutually agreeable result is not enough. . . . [F]or each of these groups, their respective corporate unity is one of the *reasons for action*—unity is one of the goods being aimed at."[73]

Responding to *Dale*, Andrew Koppelman and Tobias Barrington Wolff argue that the Court's recent freedom of association cases have gone "horribly wrong, producing a cure for the problem that is much worse than the disease."[74] If not as hostile to claims of freedom of association as Koppelman and Wolff, much of the scholarship on freedom of association follows them in struggling to account for associations within a liberal framework.[75] Will Kymlicka, for example, argues that "even 'miminal' conceptions of citizenship impose significant obligations and constraints on individual and group behavior," which results in a tension between the state and the associations of civil society.[76]

Church Autonomy

In addition to the freedom of association, there is a distinctive constitutional doctrine of church autonomy (freedom of *religious* association) based in the religion clauses,[77] most prominently reflected in the so-called "ministerial exception." The ministerial exception is a judicially created doctrine by which religious institutions are immune from antidiscrimination law with respect to employment decisions about "ministers." The federal courts of appeal have all held that the exception is required by the First Amendment, and the Supreme Court recognized the ministerial exception for the first time in 2012 in *Hosanna-Tabor Evangelical Lutheran Church and School* v. *EEOC*.[78]

A District of Columbia Circuit Court of Appeals case from 1996, *EEOC* v. *Catholic University of America*,[79] is a typical and frequently cited case recognizing the ministerial exception as applied by the federal courts of appeal. In the case, a member of Catholic University's (CUA's) Canon Law Department, Sister Elizabeth McDonough, O.P., was denied tenure. CUA was founded in 1887 under a pontifical (*i.e.*, papal) charter, and two departments (Theology and Canon Law) were, at the time of the litigation, still "ecclesiastical faculties." In those departments, a faculty member seeking tenure was required—in addition to the usual layers of tenure review by the faculty member's department, school, and the university senate—to receive approval from the Chancellor of CUA, who was (and still is) *ex officio* the Archbishop of Washington. The Chancellor, furthermore, was required by the canonical statutes of CUA to consult with the bishops on CUA's Board of Trustees to ensure that "there is no impediment to the appointment."

After repeated, unsuccessful attempts to secure approval of her tenure application from her department, Sister McDonough filed a complaint with the EEOC alleging that she had been subject to gender discrimination. In particular, Sister McDonough claimed that two male colleagues had recently been granted tenure with similar credentials. The EEOC found cause in her complaint and filed suit against CUA. CUA defended the case on the grounds both that the decision to deny tenure to Sister McDonough was justified and that the employment discrimination claim was barred under the ministerial exception. The district court agreed and dismissed the suit. On appeal, the D.C. Circuit affirmed the district court in a lengthy opinion by Judge James Buckley.

The case presented a "collision," in Judge Buckley's words, between two important government interests, "the Government's interest in eradicating discrimination in employment and the constitutional right of a church to manage its own affairs free from governmental interference."[80] For the latter proposition, the usual citation is to the Supreme Court's holding in *Kedroff* v. *St. Nicholas Cathedral of the Russian Orthodox Church in North America*, to the effect that the First Amendment protects the ability of religious institutions "to decide for themselves, free from state interference, matters of church government as well as those of faith and doctrine."[81]

Although Sister McDonough was not an ordained member of the Catholic clergy, *CUA* v. *EEOC* is also an illustration of the application of the ministerial exception to "ministers" beyond the category of clergy. A series of courts has held that the exception applies to those whose "primary duties consist of teaching, spreading the faith, church governance, supervision of a religious order, or supervision or participation in religious ritual and worship."[82] The D.C. Circuit also held that the ministerial exception survived the Supreme Court's decision in *Smith*, even though employment anti-discrimination laws would appear to be neutral and generally applicable. So also the form of church organization is irrelevant.[83]

The state cannot interfere with the ministerial employment decisions of churches, but not because the *state* has granted an exemption from an otherwise generally applicable law. Rather, the state simply has no jurisdiction over such claims because churches have a right to govern their internal affairs free of state interference.[84] If this seems implausible as a "rights" question, consider the "remedy" issue. Roughly speaking, remedies in employment discrimination cases take two forms: reinstatement to employment or payment of damages. But both would pose significant problems if applied to religious institutions. If a civil court ordered reinstatement of a minister, then the state would be, in effect, imposing a minister on an unwilling religious body, which is a classic establishment or entanglement problem. Damages, while arguably less intrusive, would constitute an interference with religion as well insofar as damages operate effectively as a prohibition on a practice.

Constitutional protection for the ministerial exception was affirmed by the U.S. Supreme Court in *Hosanna-Tabor*. Hosanna-Tabor, a Lutheran church and school, discharged one of its teacher-employees, Cheryl Perich, after Perich threatened to bring a claim under the Americans with Disabilities Act because the church was unwilling to rehire her after a leave of absence following a diagnosis for narcolepsy. Perich eventually filed a charge with the Equal Employment Opportunity Commission ("EEOC"), which, in turn, brought suit against Hosanna Tabor on her behalf. Hosanna-Tabor raised the defense of the ministerial exception, claiming that Perich's threats of legal action had resulted in her termination because the church believed that Christians should resolve disputes without resort to litigation. The district court granted summary judgment in favor of Hosanna-Tabor's position that the ministerial exception applied. The Sixth Circuit reversed on the ground that Perich was not a "minister" for purposes of the exception because she performed both religious and secular functions as a teacher.[85]

The Supreme Court reversed the Sixth Ciruit, holding that Perich's position as a "called teacher"—a designation the church applies to those who complete theological training and are then "called" by the church ("lay" teachers require no theological training nor must they be Lutheran to be employed)—was enough to characterize her as a "minister" and her employment as "ministerial," thereby invoking the ministerial exception and barring her discrimination claim. The Court did not go any further in defining which employees of religious institutions can or should be characterized as "ministers," and left the question open to be decided on a case-by-case basis.[86]

Chief Justice Roberts's opinion for a unanimous Court reasoned that:

> Requiring a church to accept or retain an unwanted minister, or punishing a church for failing to do so, intrudes upon more than a mere employment decision. Such action interferes with the internal governance of the church, depriving the church of control over the selection of those who will personify its beliefs. By imposing an unwanted minister, the state infringes the Free Exercise Clause, which protects a religious group's right to shape its own faith and mission through its appointments. According the state the power to determine which individuals will minister to the faithful also violates the Establishment Clause, which prohibits government involvement in such ecclesiastical decisions.[87]

The *Hosanna-Tabor* Court, like the D.C. Circuit court in the *CUA* case, rejected the EEOC's and the plaintiff's arguments that *Smith* precludes recognition of a ministerial exception. Even if the ADA's prohibition on retaliation (providing that an employer may not terminate an employee due to that employee's asserting a claim under the ADA), like

Oregon's prohibition on peyote use, were a valid and neutral law of general applicability, the Court drew a distinction between internal ordering of an institution and outward conduct. *Smith*, the Court explained, involved government regulation of outward physical acts, while applying anti-discrimination law to claims by ministerial employees would constitute government interference with an internal church decision that affects the faith and the mission of the church itself. Therefore, the court rejected the argument that the holding in *Smith* precludes recognition of a ministerial exception rooted in the religion clauses.[88]

Finally, the Court rejected in *Hosanna-Tabor* the claim that Perich should receive any compensatory or punitive damages, because damage awards would penalize the church for terminating an unwanted minister and would be "no less prohibited by the First Amendment than an order overturning the termination. Such relief would depend on a determination that Hosanna-Tabor was wrong to have relieved Perich of her position, and it is precisely such a ruling that is barred by the ministerial exception."[89] The court also pointed out that a religious institution may safely (under the ministerial exception) decide to terminate a minister's employment for any number of reasons, and does not require that the religious institution prove that termination was carried out for a solely religious reason.[90]

The enormous challenge for vindicating institutional conscience is to find ways of reshaping what is now a relatively narrow but important doctrine—the ministerial exception and related areas of church autonomy—into a more general norm of group autonomy.

Conclusion: From Conscience to Institutional Liberty

The cases discussed in the opening section of this essay suggest the difficulty of bringing claims of conscience under current First Amendment free exercise doctrine. Set against a background of *ad hoc* statutory protections and confusing constitutional doctrine, those seeking to limit state encroachments rightly worry about the scope of protection for "conscience," whether individual or institutional. Part of the problem, I suspect, is that our constitutional doctrine surrounding freedom of conscience—both individual and institutional—reflects deeper and more pervasive philosophical confusion about the very notion of "conscience." In a series of articles, constitutional law scholar Steven D. Smith has echoed such skepticism about conscience. In "The Tenuous Case for Conscience," for example, Smith concludes that "the modern invocation of freedom of conscience is partly parasitic on older ways of thinking that many of those who invoke conscience today might find problematic. . . . [I]f we look closely at the modern invocations of conscience we will find uncertainty, confusion, and perhaps even a kind of degradation."[91] These problems are all the more pressing when claims of *institutional* conscience arise, as they will always be derivative—and perhaps problematically so—of individual conscience.

Better to reflect, I submit, on the possibility that religious corporations are free and autonomous groups within the state. "What we actually see in the world," John Neville Figgis claimed, "is not on the one hand the State, and on the other a mass of unrelated individuals; but a vast complex of gathered unions, in which alone we find individuals."[92] My conclusion inverts the historical trend by which the idea of the freedom of the church declined and was replaced by individual conscience. In his book *We Hold These Truths*, theologian John Courtney Murray traces the demise of the concept of freedom of the church. Dating from Gelasius's 494 A.D. letter to Anastasius I, the freedom of the church, classically understood, insisted that there were things that were not Caesar's. In modern politics, Murray argues, the freedom of the church was displaced, and the freedom of the individual conscience filled the void. Appeals to freedom of conscience were, in Murray's view, historically an aspect of the systematic undermining of the freedom of the church. As Murray writes, "[t]he key to the whole new political edifice was the freedom of the individual conscience. . . . The freedom of the individual conscience, constitutionally guaranteed, would supply the armature of immunity to the sacred order, which now became, by modern definition, precisely the order of the private conscience."[93] "It was an essential part of modernity's hope," Murray concludes, "that the moral consensus upon which every society depends for its stability and progress could be sustained and mobilized simply in terms of a fortunate coincidence of individual private judgments, apart from all reference to a visibly constituted spiritual and moral authority."[94] The visible, institutional faces of religious authority—the churches—were relegated to a voluntary association. So it is that today freedom of *association*—the happy coincidence of several individuals gathered for an associational purpose—and not freedom of *conscience* provides the most promising basis for constitutional recognition of institutional liberty.

ENDNOTES

1   John M. Finnis, "Conscience, Infallibility and Contraception," *The Month* 11 (1978): 410, 410.

2   I leave to others to discuss whether and to what extent "institutional conscience" is a meaningful term. Most of the philosophical and theological literature on "conscience" proceeds on the unexamined assumption that conscience is a faculty or possession (a "habit," in the older sense) of individuals. See Eric D'Arcy, *Conscience and its Right to Freedom* (New York: Sheed & Ward, 1961). Paul Ramsey may have popularized the phrase when he discussed "institutional conscience" in the context of hospitals' refusals to perform abortions. See Paul Ramsey, *Ethics at the Edges of Life: Medical and Legal Intersections* (New Haven: Yale University Press, 1978), 62–82. For a pervasively institutional account of conscience, see Robert K. Vischer, *Conscience and the Common Good: Reclaiming the Space between Person and State* (New York: Cambridge University Press, 2009).

3   132 S.Ct. 694 (2012).

4   494 U.S. 872 (1990) (characterizing the Court's free exercise cases as "consistently [holding] that the right of free exercise does not relieve an individual of the obligation to comply with a valid and neutral law of general applicability on the ground that the law proscribes (or prescribes) conduct that his religion prescribes (or proscribes)") (internal quotation omitted).

5   *See* Michael McConnell, "The Origins and Historical Understanding of Free Exercise of Religion," *Harvard Law Review* 103 (1990): 1409, and Philip A. Hamburger, "A Constitutional Right of Religious Exemption: An Historical Perspective," *George Washington Law Review* 60 (1992): 915.

6   Even accepting *Smith* as settled doctrine, several leading scholars have sought to avoid overly broad interpretations of *Smith* and to limit its effect on such doctrines as church autonomy. See, *e.g.*, Douglas Laycock, "Theology Scholarships, the Pledge of Allegiance, and Religious Liberty: Avoiding the Extremes but Missing the Liberty," *Harvard Law Review* 118 (2004): 155, and Kathleen A. Brady, "Religious Organizations and Free

Exercise: The Surprising Lessons of *Smith*," *BrighamYoungUniversity Law Review* 2004: 1633.

7   374 U.S. 398 (1963).

8   For the most comprehensive and detailed survey of the free exercise exemption cases, see Kent Greenawalt, *Religion and the Constitution*, vol. 1, *Free Exercise and Fairness* (Princeton: Princeton University Press, 2006).

9   Such strict scrutiny is still available in cases brought under federal or state religious freedom restoration acts (RFRAs), which I leave to discussions of available statutory accommodations of institutional conscience. See *Gonzales* v. *O Centro Espirita Beneficente Uniao do Vegetal*, 546 U.S. 418, 430–31 (2006) ("RFRA requires the Government to demonstrate that the compelling interest test is satisfied through application of the challenged law "to the person"—the particular claimant whose sincere exercise of religion is being substantially burdened. RFRA expressly adopted the compelling interest test as set forth in *Sherbert* v. *Verner* and *Wisconsin* v. *Yoder*.") (internal citations and quotation omitted).

10   *Goldman* v. *Weinberger*, 475 U.S. 503 (1986).

11   *Lyng* v. *Northwest Indian Cemetery Protective Association*, 485 U.S. 439 (1988). In *Lyng*, part of the reason for the Court's rejection of the free exercise claim was that such claims should not affect how the government conducts its own programs. See also *Bowen* v. *Roy*, 476 U.S. 693 (1986).

12   See *Frazee* v. *Ill. Dept. of Employment Sec.*, 489 U.S. 829 (1989); *Hobbie* v. *Unemployment Appeals Comm'n of Fla.*, 480 U.S. 136 (1987); and *Thomas* v. *Review Bd. of Ind. Employment Sec. Div.*, 450 U.S. 707 (1981).

13   406 U.S. 205 (1972).

14   494 U.S., at 879 (internal quotation omitted).

15   508 U.S. 520 (1993).

16   Laycock, "Theology Scholarships," 202. Note that this does not necessarily require a showing of bad motive or discriminatory intent. See *ibid.* at 210:

The persistent effort to read a bad motive requirement into the *Smith-Lukumi* rules distorts the structure of those rules. Bad motive may be one way to prove a violation, but first and foremost, *Smith-Lukumi* is about objectively unequal treatment of religion and analogous secular activities. The protection for religious liberty under the *Smith-Lukumi* rules lies in their effect on the political process. Legislatures can impose on religious minorities only those laws that they are willing to impose on all their constituents....

Even narrow secular exceptions rapidly undermine this interest. If the legislature can exempt those secular groups with the greatest motivation or ability to resist a proposed law, then the effective secular opposition would be left with no reason to continue its opposition, and the religious minority would be left without political protection in the legislature. And if these secular exceptions do not trigger strict scrutiny under *Smith-Lukumi*, the religious minority would also be left without the protection of judicial review. The focus on secular exceptions is thus an integral part of the *Smith-Lukumi* rules.

17 85 P.3d 67 (Cal. 2004).

18 Cal. Health & Saf. Code § 1367.25.

19 *Catholic Charities*, 85 P.3d at 76.

20 *Catholic Charities* v. *Serio*, 859 N.E.2d 459 (N.Y. 2006).

21 *Catholic Charities* v. *California,* 543 U.S. 816 (2004), and *Catholic Charities* v. *Dinallo*, 552 U.S. 816 (2007).

22 See Kathleen A. Brady, "Religious Group Autonomy: Further Reflections about What Is at Stake," *Journal of Law & Religion* 22 (2006–07): 153 , and "Religious Organizations and Free Exercise."

23 *Catholic Charities*, 85 P.3d at 99–100 (internal citations omitted):

This case involves a religious organization and not an individual. Perhaps more importantly, it does not deal with the denial of a benefit because of a violation of existing law. Rather, it attempts to assess the constitutional implications of a law that requires a religious organization to provide a benefit despite its theological objections. These fundamental differences are simply ignored in the majority's analysis.

Under *Smith*, the right of free exercise does not relieve an individual of the obligation to comply with a valid and neutral law of general applicability even if the law requires conduct that contravenes a religious belief, but "[i]t does not follow . . . that *Smith* stands for the proposition that a church may never be relieved from such an obligation."

The majority may have made an abortive attempt to deal with this obvious distinction by citing, and dismissing, the so-called ministerial exception. It is true, as the majority notes, that the ministerial exception is not directly at issue here. Likewise, it is certainly debatable whether the legislative action challenged here invades the narrow domain labeled church autonomy. And yet, the logic of these cases suggests that the constitutionally protected space for religious organizations is actually broader than these obvious categories. In short, the ministerial exception and the church autonomy doctrine are ways of describing spheres of constitutionally required protection, but these categories are not exhaustive.

24 Roderick M. Hills, Jr., "The Constitutional Rights of Private Governments," *New York University Law Review* 78 (2003): 144, 159–60:

[T]here is another, rival intuition repeatedly enforced by the U.S. Supreme Court that at least private governments must enjoy some constitutional liberties because such organizations are the fora in which individual liberties are typically exercised. Newspapers, churches, universities, unions, political parties, and advocacy groups like Common Cause or the National Rifle Association are all sites for individuals' exercise of core constitutional liberties such as the rights to petition government and to speak freely. To say that such organizations have no constitutional rights or that such rights have nothing to do with individual rights seems odd, even though anticoercion theory seems to suggest such a conclusion.

25 530 U.S. 640 (2000).

26 515 U.S. 557 (1995).

27 Richard W. Garnett, "John Courtney Murray on the 'Freedom of the Church,'" *Journal of Catholic Social Thought* 4 (2007): 59, 63.

28 *Ibid.*, 86.

29 See, *e.g., Serbian E. Orthodox Diocese* v. *Milivojevich*, 426 U.S. 696 (1976), *Kedroff* v. *Saint Nicholas Cathedral of the Russian Orthodox Church*, 344 U.S. 94 (1952), and *EEOC* v. *Catholic Univ. of Am.*, 83 F.3d 455 (D.C. Cir. 1996).

30 Garnett, "John Courtney Murray," 64.

31 *Lukumi*, 508 U.S. at 535–36 ("[A]lmost the only conduct subject to Ordinances 87–40, 87–52, and 87–71 is the religious exercise of Santeria church members. The texts show that they were drafted in tandem to achieve this result. We begin with Ordinance 87–71. It prohibits the sacrifice of animals, but defines sacrifice as 'to unnecessarily kill…an animal in a public or private ritual or ceremony not for the primary purpose of food consumption.' The definition excludes almost all killings of animals except for religious sacrifice.") (second alteration in original) (internal citation omitted).

32 See, *e.g.*, Mass. Gen. Laws. ch. 111, § 70E(o) (requiring all covered facilities to provide to female rape victims of childbearing age "accurate written information about emergency contraception from any facility, including any private or state run hospital, to be promptly offered the same, and to be provided with emergency contraception upon request").

33 102 Mass. Code Regs. 1.03(1) (2007) (requiring adoption agencies to obtain a state license and prohibiting discrimination "on the basis of race, religion, cultural heritage, political beliefs, national origin, marital status, sexual orientation or disability").

34 See Helen Watt, ed., *Cooperation, Complicity, and Conscience: Problems in Healthcare, Science, Law and Public Policy* (London: Linacre Centre,

2005) and Henry Davis, S.J., *Moral and Pastoral Theology* (New York: Sheed & Ward, 1949), vol. 1, 341–52.

35 Daniel Sulmasy, "Emergency Contraception for Women Who Have Been Raped: Must Catholics Test for Ovulation, or Is Testing for Pregnancy Morally Sufficient?" *Kennedy Institute of Ethics Journal* 16 (2006): 305.

36 In both the California and New York litigation, Catholic Charities argued that it believed it was required as a matter of social justice to provide health benefits, including prescription drug benefits, to its employees. *Catholic Charities v. Superior Court*, 85 P.3d 67, 91–92 (Cal. 2004).

37 Douglas Laycock, "Towards a General Theory of the Religion Clauses: The Case of Church Labor Relations and the Right to Church Autonomy," *Columbia Law Review* 81 (1981): 1373, 1390.

38 I will leave aside the difficult question of the precise constitutional basis for freedom of association. *See* John D. Inazu, "The Strange Origins of the Constitutional Right of Association," *Tennessee Law Review* 77 (2010): 485.

39 530 U.S. 567 (2000).

40 530 U.S. 640 (2000).

41 130 S.Ct. 876 (2010). An extended discussion of *Citizens United* would, of course, take us far afield into election law and freedom of speech in political campaigns. I mention the case here only to signal the relevance of the corporate or group personality question across different areas of constitutional doctrine.

42 625 F.3d 1247 (10th Cir. 2010).

43 468 U.S. 609 (1984).

44 515 U.S. 557 (1995).

45 530 U.S. 640 (2000).

46 I am passing over the most recent case in which freedom of association was asserted as the basis for exclusion of unwanted members, *Christian Legal Society v. Martinez*, 130 S. Ct. 2971 (2010), because the freedom of association claim there was reduced (mistakenly, in my view) to the "limited public forum" analysis under freedom of speech.

47 *Roberts*, 468 U.S. 609.

48 *Ibid.* at 617–18.

49 *Ibid.* at 618.

50 *Ibid.*

51 *Ibid.*

52 *Ibid..*

53 *Ibid.,* at 622 (emphasis added).

54 *Ibid.*, at 623.
55 *Ibid.*
56 *Ibid.*, at 627.
57 *Irish-American Gay, Lesbian and Bisexual Group of Boston* v. *City of Boston*, 636 N.E.2d 1293 (Mass. 1994).
58 *Hurley* v. *Irish-American Gay, Lesbian, and Bisexual Group of Boston*, 515 U.S. 557, 568 (1995).
59 *Ibid.*
60 *Ibid.*, at 569–70.
61 *Ibid.*, at 572–73.
62 *Dale* v. *Boy Scouts*, 734 A.2d 1196, 1221 (N.J. 1999) (internal quotation omitted).
63 *Ibid.*, at 1229.
64 *Boy Scouts* v. *Dale*, 530 U.S. 640, 648 (2000).
65 *Ibid.*, at 651.
66 *Ibid.*, at 653.
67 *Ibid.*, at 654.
68 *Ibid.*, at 655.
69 *Ibid.*, at 656.
70 John H. Garvey, *What Are Freedoms For?* (Cambridge: Harvard University Press, 1996).
71 *Ibid.*, at 133.
72 *Ibid.*, at 137.
73 Russell Hittinger, "Society, Subsidiarity, and Authority in Catholic Social Thought," in *Civilizing Authority: Society, State, and Church*, ed. Patrick McKinley Brennan (Lanham, MD: Lexington, 2007), 122.
74 Andrew Koppelman, with Tobias Barrington Wolff, *A Right to Discriminate? How the Case of* Boy Scouts of America v. James Dale *Warped the Law of Free Associations* (New Haven: Yale University Press, 2009), 24.
75 See, *e.g.*, Amy Gutmann, ed., *Freedom of Association* (Princeton: Princeton University Press, 1998) and Nancy Rosenblum, *Membership and Morals: The Personal Uses of Pluralism in America* (Princeton: Princeton University Press, 1998). As George Kateb notes, "Only rarely does freedom of association receive a defense that honors it as integral to a free human life, to being a free person." George Kateb, "The Value of Association," in Gutmann, Freedom of Association, 35–36.
76 Will Kymlicka, "Civil Society and Government: A Liberal-Egalitarian Perspective," in *Civil Society and Government*, ed. Nancy L. Rosenblum and Robert C. Post (Princeton: Princeton University Press, 2002), 102–03.

77 Indeed, there is lingering uncertainty about whether church autonomy is a free exercise or establishment doctrine. My argument here is that it is both more and different than merely a free exercise doctrine. As shown by such early cases as *Watson* v. *Jones* and more recent cases such as *Kedroff* and *Serbian Orthodox*, the ministerial exception—and other church autonomy doctrines—are part of a larger account of state authority and jurisdictional limitations.

78 132 S.Ct. 694 (2012).

79 83 F.3d 455 (D.C. 1996).

80 *Ibid.*, at 460.

81 344 U.S. 94, 116 (1952).

82 *Rayburn* v. *General Conference of Seventh-day Adventists*, 772 F.2d 1164, 1169 (4th Cir.1985) (internal quotation marks and citation omitted).

83 Douglas Laycock, "Towards a General Theory," 1414:

The right of church autonomy is the right to keep decisionmaking authority over church operations within the church, free of outside control; how that authority is allocated internally is irrelevant. Churches may be hierarchical or congregational, episcopal or democratic, clerical or lay, incorporated or informally associated, a single entity or a network of subsidiaries and affiliates-all are entitled to autonomy by the free exercise clause. Unavoidable secular inquiry into church organization in some cases implementing the right of church autonomy does not justify distinctions based on church organization in determining the scope of the right or the strength of a church's interest in it.

84 For a defense of the view that the ministerial exception is a subject matter jurisdictional defense (not a challenge to the legal sufficiency of a plaintiff's claim), see Gregory A. Kalscheur, S.J., "Civil Procedure and the Establishment Clause: Exploring the Ministerial Exception, Subject-Matter Jurisdiction, and the Freedom of the Church," *William & Mary Bill of Rights Journal* 17 (2008): 43.

85 597 F.3d 769 (6th Cir. 2010).

86 132 S.Ct., at 707.

87 *Ibid.*, at 706.

88 *Ibid.*

89 *Ibid.*, at 709.

90 *Ibid.*

91 Steven Smith, "The Tenuous Case for Conscience," *Roger Williams University Law Review* 10 (2005): 325, 358.

92 John Neville Figgis, *Churches in the Modern State* (London: Longmans Green, 1913), 70.

93 John Courtney Murray, *We Hold These Truths: Catholic Reflections on the American Proposition* (New York: Sheed & Ward, 1960; reprint, Lanham, MD: Rowman & Littlefield, 2005), 190.

94 *Ibid.*, at 196.

Chapter Nine
The Precarious Freedom of the Church
Steven D. Smith

Introduction

The church, we are told, lives like a pilgrim in this world.[1] But just as a pilgrim may seek secure lodgings along the way, the church may try to secure favorable arrangements with the mundane regimes through which it passes. Because the assumptions and aspirations of the church are not those of the world, however, accommodations offered by worldly sovereigns are likely to be constrictive and contested. This condition of contestation sometimes erupts into a struggle for "freedom of the church."

One celebrated chapter in this struggle commenced almost a millennium ago in what is sometimes called the Papal Revolution,[2] with a dispute over the prerogative claimed by kings to participate in the appointment of bishops. The most vivid image from that struggle is of King Henry IV of France waiting in the snow outside the castle at Canossa for three days, ragged and barefoot, weeping and pleading for Pope Gregory VII's pardon. But the more ominous episode occurred several years later when Henry, pardoned and once again powerful, ordered his men of might to invade Rome, forcing the Pope to flee for his life.[3] Despite this setback, the campaign for freedom of the church pressed by Gregory and carried on by, among others, martyrs like Thomas Becket, achieved some significant success (and possibly practiced some overreaching)[4] over the next several centuries.

That success was largely undone, though, beginning in the fourteenth century, and especially following the Reformation. The execution of Thomas More and the assumption by Henry VIII of control over the church in England augured a long Erastian servitude in which the church—the "visible church," anyway—would be subjected to the domination of the secular state.[5]

The church's fortunes (or at least its legal freedom) revived with the inauguration of the American republic. We typically attribute this achievement to the Constitution and the First Amendment.[6] But even more important, probably, were the political attitudes and general conditions that prevailed in the new republic. There was a fervent commitment to liberty. And there was land to be settled, and a need to attract settlers to this land, and hence a reluctance to discourage settlement by religious restrictions. The abundance of land and frontier also gave the devotees of more controversial faiths a place to which to escape—as the Pilgrims did in the seventeenth century, and as the Mormons did in the nineteenth.

Today the situation is different. The Erastian servitude, and the anti-Erastian function of the First Amendment in ending that servitude, have receded from the memories of most Americans. "Separation of *church and state*" has transmogrified into "separation of *government from religion*." Free exercise doctrine that might once have offered the church some constitutional immunity has been significantly curtailed. Even more importantly, perhaps, background conditions have changed: the frontier has long since been filled in, and the revolutionary generation's rage for freedom has been domesticated under the ministrations of the secular regulatory state. That regime is animated by an increasingly imperious egalitarianism that is at odds in important particulars with the views and practices of many churches.[7]

For these reasons, the ample if imperfect freedom that the church has enjoyed through much of American history seems vulnerable today. The devout (and perhaps even the less than devout) would do well to notice looming challenges, and to ask whether and how these challenges might be addressed.

Contemporary Obstacles to Freedom of the Church

Consider two major contemporary problems for a commitment to freedom of the church. The first problem is troublesome but perhaps not insuperable. The second seems more intractable.

Many Churches

One objection to "freedom of the church" in its classical sense is that the idea is anachronistic because there is nothing today that answers to the description of "*the* church." In the year 1200, say, or even 1500, if reference was made to "the church," people in Western nations could be reasonably sure what institution was being identified. But today there is no "the church"; instead there are scores upon scores of church*es*. Thus, Nicholas Wolterstorff explains that in the older world of Christendom, "within a given political jurisdiction, virtually all subjects of the state were also members of the church. Hence it was that church and state were distinguished not as two distinct communities but as two authority structures over one community." But this conception does not fit today's conditions, Wolterstorff contends. "The religious fragmentation of Europe by the Reformation had the consequence that, by the time of Madison and Jefferson, this way of thinking was simply no longer possible."[8]

And yet despite the momentous changes that Wolterstorff notes, the practice of referring to "the church," in the singular, persists. (I am following the practice in this essay.) Nor is that practice merely an anachronistic holdover; it captures something crucial in (many) Christians' self-understanding. Under the familiar view in which *the church* refers in part and perhaps most centrally to something like "the invisible church" and the various observable *churches* are understood to be instantiations or manifestations of that more mystical entity,[9] it is still meaningful to refer to "the church" in the singular. Theologians have developed sophisticated ecclesiologies that emphasize the underlying or immanent unity in the midst of the conspicuous plurality.[10] In this vein, Gilbert Meilander writes:

> For my part, I believe that the Church's genuine oneness need not be translated into institutional unity. If this commits me to believing that the one holy catholic and apostolic Church is "invisible," that's all right. Invisibility in this sense is not a way of escaping from time, place, and embodiment. On the contrary, it is a way of taking time, place, and embodiment

seriously, a way of recognizing the multiform manner in which the one Church— under, surely, the governance of the Holy Spirit— has taken shape in human history.[11]

This is a view that churches and the state conceivably might take, for public purposes at least, even if some Christians have theological reservations.[12] There would be classification issues, of course, but not, perhaps, insuperable ones. Once again, theologians have reflected insightfully on the "signs" or "marks" of the church.[13] Such reflections point to indicia that might serve to provide a method, good enough for government work anyway, for distinguishing "churches"—franchises of "the church," so to speak—from other organizations and from mere religious associations (like Bible study groups) that are not "the church." The task would not be easy, but it might be manageable if the motivation were present.

That is an insecure "if," however, and it brings us up against a more formidable obstacle to recognition of freedom of the church in today's political environment.

The Secular Framework

Legal recognition of freedom of the church inevitably entails limitations on the power of secular government, and thus limitations on the ability of government to promote valued policies and objectives. Today, for example, freedom of the church could potentially impede widely-supported efforts to eliminate, say, gender discrimination, or sexual exploitation of children, or the promotion of certain views of equal treatment for homosexuals. Given these costs, a proposal to protect freedom of the church carries a burden of justification.

But it is not easy to see exactly how that burden can be carried. I have already suggested that the struggle for freedom of the church began in a sustained way in the eleventh century—there were important but more sporadic skirmishes much earlier—and has persisted ever since. In one central respect, though, the modern challenge is essentially the opposite of the one faced by Gregory VII. *Then* the relevant political and ecclesiastical actors largely shared a Christian worldview and Christian premises. So the problem was to fend off interference from rulers—like

Henry IV, Gregory's nemesis—who themselves claimed to be acting as God's representatives and even as the guardians of God's church.[14] (This was hardly a preposterous claim, by the way: it could invoke the precedents of Constantine and Charlemagne—or, more recently, of Henry's father, Henry III, who had played a prominent role in helping to rescue the papacy from a period of violence and scandal.)[15] In any case, the justificatory challenge for Gregory and his successors was to show, using the same kinds of Christian authorities and premises that rulers and subjects generally accepted, that God had so ordained the temporal and spiritual jurisdictions that kings and princes should not meddle in, say, the selection of bishops.

Today the challenge of justification is utterly different. The problem now is the pervasive assumption that government and political discourse must be secular in nature—"secular" in the sense of "not religious." And judges and scholars take it as axiomatic that governments cannot make judgments about the truth of religious propositions, which seemingly means that governmental decisions and policies cannot be based on such propositions. These assumptions effectively exclude the kinds of reasons that were offered over the centuries for treating the church as in some sense a separate jurisdiction. The hard question is whether it is possible to give justifications for freedom of the church without invoking the special features and claims—"religious" features and claims—that make the church a distinctive institution.

It is not surprising, probably, that after a span of almost a millennium, the claims asserted in the *Dictatus Papae*, Gregory's declaration of papal powers,[16] do not translate easily into American constitutional discourse. But consider a more recent example: Jacques Maritain's *The Things That Are Not Caesar's*. In this book Maritain offered a spirited defense of freedom of the church (and of the church's "indirect power" over temporal matters). That defense was premised on the contention that "[e]ach of us . . . belongs to two States—a terrestrial State whose end is the common temporal good, and the universal State of the Church whose end is eternal life."[17] The church's freedom arises from the fact that its authority transcends that of the state, and this transcendence reflects the church's character as "a supernatural mystery."

> [T]he Church is not only a visible and apparent reality but also an object of faith, not a system of administrative cogwheels but the Body of Christ whose living unity, incomparably more elevated and strong than in this world we describe as moral personality, is guaranteed by the action of the Holy Ghost.[18]

These claims were patently theological in character; it is hard to imagine them being offered, much less comprehendingly received, in an environment committed to exclusively secular public decision-making.[19]

This difficulty applies not just to the church but to religious freedom generally. I have argued elsewhere that it is difficult to justify a special constitutional commitment to religious freedom without invoking the kinds of essentially theological justifications that historically were the basis of that commitment—the kinds of justifications offered in the first section of James Madison's Memorial and Remonstrance and in Thomas Jefferson's Virginia Statute for Religious Freedom. ("Almighty God hath created the mind free . . . .")[20] This difficulty is apparent, I believe, in the increasingly reductionist tendencies that courts and scholars exhibit toward religious freedom generally.[21]

Even so, freedom of the church presents especially daunting difficulties. The commitment to *individual religious freedom* seems to be deeply entrenched in our political tradition. That commitment can accordingly claim the support of longstanding tradition even when explicit justifications seem feeble. In the American tradition, by contrast, *freedom of the church* has no deep resonance. By the time our Constitution was being shaped, the medieval struggle for freedom of the church had largely been redirected, in Protestant societies anyway, into a campaign for "freedom of conscience." And many Americans, even including "religious" Americans, harbor an instinctive resentment toward "organized religion," or churches.[22]

There is, to be sure, a venerable American commitment to "separation of church and state." This commitment *could*– and to some extent probably *does*—support "freedom of the church."[23] Unfortunately, though, as noted already, the slogan of "separation of church and state" has to a significant extent been commandeered by advocates who use it mainly to advocate governmental secularism, and to oppose any sort of governmental support for religion. By this view, the sorts of theological claims or distinctive immunities that might be associated with freedom of the church are likely to be regarded as deviating from secularism and as promoting religion—and hence, ironically, as *precluded* by the "separation of church and state." Paradoxically, perhaps, "separation of church and state" in its modern secularist make-over actually works to subvert "separation of church and state" in its more classical sense.

In short, the secular framework that prevails in legal, academic, and a good deal of public discourse makes it difficult to justify the classical commitment to freedom of the church. But the difficulty runs still deeper. In a thoroughly secular context, the commitment can seem not only unjustifiable, but almost unintelligible. Secular citizens, scholars, and jurists (and for that matter "religious" citizens, scholars, and jurists who have been formed in a secular environment) may find it difficult to fathom the character of the church as the "body of Christ" and "a supernatural mystery"[24] that is in some important sense beyond the jurisdiction of the secular state,[25] analogous to the way that a foreign embassy is to some extent beyond domestic jurisdiction. Instead, the church is likely to appear as simply a human association formed under the state's laws for particular purposes—purposes that happen to be "religious"—and claiming legal rights and immunities in much the way other human associations may claim them. Some people congregate to hear chamber music or play poker, and others get together for praying or preaching: the purpose that animates their associating is mostly not the state's concern.

These difficulties were clearly discerned over two decades ago in a penetrating article by Gerard Bradley. Bradley suggested the need "to recover what 'separation of church and state' means."

> It symbolizes the permanent tension in Western societies between the exigencies of pragmatic existence in history and the consciousness of divine order arising in men's souls. The reality so constituted is, most precisely, a field of tension bordered by two pulls, denoted "world" and "divine."[26]

}184{

Within this reality,

> [m]an's destination is eternal life in beatific vision. His
> earthly existence then becomes a journey of sanctification
> which can no longer be symbolically represented by political
> society, but only by the church. The church becomes a flash
> of that eternity into time, a community ahead of itself, the
> "already" of the "already but not yet," the vessel and the
> means of that sanctification which carries on after death.[27]

Maintaining the autonomy of the church, Bradley suggested, "should
be the flagship issue of church and state."[28] Sadly, the field is enveloped
by "an intellectual haze that fundamentally obscures the combatants'
line and that transforms the fray into an almost undirected melee."[29]
Thus, the Supreme Court has never "squarely held that religious organizations possess constitutional rights" at all, and constitutional doctrines
and prevailing liberal thought lack the cognitive resources to grasp or
ground a sound doctrine of church autonomy.[30] The stark truth is that
"what we call 'church-state' arises and can only be discussed within an
intellectual field that presupposes religious, particularly Christian con-
cepts."[31] Estranged from that context, "we constitutionalists are not con-
structively engaging the church-state issue and have practically
obliterated it."[32] The situation did not bode well for the church in a world
in which, as Bradley presciently warned, "the muscular maturity of
nondiscrimination still awaits us."[33]

Bradley's assessment points to a dilemma that the church and those
who would defend its freedom currently face.

The Church's Dilemma

In the prevailing secular legal environment, what possibilities are available for defending the freedom of the church? One strategy would adhere
steadfastly to the kinds of theological rationales embraced by Bradley,
Maritain, and their predecessors.[34] We have already noticed the major
disadvantage of this strategy: theological rationales are likely to seem
unpersuasive, inadmissible, and even unintelligible to the broad mass of
political and legal actors.

The other obvious alternative, it seems, is to reconceive the freedom of the church in secular terms and to defend it on secular grounds. This seems at the moment to be the strategy of choice. Some advocates adopt it enthusiastically; others find themselves reluctantly drawn into it, or at least drawn towards it. But again there is a worry: as we will consider shortly, it is doubtful that this secularizing strategy is capable of supporting any substantial protection for freedom of the church.

So each alternative has its drawbacks. Actually, this dilemma remains largely hidden so long as we treat the problem as merely one of positive constitutional law. On that level, advocates of freedom of the church may simply look for a constitutional provision or doctrine to which the freedom can be attached. Thus, in an important article published three decades ago, Douglas Laycock argued that church autonomy falls within the protective scope of free exercise of religion.[35] Free exercise is assured by the Constitution, or so Laycock assumed, and so if church autonomy can be fastened to free exercise, constitutional protection for church autonomy will have been secured. Laycock accordingly made little effort to offer any deeper justification for either free exercise or church autonomy.

Even if it is persuasive on its own terms, though, Laycock's argument now seems insufficient. For one thing, in *Employment Division* v. *Smith* free exercise doctrine was restructured, so that it no longer requires accommodation of religion as against generally applicable and religiously neutral regulations.[36] But the major current threats to church autonomy, such as anti-discrimination laws, are likely to be generally applicable and religiously neutral: so free exercise doctrine offers little assistance. To be sure, advocates can try to argue that free exercise still protects religious institutions against even such generally applicable laws—we will consider one such effort shortly—but this position seems a bit topsy-turvy. Before *Smith*, it was a contested question whether religious *institutions*, as opposed to *individuals*, enjoyed any free exercise protection at all in their own right. (This uncertainty was of course what made Laycock's article important.) Protection for individuals seemed primary; protection for institutions was arguably derivative. So how would it happen that the retrenchment implemented in *Smith* left institutions with *more* protection than individuals receive?

The tactic of simply attaching church autonomy to free exercise seems insufficient for a second reason as well. Scholars have lately focused on the problem of providing justifications for a special constitutional commitment to religious freedom, as additional to or distinct from a general freedom of association. And for reasons that I have discussed elsewhere,[37] they have often concluded that such justifications are lacking. In the absence of persuasive justifications, however, the commitment may lose its vigor. And indeed, some respected scholars have recently concluded that the special constitutional commitment to religious freedom should be relaxed or abandoned.[38]

Given the truncated condition of free exercise doctrine and the difficulties of providing persuasive justifications for special protection for religion, proponents of church autonomy may turn to other constitutional provisions—especially the freedom of association.[39] In a similar vein, John Inazu argues for grounding church autonomy in the freedom of assembly. Inazu himself is not averse to theological reflection; indeed, his article contains a good deal of such reflection, appealing to the strong and distinctive ecclesial views of Stanley Hauerwas. But Inazu does not think these theological views can be absorbed or accepted in constitutional law. "[A]rguments for the constitutional distinctiveness of religious groups are less convincing today than they have been in past years," he observes, "and they are likely to be even less salient in the future." Consequently, "[p]roponents of religious freedom . . . are better off embracing recent arguments that move away from the constitutional distinctiveness of religious groups."[40]

A more reluctant version of this strategy is evident in a thoughtful, somewhat Hamlet-like article by Kathleen Brady,[41] a legal academic with much more than the usual theological sophistication (or than my own).[42] Brady sets out to show that *Employment Division* v. *Smith* actually supports a broad right of church autonomy, and she offers two main arguments for this counterintuitive interpretation.

First, Brady observes that *Smith* retained the proposition from earlier decisions that freedom of religious *belief* (as opposed to religious conduct) enjoys "absolute" constitutional protection. But belief is formed in religious associations, she reasons, so the strong protection for freedom of belief should extend to the associations that nurture such belief.[43]

Yet this argument seems to turn on a *non sequitur*. After all, people have rights to do things that they ought not to do, and that we wish they wouldn't do. People have a right to hold racist beliefs, probably, but it hardly follows that government must affirmatively cultivate the conditions conducive to such beliefs. Similarly, someone might without inconsistency concede that people have a right to their religious beliefs while ardently wishing that such beliefs would wither away (as they were long since supposed to have done, according to the now largely discredited secularization thesis). In this vein, Michael Smith describes Felix Frankfurter and Alexander Bickel as holding the view that religion is a "public nuisance" but that "we are bound to suffer it."[44]

> Brady herself acknowledges the basic problem. I have argued that full freedom of religious belief requires at least some special protection for groups, but perhaps that was the wrong starting point. After all, *Smith* does not guarantee a diversity of religious perspectives or that religious belief will be unaffected by government action. *Smith* states that government may not regulate beliefs as such, but the decision requires nothing further. The *Smith* Court may envision a world of diverse religious beliefs unimpeded by government action, but it did nothing to ensure such an environment.[45]

Exactly. So Brady offers a second argument. While eliminating mandatory free exercise exemptions, she observes, *Smith* allowed that legislatures are still free to offer such accommodation. This position, by leaving the issue of accommodation to the more democratic institutions, implicitly presupposes the efficacy of democracy. But democracy flourishes best, Brady argues, in a civil society that sustains a variety of "mediating structures" and associations. And religious associations are an important ingredient in this mediating mix, Brady argues; as a historical matter they have often served a "prophetic" role in, for example, opposing slavery and supporting civil rights.[46] Thus, religious associations can claim the protection of the democracy-grounded "right of association."[47]

One reservation about this "mediating structures" rationale is that it may seem to apply as much to nonreligious as to religious mediating associations. Far from resisting this conclusion, Brady appears to embrace it. "The proper response to this concern," she says, "is not to diminish protections for religious organizations but expand them for secular associations that play similar roles in the lives of individuals and the larger community."[48] The concession effectively sacrifices any *distinctive* protection for freedom of the church.

In a poignant conclusion, Brady indicates that neither of the arguments offered for church autonomy is the argument she would prefer to give. Her deeper view, she suggests, grows out of

> a faith in a transcendent reality which grounds, guides and communicates with the temporal world. It is this transcendent point of reference that is the source of truths for individual conduct, social relationships and political life, and these truths are, in turn, the basis for legal and political legitimacy.[49]

This view, Brady suggests, is not just special pleading on behalf of religious believers; freedom of religion, including freedom for churches, blesses even those who reject the faith it protects. "God's grace extends to those who do not know Him by name."[50]

But Brady offers these more faith-filled observations tentatively, even apologetically,[51] because she perceives that although at one time religious freedom was defended on religious premises, "this type of argument is not persuasive today." So Brady rests her case not on these wistful parting reflections, but rather on a secularized and democratic "freedom of association" under which religious groups are entitled to the same constitutional protections– no more, and no less—than comparable non-religious associations enjoy.[52]

So, should proponents of freedom of the church eschew reliance on theological justifications, relinquish any special claim to freedom of *the church*, and instead rely on the more generic freedom of association? One drawback of this approach, it might seem, is that the approach misrepresents the nature of the church, treating it as if it were merely another human association. Gerard Bradley deplores the tendency to treat churches as simply voluntary associations, "as if the Jaycees and the Roman Catholic Church were analytically fungible entities."[53] Alluding to *Boy Scouts* v. *Dale*,[54] a case on which scholars like Brady rely, Richard

Garnett remarks that freedom of the church is "an idea that, with all due respect to the Boy Scouts, is bigger than 'be prepared.'"[55]

Still, it might be that the more mundane conception of the church is not so much false as incomplete. The church today *is* a voluntary association, even if it is much more than that. And in any case, it would be unrealistic, as Maritain acknowledged, to expect a secular observer (and perhaps *any* mere mortal, secular or not) to grasp the full nature of the church. So if the practical consequences of dissolving church freedom into the freedom of association were favorable, the incomplete comprehension of the church might be tolerable.

But *will* the consequences be favorable?

The Feeble Freedom of Association

Freedom of association, though acknowledged in a number of modern judicial decisions, seems a half-baked and half-hearted constitutional commitment. The right of association is nowhere named, in so many words at least, in the text of the Constitution. Seeking some textual home, the modern Supreme Court has mostly tried to house the right in the free speech clause.[56] People often join together to express themselves and to spread their messages, the reasoning runs; hence, a right to freedom of association is an aspect or corollary of the freedom of expression.[57] The logic of this expression-based approach to freedom of association may be plausible as far as it goes, but it has turned out to support only a feeble association right, for at least three reasons.

First, the Justices have on occasion shown themselves to be startlingly (or perhaps opportunistically) insouciant regarding the institutional dynamics that connect association to expression. Thus, in *Roberts v. United States Jaycees*,[58] the seminal modern case, the Court accepted the Jaycees' self-description as an organization devoted to advancing the business interests of young men, but then blithely asserted that the legally compelled admission of women as full members need not alter or negate this male-oriented purpose and message.[59] And as a purely abstract matter, we can perhaps conceive of an organization composed of men and women of equal status devoted to advancing the interests of men—just as we can conceive of an association of oil drillers and environmentalists working to promote the interests of drillers. Such things are *conceivable*—conceivable in the sense that they are not logically impossible—but it is also wholly unrealistic to expect real human associations to behave in this way, in our society at least. Thus, Seana Shiffrin characterizes the *Roberts* Court's position as "naive" and "bizarre."[60] George Kateb observes that "where sex is a salient element, [Justice William] Brennan's claim that young women may, after their compulsory admission, contribute to the allowable purpose of 'promoting the interests of young men' is absurd."[61]

In a similar vein, Justice John Paul Stevens' claim for himself and three other Justices in *Boy Scouts* v. *Dale* that a Boy Scout troop could retain as scoutmaster a man who was publicly serving as the president of a local Lesbian/Gay Alliance without thereby compromising its teaching opposing homosexual conduct[62] seems woefully if conveniently oblivious to the ways in which an organization like the Boy Scouts seeks to inculcate its values by informal interaction and role modeling.[63]

A second reason why the speech-derived freedom of association provides scant protection in practice is that the right can be overcome by a "compelling" state interest. There is of course no metric for calibrating the compellingness of asserted state interests. But the Court has had little difficulty concluding that the state's interest in eliminating disfavored forms of discrimination satisfies that standard.[64]

Perhaps the most serious shortcoming of freedom of association, though, is that the right has been constructed, perhaps inadvertently, to provide almost no protection in the situations where protection is most needed. This construction results from the fact that freedom of association has been derived from freedom of speech, together with the shape that the Supreme Court has given to free speech doctrine over the past several decades. In speech cases, the Supreme Court has developed a two-track approach in which the level of protection depends on whether a law burdening expression is directed at the *suppression of expression*. Such laws are presumptively unconstitutional; by contrast, laws that "incidentally" burden speech but are viewpoint-neutral and "unrelated to the suppression of expression" receive only minimal scrutiny. Whether or not this approach is sensible for the protection of speech, its implications for freedom of association are devastating. That is because the laws most threatening to freedom of association—anti-discrimination laws, primarily, but also other sorts of regulations such as tort or labor laws—are typically directed not at *expression*, but rather at *conduct*. Insofar as freedom of association is thought to be merely a corollary of freedom of expression, it may seem to follow that freedom of association is not significantly implicated by such laws.

To be sure, this construction of the right is not inevitable. If freedom of association were viewed as an independent right and not as a mere aspect or corollary of freedom of speech, then the "two-track" reasoning of the speech cases would point to a different sort of parallel. Just as laws that aim to regulate *expression* presumptively violate the freedom of expression, so laws that aim to regulate *association* would be deemed presumptive violations of the freedom of association. And of course anti-discrimination laws in particular *do* directly and intentionally regulate association; that is precisely their purpose. So such laws would receive heightened scrutiny, at least as applied to the class of associations that are deemed to enjoy this constitutional protection.[65]

The decision in *Boy Scouts* v. *Dale* in fact seemed to comprehend this association-oriented logic.[66] But hostile critics did not or would not grasp the logic, so they sharply criticized the Court for treating the Boy Scouts' constitutional defense as worthy of heightened protection against a generally applicable law that was aimed at conduct, not expression.[67] And in 2011, in *Christian Legal Society* v. *Martinez*,[68] the Supreme Court seemed to adopt the more deflationary view. Thus, the Court indicated that since the right of association is derived from freedom of speech, that right could not prevail where a free speech right would not, and the Court accordingly explicitly declined even to give any separate consideration to the plaintiffs' freedom of association claim.[69] Finding that Hastings' proclaimed "all-comers" policy for student associations was a viewpoint-neutral regulation not aimed at expression, the Court concluded that at least for public forum purposes the Christian Legal Society had no constitutional right to limit its membership to students who shared its core beliefs and commitments.

When a Christian association that limits its membership and officers to Christians can for that reason be singled out and denied access to a law school's public forum, the freedom of association does not amount to very much. As understood (or misunderstood) in *Martinez*, freedom of association becomes as useless for protecting church autonomy as free exercise doctrine has become, and for essentially the same reason. Both doctrines assume that the only political or legal threats against which churches need heightened constitutional protection are measures that *single out* religion or religious associations for hostile or unfavorable treatment. But that position offers no immunity against what is in fact the major contemporary threat to religious associations; namely, increasingly insistent governmental efforts to impose general regulations, and especially a secular egalitarian orthodoxy, on institutions of all sorts.

To be sure, some scholars are currently arguing for a more meaningful and vigorous conception of the freedom of association; quite apart from concerns of the church, this project seems to me a worthy one.[70] But in the current climate of political and jurisprudential opinion, there is little cause for confidence about the project's success. In the meantime, if freedom of the church is something worth preserving and protecting, the strategy of acquiescing in a secular approach—of dissolving freedom of the church into a more general freedom of association—seems unpromising.

Conclusion

But *is* freedom of the church worth preserving? On that question, obviously, views differ, both among religious believers and nonbelievers. It would be futile for me to assert any particular answer here. So I will venture only one tentative parting observation: it may well be that legal protection for freedom of the church is ultimately more important to secular society– at least to a secular society that values liberal freedoms—than to the church itself.

The church, after all, if it is in fact the transcendent reality that it claims to be, is in an important sense beyond the reach of the secular state anyway. It can no more be destroyed by the state's power than Shadrach, Meshach, and Abednego could be consumed by Nebuchadnezzar's exquisitely kindled fire. Over the centuries, of course, the state has often visited injury on the "visible" instantiations of the church. But the church itself has persisted: the gates of hell, it is said, will not prevail against it.[71] And although the church's followers can be persecuted in ways that they may not (or, sometimes, perhaps perversely, *may*)[72] welcome, they have been warned to expect such treatment, and have been consoled with promised rewards for enduring it.[73]

Conversely, it is not obvious that the state—or at least the liberal democratic state that Americans have come to cherish—can prosper, over the long run, without the church. I understand that this suggestion will strike secular liberals as profoundly implausible, even perverse. There is a long tradition, going back at least to the Enlightenment, of regarding the church as a, or even *the*, leading opponent of liberty, democracy, and freedom of thought. Evidence might be cited—*has* been cited, over and over again—in support of that view.

Even so, someone might plausibly argue (although this is not the place to lay out the full argument)[74] that the political and legal benefits that Americans enjoy today—in particular the benefits of limited government and of freedom of speech and thought—are the heritage of the Western tradition of dual jurisdictions that cooperate but also compete with and thus check and limit each other. The state supervises the temporal domain. But there is a spiritual domain that the state not merely *ought to* respect but over which the state has no jurisdiction—*no power*—because the jurisdiction belongs to a different sovereign. This idea of dual and hence limited *jurisdictions* is not the same as the notion that has largely displaced it in modern constitutional thought—namely, that the state ought to operate (and to restrain itself) in accordance with principles of justice or political morality. And the jurisdictional idea arguably is the foundation upon which modern notions of liberal and limited government are based.

The idea has worked itself out over the course of centuries.[75] The *freedom of the church*, vigorously defended in the Papal Revolution, is the first important manifestation of that idea of divided and hence limited jurisdictions. Freedom of the church in due course begets *freedom of conscience*—the individual conscience being, as it were, the inner church, or the church of one—and freedom of conscience grows into a more general *freedom of thought and expression*. "My own mind is my own church,"[76] the truculent, irreverent, liberty-loving Thomas Paine declares, thereby inadvertently acknowledging the continuing influence of the concept of the church in the defense of a domain beyond the jurisdiction of collective control.

The seminal conception of dual jurisdictions—and hence of a limited secular jurisdiction—is not the same, I have already suggested, as the idea reflected in so much contemporary theorizing that government ought to act rationally and justly and reasonably. But can't the idea of limited jurisdiction be defended, and can't totalitarian tendencies—tendencies to which secular and (in their own estimation) enlightened governments are hardly immune—be resisted, without positing that the other side of the jurisdictional line is occupied by *the church,* an institution that in its human manifestations is famously prone to its own kinds of authoritarian proclivities?

The answer to that question, I submit, is not obvious. It is one thing to declare a boundary: "Thus far and no farther." But power, like nature, abhors a vacuum: if the territory on the other side of the boundary is not actively occupied and defended, encroachment and expansion are likely to ensue. And while individuals may assert the rights the state has seen fit to grant them, their claim to a limited immunity from the state's power is strongest, as Madison understood, when they are understood to be dual citizens able to invoke the protection of another sovereign as well.[77] Stripped of that dual citizenship, individuals (in themselves manifestly subjects of the state) have difficulty articulating why they or their interests are beyond the state's plenary *jurisdiction.*

John Stuart Mill seems to have understood or at least sensed this difficulty, and his celebrated "harm principle" can be seen as a modern secular attempt to draw a jurisdictional line that would substitute for the jurisdictional boundaries once drawn and defended on theological grounds and in the name of freedom of the church. Indeed, Mill explicitly described his principle as an attempt to limit the state's "jurisdiction."[78] And the wide-ranging attractiveness of the harm principle, despite its deficiencies, may well reflect a corresponding sense of the need for such a jurisdictional line. But the "harm principle" is wonderfully flexible, to put the point gently, and its justifications and applications arguably rest on a series of contestable assumptions and bald equivocations.[79] Whether the principle or something like it is realistically capable of preserving the legacy of political liberty over the long run is open to doubt.

In sum, the freedom of the church may continue to be a necessary notion and commitment—necessary as much for liberal democracy as for the church itself. The fact that something is necessary, however, does not assure that it is possible, or available: a man lost in the desert may need water but not get it. As we have seen, it is not easy to see how freedom of the church can be persuasively justified under current circumstances and in our current climate of opinion. Alasdair MacIntyre famously ended a bleak and provocative analysis of modern moral philosophy by suggesting that we are "waiting not for a Godot, but for another—doubtless very different—St. Benedict."[80] It may be that in jurisprudence and constitutional law we are waiting for another—doubtless very different—Gregory VII.

ENDNOTES

1   See St. Augustine, *City of God*, XIX. 17 (tr. Marcus Dods) ("This heavenly city, then, while it sojourns on earth, calls citizens out of all nations, and gathers together a society of pilgrims . . ."). Cf. Hebrews 13:14 ("For we have not here an abiding city, but we seek after the city which is to come.") (American Standard Version).

2   Harold J. Berman, *Law and Revolution: The Formation of the Western Legal Tradition* (Cambridge: Harvard University Press, 1983), 85–113.

3   The conflict is described in Brian Tierney, *The Crisis of Church and State 1050–1300* (Toronto: University of Toronto Press, 1988; orig. pub. Englewood Cliffs, NJ: Prenctice-Hall, 1964), 53–55.

4   See *ibid.*, 182–83 (discussing conflicting interpretations of the far-reaching claims asserted by Pope Boniface VIII).

5   Jose Casanova observes that following the Reformation, "[t]he churches attempted to reproduce the model of Christendom at the national level, but all the territorial national churches, Anglican as well as Lutheran, Catholic as well as Orthodox, fell under the caesaropapist control of the absolutist state." Jose Casanova, *Public Religions in the Modern World* (Chicago: University of Chicago Press, 1994), 22.

6   I argue elsewhere that the Amendment's religion clauses can be interpreted as ending the Erastian regime and thereby restoring the classical freedom of the church together with its younger corollary, the freedom of conscience. Steven D. Smith, "The Establishment Clause and the 'Problem of the Church,'" forthcoming.

7   See Steven D. Smith, "Religious Freedom and its Enemies," *Cardozo Law Review* 32 (2011): 2033. To be sure, courts have continued to recognize the so-called "ministerial exemption" that insulates churches from some aspects of anti-discrimination law. But as both its supporters and critics recognize, the ministerial exemption is an awkward anomaly in current constitutional doctrine. Statutes like the Religious Land Use and Institutionalized Persons Act of 2000 extend further exemptions. But statutes that run contrary to dominant philosophies can easily be repealed, or interpreted away.

8   Nicholas Wolterstorff, "Escaping the Cage of Secular Discourse: A Review Essay," *Christian Scholar's Review* 40 (2010): 93, 97.

9   See, e.g., Veli-Matti Kärkkäinen, *An Introduction to Ecclesiology* (Downers Grove, IL: IVP Academic, 2002), 51–53, 168–69. Cf. Brigham Young, *Discourses of Brigham Young*, ed. John A. Widtsoe (Salt Lake City: Deseret Book Co., 1976), 441 ("When this Kingdom is organized in any age, the Spirit of it dwells in the hearts of the faithful, while the visible department exists among the people, with laws, ordinances, helps, governments, officers, administrators, and every other appendage necessary for its complete operation to the attainment of the end in view.").

10   See, e.g., Roger Haight, , *Christian Community in History*, vol. 3, *Ecclesial Existence* (New York: Continuum, 2008).

11   Gilbert Meilander, "The Catholic I Am," *First Things*, February 2011, 27, 28.

12   See, e.g., Henri de Lubac, *The Splendor of the Church*, tr. Michael Mason (New York: Sheed & Ward 1953), 84–102.

13   See, e.g., Gordon W. Lathrop and Timothy J. Wengert, *Christian Assembly: Marks of the Church in a Pluralistic Age* (Norristown, PA: Augsburg Fortress, 2004).

14   See William Chester Jordan, *Europe in the High Middle Ages* (New York: Viking, 2001), 85–87. Consider one of Henry IV's letters in the dispute with Gregory VII. The letter begins by stating that it is from "Henry, King not by usurpation, but by the pious ordination of God," and it goes on to protest:

> [Y]ou were emboldened to rise up even against the royal power itself, granted to us by God. You dared to threaten to take the kingship away from us—as though we had received the kingship from you, as though kingship and empire were in your hand and not in the hand of God.
> Our Lord, Jesus Christ, has called us to this kingship . . . .

Tierney, *Crisis of Church and State*, 59–60. The letter also accused Gregory of interfering with "the rectors of the holy Church– the archbishops, the bishops, and the priests– but you have trodden them underfoot like slaves . . . ." *Ibid.*

15 Eamon Duffy, *Saints and Sinners: A History of the Popes* (New Haven: Yale University Press, 2001), 110–12.

16 Tierney, *Crisis of Church and State*, 49–50.

17 Jacques Maritain, *The Things That Are Not Caesar's*, trans. J.F. Scanlan (New York: Scribner, 1930), 5.

18 *Ibid.*, 31.

19 Maritain acknowledged as much:

> Here we stand at the parting of the ways where every human conception of the Church, however elevated, proved inadequate. I can understand that so extensive a power should scandalise unbelievers and heretics. . . . [I]t would even be absurd for those who do not and those who do know what the Church is to form the same idea of what her rights are.

> *Ibid.*, 24.

20 Both documents are reprinted in Bruce Frohnen, ed., *The American Republic: Primary Sources* (Indianapolis: Liberty Fund, 2002), 327–31.

21 See Steven D. Smith, *The Disenchantment of Secular Discourse* (Cambridge: Harvard University Press, 2010), 107–50; Steven D. Smith, "Discourse in the Dusk: The Twilight of Religious Freedom," *Harvard Law Review* 122 (2009): 1869.

22 Cf. Kärkkäinen, *Introduction to Ecclesiology*, 7 (observing that "the term *church* for better or worse reasons has been loaded with so many unfortunate connotations from authoritarianism to coercion to antiquarianism").

23 See Richard W. Garnett, "Religion and Group Rights: Are Churches Just Like the Boy Scouts? *St. John's Journal of Legal Commtary* 22 (2007): 515.

24 See Avery Dulles, *Models of the Church*, expanded ed. (New York: Doubleday Image, 1987), 47–75 (discussing conceptions of the church as the "Body of Christ," as a "mystical communion," and as a sacrament).

25 For an insightful (if typically rambling) discussion of the difficulty, see G.K. Chesterton, *Everlasting Man* (New York: Dodd, Mead, 1925)

26 Gerard V. Bradley, "Church Autonomy in the Constitutional Order: The End of Church and State," *Louisiana Law Review* 49 (1988–89): 1057, 1073.

27 *Ibid.*, 1084.

28 *Ibid.*, 1061.

29 *Ibid.*. 1064.

30 *Ibid.*, 1066, 1068–1073.

31 *Ibid.*, 1077.

32 *Ibid.*, 1075.

33 *Ibid.*, 1063.

34 See, e.g., Patrick McKinley Brennan, "Equality, Conscience, and the Liberty of the Church: Justifying the *Controversiale per Controversialius*," *Villanova Law Review* 54 (2009): 625.

35 Douglas Laycock, "Towards a General Theory of the Religion Clauses: The Case of Church-Labor Relations and the Right to Church Autonomy," *Columbia Law Review* 81 (1981): 1373.

36 494 U.S. 872 (1990).

37 See Smith, *Disenchantment*, 136–48.

38 See, e.g., Christopher L. Eisgruber and Lawrence G. Sager, *Religious Freedom and the Constitution* (Cambridge: Harvard University Press, 2007); James W. Nickel, "Who Needs Freedom of Religion?" *Colorado Law Review* 76 (2005): 941, 943.

39 See, e.g., Eisgruber and Sager, *Religious Freedom*, 250–52. See also Scott M. Noveck, "The Promise and Problems of Treating Religious Freedom as Freedom of Association," Gonzaga Law Review 45: (2010): 745.

40 John D. Inazu, "Freedom of the Church as Freedom of Assembly" (unpublished draft paper in author's files).

41 Kathleen A. Brady, "Religious Organizations and Free Exercise: The Surprising Lessons of Smith," *Brigham Young University Law Review* 2004: 1633.

42 See, e.g., Kathleen A. Brady, "Fostering Harmony Among the Justices: How Contemporary Debates in Theology Can Help to Reconcile the Divisions on the Court regarding Religious Expression by the State," *Notre Dame Law Review* 75: (1999): 433.

43 Brady, "Religious Organizations and Free Exercise," 1673–79.

44 Michael E. Smith, "The Special Place of Religion in the Constitution," *Supreme Court Review* 1983: 83, 112.

45 Brady, "Religious Organizations and Free Exercise," 1699.

46 *Ibid.*, 1674–79.

47 *Ibid.*, 1677.

48 *Ibid.*, 1706.

49 *Ibid.*, 1713.

50 *Ibid.*

51 See *ibid*. ("Before closing, I hope the reader will indulge me in such a [theological] argument.").

52 Brady further develops her rationales for church autonomy, and responds to criticisms, in Kathleen A. Brady, "Religious Group Autonomy: Further Reflections on What is At Stake," *Journal of Law and Religion* 22 (2006–2007): 153.

53 Bradley, "Church Autonomy," 1076.

54 530 U.S. 640 (2000).

55 Garnett, "Religion and Group Rights," 533.

56 The Court has also recognized a separate "freedom of intimate association" that seems more akin to something like privacy.

57 For a discussion of this development, see Ashutosh Bhagwat, "Associational Speech," *Yale Law Journal* 120 (2011): 978, 985–89.

58 468 U.S. 609 (1984).

59 *Ibid*., at 627–28.

60 Seana Valentine Shiffrin, "What Is Really Wrong with Compelled Association?" *Northwestern University Law Review* 99 (2005): 839, 849.

61 George Kateb, "The Value of Association," in Amy Gutmann, ed., *Freedom of Association* (Princeton: Princeton University Press, 1998), 55.

62 530 U.S. 640, 689–90 (2000) (Stevens, J., dissenting).

63 In *Dale*, to be sure, these Justices were in dissent, but in the more recent case of *Christian Legal Society* v. *Martinez* they dominated the majority.

64 In addition to *Roberts*, see *Board of Directors of Rotary International* v. *Rotary Club of Duarte*, 481 U.S. 537 (1987); *New York State Club Ass.* v. *City of New York*, 487 U.S. 1 (1988).

65 A common but contested position holds, for example, that primarily commercial associations should not enjoy such protection. See, e.g., *Roberts* v. *Jaycees*, 468 U.S. 609, 632–36 (1984) (O'Connor, J., concurring).

66 *Boy Scouts* v. *Dale*, 530 U.S. 640, 659 (2000).

67 See, e.g., Andrew Koppelman, with Tobias Barrington Wolff, *A Right to Discriminate? How the Case of* Boy Scouts of America v. James Dale *Warped the Law of Free Associations* (New Haven: Yale University Press, 2009).

68 130 S.Ct. 2971(2010).

69 130 S.Ct., at 2985.

70 See, e.g., Bhagwat, "Associational Speech" ; see also John D. Inazu, "The Unsettling 'Well-Settled' Law of Freedom of Association," *Connecticut Law Review* 43 (2010): 149.

71 Matt. 16:18.

72 Cf. Brad S. Gregory, *Salvation at Stake: Christian Martyrdom in Early Modern Europe* (Cambridge: Harvard University Press, 1999), 104 ("Certain devout Christians, particularly within post-Tridentine Catholicism, actively yearned for martyrdom.").

73 See, e.g., Matt. 5:11 ("Blessed are ye when men shall reproach you, and persecute you, and say all manner of evil against you falsely, for my sake.").

74 For a more extensive and insightful statement of the view, though, see John Courtney Murray, *We Hold These Truths: Catholic Reflections on the American Proposition* (New York: Sheed & Ward, 1960), 197–217.

75 This paragraph distills the longer exposition in Smith, *Disenchantment*, 112–27.

76 Thomas Paine, *The Age of Reason* (New York: D.M. Bennett, 1877), 6.

77 Madison stated this position clearly in his first claim in the Memorial and Remonstrance:

> Before any man can be considered as a member of Civil Society, he must be considered as a subject of the Governor of the Universe: And if a member of Civil society, who enters into any subordinate Association, must always do it with a saving of his allegiance to the general authority; much more must every man who becomes a member of any particular Civil Society, do it with a saving of his allegiance to the Universal Sovereign. We maintain therefore that in matters of Religion, no man's right is abridged by the institution of Civil Society, and the Religion is wholly exempt from its cognizance.

> James Madison, "Memorial and Remonstrance against Religious Assessments," in Frohnen, *American Republic*, 327. And Madison concluded that if this right is not secure, then all other rights are vulnerable as well. The right to religious freedom "is held by the same tenure with all our other rights. . . ."

> Either, then, we must say that the will of the Legislature is the only measure of their authority, and that in the plenitude of this authority, they may sweep away all our fundamental rights; or, that they are bound to leave this particular right untouched and sacred.

> *Ibid.*, 329.

78 John Stuart Mill, "On Liberty," in J.S. Mill, *On Liberty and Other Writings*,

ed. Stefan Collini(New York: Cambridge University Press, 1989), 76 (emphasis added).

79 For discussion, see Smith, *Disenchantment*, 70–106.

80 Alasdair MacIntyre, *After Virtue: A Study in Moral Theory*, 2nd ed. (Notre Dame, IN: University of Notre Dame Press, 1985), 263.

Chapter Ten

The Global Implications
of the Domestic Conscience Battle

Allen D. Hertzke

Introduction

In a paper presented at the XVII Plenary Session of the Pontifical Academy of Social Sciences in Rome, I noted a profound paradox of our age: at the very time the value of religious freedom is becoming manifest, the international consensus behind it is weakening.[1] Thus religious liberty is not only imperiled by sundry despotisms around the world, but by growing elite hostility in the West that jeopardizes previous gains.

Behind this sobering picture, however, lies promise. We are witnessing an historic convergence of empirical evidence and events on the ground that corroborate a key ontological reality: humans are spiritual creatures who thrive best and most harmoniously when they enjoy the freedom to express their fundamental dignity, both individually and in community with others. Religious liberty is crucial to thriving societies and is the best means of peacefully navigating the most treacherous waters of the twenty-first century: living with our differences in a shrinking world.

The fate of religious liberty in America, consequently, has huge global implications, especially because the United States has played, and continues to play, a singular role in upholding religious freedom principles contained in United Nations declarations and international covenants. It would be ironic and devastating if a nation with an official foreign policy of promoting global religious freedom saw the erosion of that liberty at home. Indeed, prominent comparative law theorists such as Cole Durham now routinely critique court rulings or political decisions in the United States that depart from robust principles of religious liberty they defend in international tribunals.[2]

That is the theme of my reflections here. If we lose the battle at home, we lose our credible voice for religious freedom around the world. If it comes to a point where American religious institutions are eliminated from doing charitable work, and religious providers are fined because the state insists that they operate in ways that violate conscience and transcendent mandates, then we will have undermined our ability to make the case for the freedom and autonomy of religious actors in societies abroad afflicted by more onerous restrictions on religious practice or even by egregious persecution. If modern "free" nations like the United States are seen as hostile toward faith, traditional marriage, and the autonomy of religious institutions, then traditional religious societies will not find our arguments for "liberty" very persuasive.

A Brief History of the Interplay Between Domestic and International Religious Freedom

The American religious heritage has deeply influenced the global scene. In the searing aftermath of the Holocaust, the United States played a leading role in developing the Universal Declaration of Human Rights, through the leadership of Eleanor Roosevelt, who chaired the U.N. committee that drafted the declaration. Article 18 of that foundational declaration, adopted by the United Nations in 1948, provides this ringing statement of principles:

> Everyone has the right to freedom of thought, conscience, and religion. This right includes freedom to change his religion or belief, and freedom, either alone or in community with others and in public or private, to manifest his religion or belief in teaching, practice, worship, and observance.

The American experience and model also profoundly influenced the eloquent embrace of religious freedom by the Catholic Church at the Second Vatican Council. As Daniel Philpott and others have documented, *Dignitatis Humanae* (1965) stands as one of the pivotal moments in the global advance of liberty because it turned the Church into the great engine of the last wave of democratization on earth.[3]

American leadership continued during the Cold War, when the denial of religious freedom was a subtext of relations between the United States and the Soviet Union. The Jackson-Vanik amendment of 1974 tied normalized trade relations to the freedom of Jews and others to emigrate from the Soviet Union. Similarly, the Helsinki Accords of 1975 tied territorial sovereignty of the Soviet Union to advancements in human rights, including religious freedom.

Most recently, of course, Congress invoked the American tradition of religious liberty in its landmark International Religious Freedom Act (IRFA) of 1998, which makes the promotion of religious freedom a "core objective" of American foreign policy. What moved Congress to act was the striking array of religious leaders backing the initiative, leaders often at odds on other issues. In interviews I discovered that a number of these leaders forged relationships with their unlikely allies through the earlier domestic campaign to reinstate heightened legal standards for religious exercise (in the wake of the *Smith* decision)[4] that produced the Religious Freedom Restoration Act of 1993. In other words, a coalition galvanized to strengthen *domestic* religious liberty helped fuel the *international* campaign. Though not yet applied vigorously by our secular State Department, IRFA's vast reporting enterprise has provided the pivotal foundation for the systematic measurement of global restrictions on religion by the Pew Forum and the path-breaking scholarship flowing from that enterprise (more about that later).

We also see instances where struggles at home gain traction through international engagement. As Sarah Barringer Gordon documents in her book *The Spirit of the Law*,[5] when President Roosevelt in 1941 included religious liberty as one of the "Four Freedoms" that conduce to world peace, it buoyed conscience claims of Jehovah's Witnesses and aided their legal victory in the *Barnette* flag salute case of 1943.[6] It seems possible, and I would certainly make the case, that the compelling work of scholars focused on global religious freedom could inform our domestic struggles. Even more, the titanic struggles against religious persecution around the world should rekindle commitment to religious liberty at home and perhaps even shame those who so blithely ignore attacks on institutional ministries.

Emerging Data: the Link Between Religious Freedom and Other Freedoms

With that in mind, it seems useful to highlight that emerging scholarship. It is stunning how mounting empirical research shows the contribution of religious freedom to other human goods. Propositions about such linkages have been advanced for centuries. But for the first time in human history we have the documentary record and the capacity to apply rigorous scientific methods to test such propositions.

That documentary record includes reports by international agencies, human rights groups, and national governments on religious conditions around the world. What turned out to be pivotal for this new scholarly enterprise, however, was the mandated U.S. government reporting under IRFA. The State Department's voluminous annual report on the status of religion in every country on earth, critiqued by advocacy groups and improved over time, provides a key resource—a raw database—for innovative methods that uncover the scope of and limits on religious practice in the world.

Brian Grim is the pioneer who developed a rigorous coding protocol for measuring objective restrictions on religion. Rather than attempting to measure some indefinable "quantity of freedom," this method instead systematically codes observable *restrictions* to create a verifiable index, which can be compared cross-nationally, replicated over time, correlated for causal explanations, and plumbed for normative conclusions.

The Pew Forum on Religion and Public Life applied this new method to provide the first systematic, quantitative measures of the global status of religious freedom. Pew's research protocol involves coding incidents of restrictions documented in numerous international reports (from less to more severe on scale of 0–10) to develop numerical indices for both governmental and social restrictions in every country on earth. The first Pew Forum report, "Global Restrictions on Religion," was issued in 2009, while the second, "Rising Restrictions on Religion," came out in 2011.[7]

These Pew Forum reports include country breakdowns by degree of restrictions, regional and religious patterns, and detailed raw data on the coding of individual countries, so that scholars can determine exactly how a particular country received its index score. The Pew team will continue to do this coding to record longitudinal trends.

A distinct feature of the Pew Forum enterprise is that it includes the United States, whose "government restrictions" index so far codes in the low category (though not the lowest). In part, this low index score reflects our constitutional protections of religious free exercise, but it also results, ironically, from the absence of systematic documentation on laws and practices in United States of the sort provided internationally. Thus, recent encroachments on institutional ministries inconceivable only a few years ago—such as actions by state authorities that forced closure of Catholic adoption agencies in Massachusetts, the District of Columbia, and Illinois—have yet to be picked up by Pew coders. But as these cases mount—and as systematic documentation on the U.S. improves—the U.S. score will show rising restrictions on religion, a sobering prospect for the nation that pioneered religious autonomy and the rights of conscience.

Armed with the Pew Forum's country data, scholars now can apply rigorous statistical analysis to probe the normative value of religious freedom. The chart below shows the robust correlations between religious freedom and political rights, press autonomy, civil liberties, longevity of democracy, women's status, economic development, health outcomes, social peace, and regional stability. Religious freedom, as Brian Grim observes, is an integral part of the "bundled commodity" of human freedoms. Remove it and the others tend to unravel.[8]

Correlation is not causation, the skeptic will retort, so these relationships do not necessarily show that religious freedom is a key driver of social goods. Perhaps it is a *result* more than a cause. Scholars, in fact, have taken up this challenge to provide persuasive theories that explain these statistical relationships, to show why religious freedom is indeed a powerful "independent variable." A growing scholarship shows, for example, that the statistical link between religious liberty and economic development makes sense because societies that protect freedom of belief and conscience tend to operate with greater transparency and less corruption. Deregulated religious markets, moreover, can contribute to an enterprising ethos and climate so vital to economic progress.[9] Based on work in India and elsewhere, Rebecca and Timothy Shah suggest further that the economic value of "spiritual capital" can operate for the very poor by enabling them to exercise agency and develop

supportive communities.[10] To the extent that the state limits the autonomy of civil society institutions, it undermines this spiritual capital.

Chart 1: Correlation of religious freedom with other freedoms and well-being within countries

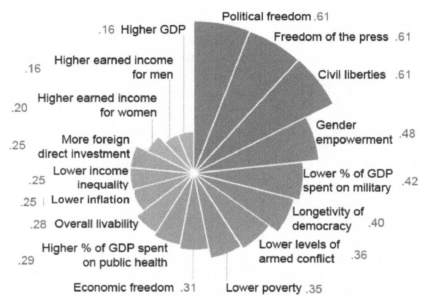

Brian J. Grim and Roger Finke, *The Price of Freedom Denied*, Chapter 7. All correlations are statistically significant, with the larger the area and number, the stronger the
direct correlation.

The pioneering explanation of the contribution of religious freedom
to human flourishing is provided by Brian Grim and Roger Finke. Their
book, *The Price of Freedom Denied*,[11] is a model of what social science
aspires to but rarely achieves: a historically-rooted theory with virtually
universal application, supported by rigorous empirical analysis of voluminous data, with application across cultures and continents. Grim and
Finke probe the timeless question of why religious liberty matters. Their
answer is theoretically elegant and empirically powerful: as religious
freedoms expand, inter-religious conflict declines, grievances lessen,
persecution wanes, societies stabilize, and mushrooming religious contributions enrich civil societies. On the other hand, as government

restrictions on religion increase, we see measurable increases in inter-religious grievances, social strife, persecution, repression, and instability. States that arrogate the role of regulating religious civil society operate with fewer checks; their abuse of power bleeds into other areas of life.

The theory also provides real guidance to policymakers because it shows why their common inclination to control religion is counterproductive. Government restrictions on religion, Grim and Finke show, trigger social hostility among religious groups, which produces more pressure for government restrictions and further religious strife in a "religious violence cycle."[12]

This cycle is elaborated in the new book, *God's Century*, by Monica Toft, Daniel Philpott, and Timothy Shah, which provides a cogent theoretical framework for understanding the relationship between religious autonomy and political theology.[13] Synthesizing a vast body of research that challenges the secular paradigm of the twentieth century, these sophisticated scholars of international relations and comparative politics show that regime attempts to repress religion induce the very militancy such efforts purport to prevent. In addition, because the dramatic resurgence of public religion around the world is irreversible, secular efforts to tame religion by privatizing it will fail. The only hope is in finding ways to channel religious energies into healthy civil society engagement and competition, a distinctive American achievement worthy of modeling and preserving.

Another vivid illustration of the impact of domestic trends on global advocacy is provided by Thomas Farr's ethnographic account of the implementation of U.S. international religious freedom policy. As former director of the State Department's Office of International Religious Freedom (and now director of the Religious Freedom Project at the Berkley Center at Georgetown University), Farr enjoys a unique vantage point. In his book, *World of Faith and Freedom*,[14] he describes how the same secular infrastructure that undermines domestic conscience rights produces a "religion deficit" among America's foreign policy elites. If religion is viewed as irrational and conflict-prone, as it often is by leaders socialized at elite academic institutions, then international progress will mean secularization, privatization, and strict separation. In fact, Farr was struck by how deeply his colleagues at the State Department operated under the spell of John Rawls about the danger of religion to liberal societies. The only way a polity is safe from fanaticism, in their view, is if religious people refrain from asserting themselves in the public square.

But Farr turns this Rawlsian argument on its head. In a pervasively religious world, he argues, the only hope for some modicum of peace lies in regimes that grant a bargain to religious communities: abandon the claim on the coercive powers of the state and in return gain full citizenship rights to promote your religious values in public policy. This bargain can only work if the United States stops peddling a form of strict separationism that would banish religion from the public square, which religionists abroad rightly see as an attempt to secularize their societies.

Here Farr is echoing the seminal work in comparative politics by Columbia political scientist Alfred Stepan. In a systematic inquiry into the institutional requirements of democracy, Stepan provides an insightful thesis about the relationship between religion and state that he terms the "twin tolerations." [15] Liberal democracy, he argues, depends on a reciprocal bargain between the institutions of religion and the institutions of the state. The state protects and thus "tolerates" the freedom of religious institutions to operate in civil society; churches, in turn, refrain from using the powers of the state to enhance their prerogatives and thus agree to "tolerate" (not squelch) competitors. If political authorities in the United States undercut the autonomy of religious institutions, they are in effect breaking the democratic bargain.

Conclusion: Waking Up Elites to the Goods of Domestic and International Religious Freedom

As this discussion suggests, there is a growing convergence of domestic and international discourses on the principles of, and threats to, religious liberty, conscience, institutional autonomy, and inter-religious amity. Take the work of Roger Finke. His theoretical framework of "religious markets" informed his global work with Brian Grim on the social value of religious freedom and the high cost of its denial. But that framework similarly directs his empirical examination of the domestic impact of Supreme Court decisions and congressional acts on the real-world scope of religious free exercise. He and his colleagues systematically analyzed more than two thousand court cases at all levels of government between 1981 and 1997, and found that religious litigants gained far more relief when authorities operated with judicial or legislative mandates to accommodate believers and religious institutions.[16]

Cole Durham's work also epitomizes this convergence of the domestic and international arenas. Employing a comparative framework to understand principles of religious liberty, his mapping of the diverse global threats to religious free exercise finds a "sweet spot" for its maximum protection in a robust policy of *accommodation*,[17] which ensures the autonomy of religious institutions and provides leverage for claimants seeking relief from policies that burden their practice. The American experience, he suggests, cultivates wide popular support for such a policy. This is indicated by numerous congressional and state-level initiatives that protect particular religious practices and mandate reasonable accommodations for religious claimants. In a summary of the status of religious liberty in the United States in the first decade of this century, for example, Durham and Smith find that since the Supreme Court's decision in *City of Boerne* v. *Flores*,[18] half of the states have either enacted their own RFRA laws or have state Supreme Court decisions providing enhanced leverage for religious claimants seeking accommodation.[19] Thus those seeking to protect institutional ministries may find valuable levers and precedents in these state actions.

But while Durham sees durable *popular* support for religious freedom in the United States, he fears that certain trends will lead to its gradual erosion, even a tipping point profoundly at odds with the American tradition. The crucial trend is secularization. Because the law operates within a wider social and political environment, Durham is particularly concerned with the absence of experiential contact with the world of faith among elite strata in American society, which will induce amnesia about the origins of religious liberty and indifference about its ultimate value. If religion is seen as passé or benighted—by judges, policymakers, or public administrators—their defense of religious rights will probably be anemic. If there is nothing *special* about faith commitments, why be concerned with the autonomy of religious institutions or the conscience rights of believers? Why treat a zoning request by a church any differently from that of a business? Or see a transcendent duty as distinct from a lifestyle choice? Why worry if new equality norms trump religious liberty?[20]

The American experience, though never perfect, provides a model to the world of how protecting broad religious exercise fosters a vibrant civil society, unleashes positive contributions by religious communities, builds citizen loyalty, and cultivates mutual respect among competing faiths. This is why the pioneering scholars mentioned here, along with a host of international champions of religious liberty, understand the peril to global advocacy if conscience rights and institutional autonomy erode in the United States.

Considerable work of international advocates, in fact, involves remonstrating with governments to relax onerous bureaucratic obstacles to the communal and institutional exercise of religious faith. Such obstacles are rightly seen as violations of the spirit and letter of U.N. declarations and international covenants. More fundamentally, advocates know that religious freedom—and the autonomous civil society that it engenders—represent a crucial check on the overweening reach, and totalizing temptation, of the modern state.

If we cannot preserve that safeguard in the cradle of liberty, then global prospects for freedom and human flourishing will diminish, a sad but eminently avoidable prospect.

ENDNOTES

1   Allen D. Hertzke, "Religious Freedom in the World Today: Paradox and Promise," forthcoming in *Universal Rights in a World of Diversity: The Case of Religious Freedom*, Pontifical Academy of Social Sciences, XVII Plenary Session.

2   W. Cole Durham Jr., "Religious Freedom in a Worldwide Setting: Comparative Reflections," in *Universal Rights in a World of Diversity: The Case for Religious Freedom*, ed. Mary Ann Glendon and Hans F. Zacher (Vatican City: Pontifical Academy of Social Sciences, 2012); W. Cole Durham Jr., and Robert T. Smith, "Religion and the State in the United States at the Turn of the Twenty-First Century," in *Law and Religion in the 21st Century*, ed. Silvio Ferrari and Rinaldo Christofori (Surrey, UK: Ashgate, 2010).

3   Daniel Philpott, "The Catholic Wave," *Journal of Democracy* 15 (April

2004); Samuel Huntington, *The Third Wave: Democratization in the Late Twentieth* Century (Norman: University of Oklahoma Press, 1991).

4   *Employment Division* v. *Smith*, 494 U.S. 872 (1990) (holding that a state could burden religion without demonstrating a "compelling state interest," if the law was "neutral" and "generally applicable.")

5   Sarah Barringer Gordon, *The Spirit of the Law: Religious Voices and the Constitution in Modern America* (Cambridge: Harvard University Press, 2010).

6   319 U.S. 624 (1943).

7   The 2009 report is here: http://pewforum.org/Government/Global-Restrictions-on-Religion.aspx; the 2011 report is here: http://pewforum.org/Government/Rising-Restrictions-on-Religion%282%29.aspx

8   Brian J. Grim, "Religious Freedom: Good for What Ails Us?" *The Review of Faith and International Affairs*6.2 (Summer 2008): 3.

9   Brian J. Grim, "God's Economy: Religious Freedom and Socioeconomic Well-Being," and Theodore Malloch, "Free to Choose: Economics and Religion," both in *Religious Freedom in the World*, ed. Paul Marshall (Lanhamc MD: Rowman & Littlefield, 2008).

10   Rebecca and Timothy Shah, "Spiritual Capital and Economic Enterprise," Oxford Centre for Religion & Public Life, 2008, http://www.ocrpl.org/?p=13.

11   Brian J. Grim and Roger Finke, *The Price of Freedom Denied: Religious Persecution and Conflict in the Twenty-First Century* (New York: Cambridge University Press, 2011).

12   Ibid., 10.

13   Monica Duffy Toft, Daniel Philpott, and Timothy Samuel Shah, *God's Century: Resurgent Religion and Global Politics* (New York: W.W. Norton, 2011).

14   Thomas F. Farr, *World of Faith and Freedom: Why International Religious Liberty is Vital to American National Security* (New York: Oxford University Press, 2008).

15   Alfred Stepan, "The Twin Tolerations," in *World Religions and Democ*racy, ed. Larry Diamond, Marc F. Plattner, and Philip J. Costopoulos (Baltimore: Johns Hopkins University Press, 2005).

16   John Wybraniec and Roger Finke, "Religious Regulation and the Courts: The Judiciary's Changing Role in Protecting Minority Religions from Majoritarian Rule, "*Journal for the Scientific Study of Religion* 40 (2001): 427–444.

17   W. Cole Durham, Jr., "Perspectives on Religious Liberty: A Comparative

Framework," in *Religious Human Rights in Global Perspective: Legal Perspectives*, edited by Johan D. van der Vyver and John Witte, JR. (The Hague, Netherlands: Martinus Nijhoff Publishers, 1996).

18 521 U.S. 507 (1997). This decision struck down the constraints on state and local governments in the federal Religious Freedom Restoration Act of 1993.

19 W. Cole Durham, Jr., and Robert T. Smith, "Religion and the State in the United States at the Turn of the Twenty-first Century," in *Law and Religion in the 21st Century: Relations between States and Religious Communities*, ed. Silvio Ferrari and Rinaldo Cristofori (Surrey, UK: Ashgate, 2010).

20 W. Cole Durham, Jr., Matthew K. Richards, and Donlu Thayer, "The Status and Threats to International Law on Religious Liberty," in *Constituting the Future: Religious Liberty, Law, and Flourishing Societies,* edited by Allen D. Hertzke, forthcoming *Oxford University Press*; see also Cole Durham's paper presented at the XVII Plenary Session of the Pontifical Academy of Social Sciences conference, 2011.